JOHN KNOX AND THE REFORMATION

By
ANDREW LANG
To Maurice Hewlett

PREFACE

In this brief Life of Knox I have tried, as much as I may, to get behind Tradition, which has so deeply affected even modern histories of the Scottish Reformation, and even recent Biographies of the Reformer. The tradition is based, to a great extent, on Knox's own "History," which I am therefore obliged to criticise as carefully as I can. In his valuable *John Knox, a Biography*, Professor Hume Brown says that in the "History" "we have convincing proof alike of the writer's good faith, and of his perception of the conditions of historic truth." My reasons for dissenting from this favourable view will be found in the following pages. If I am right, if Knox, both as a politician and an historian, resembled Charles I. in "sailing as near the wind" as he could, the circumstance (as another of his biographers remarks) "only makes him more human and interesting."

Opinion about Knox and the religious Revolution in which he took so great a part, has passed through several variations in the last century. In the *Edinburgh Review* of 1816 (No. liii. pp. 163-180), is an article with which the present biographer can agree. Several passages from Knox's works are cited, and the reader is expected to be "shocked at their principles." They are certainly shocking, but they are not, as a rule, set before the public by biographers of the Reformer.

Mr. Carlyle introduced a style of thinking about Knox which may be called platonically Puritan. Sweet enthusiasts glide swiftly over all in the Reformer that is specially distasteful to us. I find myself more in harmony with the outspoken Hallam, Dr. Joseph Robertson, David Hume, and the Edinburgh reviewer of 1816, than with several more recent students of Knox.

"The Reformer's violent counsels and intemperate speech were remarkable," writes Dr. Robertson, "even in his own ruthless age," and he gives fourteen examples. "Lord Hailes has shown," he adds, "how little Knox's statements" (in his "History") "are to be relied on even in matters which were within the Reformer's own knowledge."

In Scotland there has always been the party of Cavalier and White Rose sentimentalism. To this party Queen Mary is a saintly being, and their admiration of Claverhouse goes far beyond that entertained by Sir Walter Scott. On the other side, there is the party, equally sentimental, which musters under the banner of the Covenant, and sees scarcely a blemish in Knox. A pretty sample of the sentiment of this party appears in a biography (1905) of the Reformer by a minister of the Gospel. Knox summoned the organised brethren, in 1563, to overawe justice, when some men were to be tried on a charge of invading in arms the chapel of Holyrood. No proceeding could be more anarchic than Knox's, or more in accordance with the lovable customs of my dear country, at that time. But the biographer of 1905, "a placed minister," writes that "the doing of it" (Knox's summons) "was only an assertion of the liberty of the Church, and of the members of the Commonwealth as a whole, to assemble for purposes which were clearly lawful"—the purposes being to overawe justice in the course of a trial!

On sentiment, Cavalier or Puritan, reason is thrown away.

I have been surprised to find how completely a study of Knox's own works corroborates the views of Dr. Robertson and Lord Hailes. That Knox ran so very far ahead of the Genevan pontiffs of his age in violence; and that in his "History" he needs such careful watching, was, to me, an unexpected discovery. He may have been "an old Hebrew prophet," as Mr. Carlyle says, but he had also been a young Scottish notary! A Hebrew prophet is, at best, a dangerous anachronism in a delicate crisis of the Church Christian; and the notarial element is too conspicuous in some passages of Knox's "History."

That Knox was a great man; a disinterested man; in his regard for the poor a truly Christian man; as a shepherd of Calvinistic souls a man fervent and considerate; of pure life; in friendship loyal; by jealousy untainted; in private character genial and amiable, I am entirely convinced. In public and political life he was much less admirable; and his "History," vivacious as it is, must be studied as the work of an old-fashioned advocate rather than as the summing up of a judge. His favourite adjectives are "bloody," "beastly," "rotten," and "stinking."

Any inaccuracies of my own which may have escaped my correction will be dwelt on, by enthusiasts for the Prophet, as if they are the main elements of this book, and disqualify me as a critic of Knox's "History." At least any such errors on my part are involuntary and unconscious. In Knox's defence we must remember that he never saw his "History" in print. But he kept it by him for many years, obviously re-reading, for he certainly retouched it, as late as 1571.

In quoting Knox and his contemporaries, I have used modern spelling: the letter from the State Papers printed on pp. 146, 147, shows what the orthography of the period was really like. Consultation of the original MSS. on doubtful points, proves that the printed Calendars, though excellent guides, cannot be relied on as authorities.

The portrait of Knox, from Beza's book of portraits of Reformers, is posthumous, but is probably a good likeness drawn from memory, after a description by Peter Young, who knew him, and a design, presumably by "Adrianc Vaensoun," a Fleming, resident in Edinburgh.

There is an interesting portrait, possibly of Knox, in the National Gallery of Portraits, but the work has no known authentic history.

The portrait of Queen Mary, at the age of thirty-six, and a prisoner, is from the Earl of Morton's original; it is greatly superior to the "Sheffield" type of likenesses, of about 1578; and, with Janet's and other drawings (1558-1561), the Bridal medal of 1558, and (in my opinion) the Earl of Leven and Melville's portrait, of about 1560-1565, is the best extant representation of the Queen.

The Leven and Melville portrait of Mary, young and charming, and wearing jewels which are found recorded in her Inventories, has hitherto been overlooked. An admirable photogravure is given in Mr. J. J. Foster's "True Portraiture of Mary, Queen of Scots" (1905), and I understand that a photograph was done in 1866 for the South Kensington Museum.

A. LANG.

8 Gibson Place, St. Andrews.

CONTENTS

CHAPTER I. 6
CHAPTER II. 15
CHAPTER III. 21
CHAPTER IV. 28
CHAPTER V. 37
CHAPTER VI. 43
CHAPTER VII. 48
CHAPTER VIII. 58
CHAPTER IX. 78
CHAPTER X. 82
CHAPTER XI. 97
CHAPTER XII. 117
CHAPTER XIII. 135
CHAPTER XIV. 141
CHAPTER XV. 152
CHAPTER XVI. 165
CHAPTER XVII. 174
CHAPTER XVIII. 187
APPENDIX A. 201
APPENDIX B. 206
LITERARY ANALYSIS 208
ABOUT THE AUTHOR 213

CHAPTER I.

ANCESTRY, BIRTH, EDUCATION, ENVIRONMENT: 1513(?)-1546

"*November* 24, 1572.

"John Knox, minister, deceased, who had, as was alleged, the most part of the blame of all the sorrows of Scotland since the slaughter of the late Cardinal."

It is thus that the decent burgess who, in 1572, kept *The Diurnal* of such daily events as he deemed important, cautiously records the death of the great Scottish Reformer. The sorrows, the "cumber" of which Knox was "alleged" to bear the blame, did not end with his death. They persisted in the conspiracies and rebellions of the earlier years of James VI.; they smouldered through the later part of his time; they broke into far spreading flame at the touch of the Covenant; they blazed at "dark Worcester and bloody Dunbar"; at Preston fight, and the sack of Dundee by Monk; they included the Cromwellian conquest of Scotland, and the shame and misery of the Restoration; to trace them down to our own age would be invidious.

It is with the "alleged" author of the Sorrows, with his life, works, and ideas that we are concerned.

John Knox, son of William Knox and of --- Sinclair, his wife, unlike most Scotsmen, unlike even Mr. Carlyle, had not "an ell of pedigree." The common scoff was that each Scot styled himself "the King's poor cousin." But John Knox declared, "I am a man of base estate and condition." The genealogy of Mr. Carlyle has been traced to a date behind the Norman Conquest, but of Knox's ancestors nothing is known. He himself, in 1562, when he "ruled the roast" in Scotland, told the ruffian Earl of Bothwell, "my grandfather, my maternal grandfather, and my father, have served your Lordship's predecessors, and some of them have died under their standards; and this" (namely goodwill to the house of the feudal superior) "is a part of the obligation of our Scottish kindness." Knox, indeed, never writes very harshly of Bothwell, partly for the reason he gives; partly, perhaps, because Bothwell, though an infamous character, and a political opponent, was not in 1562-67 "an idolater," that is, a Catholic: if ever he had been one; partly because his "History" ends before Bothwell's murder of Darnley in 1567.

Knox's ancestors were, we may suppose, peasant farmers, like the ancestors of Burns and Hogg; and Knox, though he married a maid of the Queen's kin, bore traces of his descent. "A man ungrateful and unpleasable," Northumberland styled him: he was one who could not "smiling, put a question by"; if he had to remonstrate even with a person whom it was desirable to conciliate, he stated his case in the plainest and least flattering terms. "Of nature I am churlish, and in conditions different from many," he wrote; but this side of his character he kept mainly for people of high rank, accustomed to deference, and indifferent or hostile to his aims. To others, especially to women whom he liked, he was considerate and courteous, but any assertion of social superiority aroused his wakeful independence. His countrymen of his own order had long displayed these peculiarities of humour.

The small Scottish cultivators from whose ranks Knox rose, appear, even before his age, in two strangely different lights. If they were not technically "kindly tenants," in which case their conditions of existence and of tenure were comparatively comfortable and secure, they were liable to eviction at the will of the lord, and, to quote an account of their condition written in 1549, "were in more servitude than the children of Israel in Egypt." Henderson, the writer of 1549 whom we have quoted, hopes that the agricultural class may yet live "as substantial commoners, not miserable cottars, charged daily to war and slay their neighbours *at their own expense*," as under the standards of the unruly Bothwell House. This Henderson was one of the political observers who, before the Scottish Reformation, hoped for a secure union between Scotland and England, in place of the old and romantic league with France. That alliance had, indeed, enabled both France and Scotland to maintain their national independence. But, with the great revolution in religion, the interest of Scotland was a permanent political league with England, which Knox did as much as any man to forward, while, by resisting a religious union, he left the seeds of many sorrows.

If the Lowland peasantry, from one point of view, were terribly oppressed, we know that they were of independent manners. In 1515 the chaplain of Margaret Tudor, the Queen Mother, writes to one Adam Williamson: "You know the use of this country. Every man speaks what he will without blame. The man hath more words than the master, and will not be content unless he knows the master's counsel. There is no order among us."

Thus, two hundred and fifty years before Burns, the Lowland Scot was minded that "A man's a man for a' that!" Knox was the true flower of this vigorous Lowland thistle. Throughout life he not only "spoke what he would," but uttered "the Truth" in such a tone as to make it unlikely that his "message" should be accepted by opponents. Like Carlyle, however, he had a heart rich in affection, no breach in friendship, he says, ever began on his side; while, as "a good hater," Dr. Johnson might have admired him. He carried into political and theological conflicts the stubborn temper of the Border prickers, his fathers, who had ridden under the Roses and the Lion of the Hepburns. So far Knox was an example of the doctrine of heredity; that we know, however little we learn in detail about his ancestors.

The birthplace of Knox was probably a house in a suburb of Haddington, in a district on the path of English invasion. The year of his birth has long been dated, on a late statement of little authority, as 1505. Seven years after his death, however, a man who knew him well, namely, Peter Young, tutor and librarian of James VI., told Beza that Knox died in his fifty-ninth year. Dr. Hay Fleming has pointed out that his natal year was probably 1513-15, not 1505, and this reckoning, we shall see, appears to fit in better with the deeds of the Reformer.

If Knox was born in 1513-15, he must have taken priest's orders, and adopted the profession of a notary, at nearly the earliest moment which the canonical law permitted. No man ought to be in priest's orders before he was twenty-five; Knox, if born in 1515, was just twenty-five in 1540, when he is styled "Sir John Knox" (one of "The Pope's Knights") in legal documents, and appears as a notary. He certainly continued in orders and in the notarial profession as late as March 1543. The law of the Church did not, in fact, permit priests to be notaries, but in an age when "notaires" were often professional forgers, the additional security for character yielded by Holy Orders must have been welcome to clients, and Bishops permitted priests to practise this branch of the law.

Of Knox's near kin no more is known than of his ancestors. He had a brother, William, for whom, in 1552, he procured a licence to trade in England as owner of a ship of 100 tons. Even as late as 1656, there were not a dozen ships of this burden in Scotland, so William Knox must have been relatively a prosperous man. In 1544-45, there was a William Knox, a fowler or gamekeeper to the Earl of Westmoreland, who acted as a secret agent between the Scots in English pay and their paymasters. We much later (1559) find the Reformer's brother, William, engaged with him in a secret political mission to the Governor of Berwick; probably this William knew shy Border paths, and he may have learned them as the Lord Westmoreland's fowler in earlier years.

About John Knox's early years and education nothing is known. He certainly acquired such Latin (*satis humilis*, says a German critic) as Scotland then had to teach, probably at the Burgh School of Haddington. A certain John Knox matriculated at the University of Glasgow in 1522, but he cannot have been the Reformer, if the Reformer was not born till 1513-15. Beza, on the other hand (1580), had learned, probably from the Reformer, whom he knew well, that Knox was a St. Andrews man, and though his name does not occur in the University Register, the Register was very ill kept. Supposing Knox, then, to have been born in 1513-15, and to have been educated at St. Andrews, we can see how he comes to know so much about the progress of the new religious ideas at that University, between 1529 and 1535. "The Well of St. Leonard's College" was a notorious fountain of heresies, under Gawain Logie, the Principal. Knox very probably heard the sermons of the Dominicans and Franciscans "against the pride and idle life of bishops," and other abuses. He speaks of a private conversation between Friar Airth and Major (about 1534), and names some of the persons present at a sermon in the parish church of St. Andrews, as if he had himself been in the congregation. He gives the text and heads of the discourse, including "merry tales" told by the Friar. If Knox heard the sermons and stories of clerical scandals at St. Andrews, they did not prevent him from taking orders. His Greek and Hebrew, what there was of them, Knox must have acquired in later life, at least we never learn that he was taught by the famous George Wishart, who, about that time, gave Greek lectures at Montrose.

The Catholic opponents of Knox naturally told scandalous anecdotes concerning his youth. These are destitute of evidence: about his youth we know nothing. It is a characteristic trait in him, and a fact much to his credit, that, though he is fond of expatiating about himself, he never makes confessions as to his earlier adventures. On his own years of the wild oat St. Augustine dilates in a style which still has charm: but Knox, if he sowed wild oats, is silent as the tomb. If he has anything to repent, it is not to the world that he confesses. About the days when he was "one of Baal's shaven sort," in his own phrase; when he was himself an "idolater," and a priest of the altar: about the details of his conversion, Knox is mute. It is probable that, as a priest, he examined Lutheran books which were brought in with other merchandise from Holland; read the Bible for himself; and failed to find Purgatory, the Mass, the intercession of Saints, pardons, pilgrimages, and other accessories of mediæval religion in the Scriptures. Knox had only to keep his eyes and ears open, to observe the clerical ignorance and corruption which resulted in great part from the Scottish habit of securing wealthy Church offices for ignorant, brutal, and licentious younger sons and bastards of noble families. This practice in Scotland was as odious to good Catholics, like Quentin Kennedy, Ninian Winzet, and, rather earlier, to Ferrerius, as to Knox himself. The prevalent anarchy caused by the long minorities of the Stuart kings, and by the interminable wars with England, and the difficulty of communications with Rome, had enabled the nobles thus to rob and deprave the Church, and so to provide themselves with moral reasons good for robbing her again;

as a punishment for the iniquities which they had themselves introduced!

The almost incredible ignorance and profligacy of the higher Scottish clergy (with notable exceptions) in Knox's youth, are not matter of controversy. They are as frankly recognised by contemporary Catholic as by Protestant authors. In the very year of the destruction of the monasteries (1559) the abuses are officially stated, as will be told later, by the last Scottish Provincial Council. Though three of the four Scottish universities were founded by Catholics, and the fourth, Edinburgh, had an endowment bequeathed by a Catholic, the clerical ignorance, in Knox's time, was such that many priests could hardly read.

If more evidence is needed as to the debauched estate of the Scottish clergy, we obtain it from Mary of Guise, widow of James V., the Regent then governing Scotland for her child, Mary Stuart. The Queen, in December 1555, begged Pius IV. to permit her to levy a tax on her clergy, and to listen to what Cardinal Sermoneta would tell him about their need of reformation. The Cardinal drew a terrible sketch of the nefarious lives of "every kind of religious women" in Scotland. They go about with their illegal families and dower their daughters out of the revenues of the Church. The monks, too, have bloated wealth, while churches are allowed to fall into decay. "The only hope is in the Holy Father," who should appoint an episcopal commission of visitation. For about forty years prelates have been alienating Church lands illegally, and churches and monasteries, by the avarice of those placed in charge, are crumbling to decay. Bishops are the chief dealers in cattle, fish, and hides, though we have, in fact, good evidence that their dealings were very limited, "sma' sums."

Not only the clergy, but the nobles and people were lawless. "They are more difficult to manage than ever," writes Mary of Guise (Jan. 13, 1557). They are recalcitrant against law and order; every attempt at introducing these is denounced as an attack on their old laws: not that their laws are bad, but that they are badly administered. Scotland, in brief, had always been lawless, and for centuries had never been godly. She was untouched by the first fervour of the Franciscan and other religious revivals. Knox could not fail to see what was so patent: many books of the German reformers may have come in his way; no more was wanted than the preaching of George Wishart in 1543-45, to make him an irreconcilable foe of the doctrine as well as the discipline of his Church.

Knox had a sincerely religious nature, and a conviction that he was, more than most men, though a sinner, in close touch with Him "in whom we live and move and have our being." We ask ourselves, had Knox, as "a priest of the altar," never known the deep emotions, which tongue may not utter, that the ceremonies and services of his Church so naturally awaken in the soul of the believer? These emotions, if they were in his experience, he never remembered tenderly, he flung them from him without regret; not regarding them even as dreams, beautiful and dear, but misleading, that came through the Ivory Gate. To Knox's opponent in controversy, Quentin Kennedy, the mass was "the blessed Sacrament of the Altar . . . which is one of the chief Sacraments whereby our Saviour, for the salvation of mankind, has appointed the fruit of His death and passion to be daily renewed and applied." In this traditional view there is nothing unedifying, nothing injurious to the Christian life. But to Knox the wafer is an idol, a god "of water and meal," "but a feeble and miserable god," that can be destroyed "by a bold and puissant mouse." "Rats and mice will desire no better dinner than white round gods enough."

The Reformer and the Catholic take up the question "by different handles"; and the Catholic grounds his defence on a text about Melchizedek! To Knox the mass is the symbol of all that he justly detested in the degraded Church as she then was in Scotland, "that horrible harlot with her filthiness." To Kennedy it was what we have seen.

Knox speaks of having been in "the puddle of papistry." He loathes what he has left behind him, and it is natural to guess that, in his first years of priesthood, his religious nature slept; that he became a priest and notary merely that he "might eat a morsel of bread"; and that real "conviction" never was his till his studies of Protestant controversialists, and also of St. Augustine and the Bible, and the teaching of Wishart, raised him from a mundane life. Then he awoke to a passionate horror and hatred of his old routine of "mumbled masses," of "rites of human invention," whereof he had never known the poetry and the mystic charm. Had he known them, he could not have so denied and detested them. On the other hand, when once he had embraced the new ideas, Knox's faith in them, or in his own form of them, was firm as the round world, made so fast that it cannot be moved. He had now a *pou sto*, whence he could, and did, move the world of human affairs. A faith not to be shaken, and enormous energy were the essential attributes of the Reformer. It is almost impossible to find an instance in which Knox allows that he may have been mistaken: *d'avoir toujours raison* was his claim. If he admits an error in details, it is usually an error of insufficient severity. He did not attack Northumberland or Mary Stuart with adequate violence; he did not disapprove enough of our prayer book; he did not hand a heretic over to the magistrates.

While acting as a priest and notary, between 1540, at latest, and 1543, Knox was engaged as private tutor to a boy named Brounefield, son of Brounefield of Greenlaw, and to other lads, spoken of as his "bairns." In this profession of tutor he continued till 1547.

Knox's personal aspect did not give signs of the uncommon strength which his unceasing labours demanded, but, like many men of energy, he had a perpetual youth of character and vigour. After his death, Peter Young described him as he appeared in his later years. He was somewhat below the "just" standard of height, his limbs were well and elegantly shaped; his shoulders broad, his fingers rather long, his head small, his hair black, his face somewhat swarthy, and not unpleasant to behold. There was a certain geniality in a countenance serious and stern, with a natural dignity and air of command; his eyebrows, when he was in anger, were expressive. His forehead was rather narrow, depressed above the eyebrows; his cheeks were full and ruddy, so that the eyes seemed to retreat into their hollows: they were dark grey, keen, and lively. The face was long, the nose also; the mouth was large, the upper lip being the thicker. The beard was long, rather thick and black, with a few grey hairs in his later years. The nearest approach to an authentic portrait of Knox is a woodcut, engraved after a sketch from memory by Peter

13

Knox's faults

Young, and after another sketch of the same kind by an artist in Edinburgh. Compared with the peevish face of Calvin, also in Beza's *Icones*, Knox looks a broad-minded and genial character.

Despite the uncommon length to which Knox carried the contemporary approval of persecution, then almost universal, except among the Anabaptists (and any party out of power), he was not personally rancorous where religion was not concerned. But concerned it usually was! He was the subject of many anonymous pasquils and libels, we know, but he entirely disregarded them. If he hated any mortal personally, and beyond what true religion demands of a Christian, that mortal was the mother of Mary Stuart, an amiable lady in an impossible position. Of jealousy towards his brethren there is not a trace in Knox, and he told Queen Mary that he could ill bear to correct his own boys, though the age was as cruel to schoolboys as that of St. Augustine.

The faults of Knox arose not in his heart, but in his head; they sprung from intellectual errors, and from the belief that he was always right. He applied to his fellow-Christians—Catholics—the commands which early Israel supposed to be divinely directed against foreign worshippers of Chemosh and Moloch. He endeavoured to force his own theory of what the discipline of the Primitive Apostolic Church had been upon a modern nation, following the example of the little city state of Geneva, under Calvin. He claimed for preachers chosen by local congregations the privileges and powers of the apostolic companions of Christ, and in place of "sweet reasonableness," he applied the methods, quite alien to the Founder of Christianity, of the "Sons of Thunder." All controversialists then relied on isolated and inappropriate scriptural texts, and Biblical analogies which were not analogous; but Knox employed these things, with perhaps unusual inconsistency, in varying circumstances. His "History" is not more scrupulous than that of other partisans in an exciting contest, and examples of his taste for personal scandal are not scarce.

As to Andrew Lang wrote, his fault arose 'not in his heart, but in his head'. A defensive neurotic belief that he was always right; that he forced Old Testament anachronisms on his contemporaries

CHAPTER II.

KNOX, WISHART, AND THE MURDER OF BEATON: 1545-1546

Our earliest knowledge of Knox, apart from mention of him in notarial documents, is derived from his own *History of the Reformation*. The portion of that work in which he first mentions himself was written about 1561-66, some twenty years after the events recorded, and in reading all this part of his Memoirs, and his account of the religious struggle, allowance must be made for errors of memory, or for erroneous information. We meet him first towards the end of "the holy days of Yule"—Christmas, 1545. Knox had then for some weeks been the constant companion and armed bodyguard of George Wishart, who was calling himself "the messenger of the Eternal God," and preaching the new ideas in Haddington to very small congregations. This Wishart, Knox's master in the faith, was a Forfarshire man; he is said to have taught Greek at Montrose, to have been driven thence in 1538 by the Bishop of Brechin, and to have recanted certain heresies in 1539. He had denied the merits of Christ as the Redeemer, but afterwards dropped that error, when persistence meant death at the stake. It was in Bristol that he "burned his faggot," in place of being burned himself. There was really nothing humiliating in this recantation, for, after his release, he did not resume his heresy; clearly he yielded, not to fear, but to conviction of theological error.

He next travelled in Germany, where a Jew, on a Rhine boat, inspired or increased his aversion to works of sacred art, as being "idolatrous." About 1542-43 he was reading with pupils at Cambridge, and was remarked for the severity of his ascetic virtue, and for his great charity. At some uncertain date he translated the Helvetic Confession of Faith, and he was more of a Calvinist than a Lutheran. In July 1543 he returned to Scotland; at least he returned with some "commissioners to England," who certainly came home in July 1543, as Knox mentions, though later he gives the date of Wishart's return in 1544, probably by a slip of the pen.

Coming home in July 1543, Wishart would expect a fair chance of preaching his novel ideas, as peace between Scotland and Protestant England now seemed secure, and Arran, the Scottish Regent, the chief of the almost Royal House of Hamilton, was, for the moment, himself a Protestant. For five days (August 28-September 3, 1543) the great Cardinal Beaton, the head of the party of the Church, was outlawed, and Wishart's preaching at Dundee, about that date, is supposed by some to have stimulated an attack then made on the monasteries in the town. But Arran suddenly recanted, deserted the Protestants and the faction attached to England, and joined forces with Cardinal Beaton, who, in November 1543, visited Dundee, and imprisoned the ringleaders in the riots. They are called "the honestest men in the town," by the treble traitor and rascal, Crichton, laird of Brunston in Lothian, at this time a secret agent of Sadleir, the envoy of Henry VIII. (November 25, 1543).

By April 1544, Henry was preparing to invade Scotland, and the "earnest professors" of Protestant doctrines in Scotland sent to him "a Scottish man called Wysshert," with a proposal for the kidnapping or murder of Cardinal Beaton. Brunston and other Scottish lairds of Wishart's circle were agents of the plot, and in 1545-46 our George Wishart is found companioning with them. When Cassilis took up the threads of the plot against Beaton, it was to Cassilis's country in Ayrshire that Wishart went and there preached. Thence he returned to Dundee, to fight the plague and comfort the citizens, and, towards the end of 1545, moved to Lothian, expecting to be joined there by his westland supporters, led by Cassilis—but entertaining dark forebodings of his doom.

There were, however, other Wisharts, Protestants, in Scotland. It is not possible to prove that this reformer, though the associate, was the agent of the murderers, or was even conscious of their schemes. Yet if he had been, there was no matter for marvel. Knox himself approved of and applauded the murders of Cardinal Beaton and of Riccio, and, in that age, too many men of all creeds and parties believed that to kill an opponent of their religious cause was to imitate Phinehas, Jael, Jehu, and other patriots of Hebrew history. Dr. M'Crie remarks that Knox "held the opinion, that persons who, according to the law of God and the just laws of society, have forfeited their lives by the commission of flagrant crimes, such as notorious murderers and tyrants, may warrantably be put to death by private individuals, provided all redress in the ordinary course of justice is rendered impossible, in consequence of the offenders having usurped the executive authority, or being systematically protected by oppressive rulers." The ideas of Knox, in fact, varied in varying circumstances and moods, and, as we shall show, at times he preached notions far more truculent than those attributed to him by his biographer; at times was all for saint-like submission and mere "passive resistance."

The current ideas of both parties on "killing no murder" were little better than those of modern anarchists. It was a prevalent opinion that a king might have a subject assassinated, if to try him publicly entailed political inconveniences. The Inquisition, in Spain, vigorously repudiated this theory, but the Inquisition was in advance of the age. Knox, as to the doctrine of "killing no murder," was, and Wishart may have been, a man of his time. But Knox, in telling the story of a murder which he approves, unhappily displays a glee unbecoming a reformer of the Church of Him who blamed St. Peter for his recourse to the sword. The very essence of Christianity is cast to the winds when Knox utters his laughter over the murders or misfortunes of his opponents, yielding, as Dr. M'Crie says, "to the strong propensity which he felt to indulge his vein of humour." Other good men rejoiced in the murder of an enemy, but Knox chuckled.

Nothing has injured Knox more in the eyes of posterity (when they happen to be aware of the facts) than this "humour" of his.

Knox might be pardoned had he merely excused the murder of "the devil's own son," Cardinal Beaton, who executed the law on his friend and master, George Wishart. To Wishart Knox bore a tender and enthusiastic affection, crediting him not only with the virtues of charity and courage which he possessed, but also with supernormal premonitions; "he was so clearly illuminated with the spirit of prophecy." These premonitions appear to have come to Wishart by way of vision. Knox asserted some prophetic gift for himself, but never hints anything as to the method, whether by dream, vision, or the hearing of voices. He often alludes to himself as "the prophet," and claims certain privileges in that capacity. For example the prophet may blamelessly preach what men call "treason," as we shall see. As to his actual predictions of events, he occasionally writes as if they were mere deductions from Scripture. God will punish the idolater; A or B is an idolater; therefore it is safe to predict that God will punish him or her. "What man then can cease to prophesy?" he asks; and there is, if we thus consider the matter, no reason why anybody should ever leave off prophesying.

But if the art of prophecy is common to all Bible-reading mankind, all mankind, being prophets, may promulgate treason, which Knox perhaps would not have admitted. He thought himself more specially a seer, and in his prayer after the failure of his friends, the murderers of Riccio, he congratulates himself on being favoured above the common sort of his brethren, and privileged to "forespeak" things, in an unique degree.

"I dare not deny . . . but that God hath revealed unto me secrets unknown to the world," he writes ; and these claims soar high above mere deductions from Scripture. His biographer, Dr. M'Crie, doubts whether we can dismiss, as necessarily baseless, all stories of "extraordinary premonitions since the completion of the canon of inspiration." Indeed, there appears to be no reason why we should draw the line at a given date, and "limit the operations of divine Providence." I would be the last to do so, but then Knox's premonitions are sometimes, or usually, without documentary and contemporary corroboration; once he certainly prophesied after the event (as we shall see), and he never troubles himself about his predictions which were unfulfilled, as against Queen Elizabeth.

He supplied the Kirk with the tradition of supernormal premonitions in preachers—second-sight and clairvoyance—as in the case of Mr. Peden and other saints of the Covenant. But just as good cases of clairvoyance as any of Mr. Peden's are attributed to Catherine de Medici, who was not a saint, by her daughter, La Reine Margot, and others. In Knox, at all events, there is no trace of visual or auditory hallucinations, so common in religious experiences, whatever the creed of the percipient. He was not a visionary. More than this we cannot safely say about his prophetic vein.

The enthusiasm which induced a priest, notary, and teacher like Knox to carry a claymore in defence of a beloved teacher, Wishart, seems more appropriate to a man of about thirty than a man of forty, and, so far, supports the opinion that, in 1545, Knox was only thirty years of age. In that case, his study of the debates between the Church and the new opinions must have been relatively brief. Yet, in 1547, he already reckoned himself, not incorrectly, as a skilled disputant in favour of ideas with which he cannot have been very long familiar.

Wishart was taken, was tried, was condemned; was strangled, and his dead body was burned at St. Andrews on March 1, 1546. It is highly improbable that Knox could venture, as a marked man, to be present at the trial. He cites the account of it in his "History" from the contemporary Scottish narrative used by Foxe in his "Martyrs," and Laing, Knox's editor, thinks that Foxe "may possibly have been indebted for some" of the Scottish accounts "to the Scottish

Reformer." It seems, if there be anything in evidence of tone and style, that what Knox quotes from Foxe in 1561-66 is what Knox himself actually wrote about 1547-48. Mr. Hill Burton observes in the tract "the mark of Knox's vehement colouring," and adds, "it is needless to seek in the account for precise accuracy." In "precise accuracy" many historians are as sadly to seek as Knox himself, but his peculiar "colouring" is all his own, and is as marked in the pamphlet on Wishart's trial, which he cites, as in the "History" which he acknowledged.

There are said to be but few copies of the first edition of the black letter tract on Wishart's trial, published in London, with Lindsay's "Tragedy of the Cardinal," by Day and Seres. I regard it as the earliest printed work of John Knox. The author, when he describes Lauder, Wishart's official accuser, as "a fed sow . . . his face running down with sweat, and frothing at the mouth like ane bear," who "spat at Maister George's face, . . . " shows every mark of Knox's vehement and pictorial style. His editor, Laing, bids us observe "that all these opprobrious terms are copied from Foxe, or rather from the black letter tract." But the black letter tract, I conceive, must be Knox's own. Its author, like Knox, "indulges his vein of humour" by speaking of friars as "fiends"; like Knox he calls Wishart "Maister George," and "that servand of God."

The peculiarities of the tract, good and bad, the vivid familiar manner, the vehemence, the pictorial quality, the violent invective, are the notes of Knox's "History." Already, by 1547, or not much later, he was the perfect master of his style; his tone no more resembles that of his contemporary and fellow-historian, Lesley, than the style of Mr. J. R. Green resembles that of Mr. S. R. Gardiner.

hove into view, and on June 30 summoned the castle to surrender. The siege of St Andrews Castle, from the sea, by the French then began, but the garrison and castle were unharmed, and many of the galley slaves and some French soldiers were slain, and a ship was driven out of action. The French "shot two days" only. On July 19 the siege was renewed by land, guns were mounted on the spires of St. Salvator's College chapel and on the Cathedral, and did much scathe, though, during the first three weeks of the siege, the garrison "had many prosperous chances." Meanwhile Knox prophesied the defeat of his associates, because of "their corrupt life." They had robbed and ravished, and were probably demoralised by Knox's prophecies. On the last day of July the castle surrendered. Knox adds that his friends would deal with France alone, as "Scottish men had all traitorously betrayed them."

Now much of this narrative is wrong; wrong in detail, in suggestion, in omission. That a man of fifty, or sixty, could attribute the attacks on Beaton's murderers to mere revenge, specially to that of a "wanton widow," Mary of Guise (who had, we are to believe, so much of the Cardinal's attentions as his mistress, Mariotte Ogilvy, could spare), is significant of the spirit in which Knox wrote history. He had a strong taste for such scandals as this about the "wanton widow."

Wherever he touches on Mary of Guise (who once treated him in a spirit of banter), he deals a stab at her name and fame. On all that concerns her personal character and political conduct, he is unworthy of credit when uncorroborated by better authority. Indeed Knox's spirit is so unworthy that for this, among other reasons, Archbishop Spottiswoode declined to believe in his authorship of the "History." The actual facts were not those recorded by Knox.

As regards the "Appointment" or arrangement of the Scottish Government with the Castilians, it was not made late in January 1547, but was at least begun by December 17-19, 1546. On January 11, 1547, a spy of England, Stewart of Cardonald, reports that the garrison have given pledges and await their absolution from Rome. With regard to Knox's other statements in this place, it was not *after* this truce, first, but before it, on November 26, that Arran invited French assistance, if England would not include Scotland in a treaty of peace with France. An English invasion was expected in February 1547, and Arran's object in the "Appointment" with the garrison was to prevent the English from becoming possessed of the Castle of St. Andrews. Far from desiring a papal pardon—a mere pretext to gain time for English relief—the garrison actually asked Henry VIII. to request the Emperor, to implore the Pope, "to stop and hinder their absolution." Knox very probably knew nothing of all this, but his efforts to throw the blame of treachery on his opponents are obviously futile.

As to the honesty of his associates—before the death of Henry VIII. (January 28, 1547), the Castilians had promised him not to surrender the place without his consent, and to put Arran's son in his hands, promises which they also made, on Henry's death, to the English Government; in February they repeated these promises, quite incompatible with their vow to surrender if absolved. Knox represents them as merely promising to Henry that they would return Arran's son, and support the plan of marrying Mary Stuart to Prince Edward of Wales! In March 1547, English ships gathered at Holy Island, to relieve the castle. Not on June 21, 1547, as Knox alleges, but before April 2, the papal absolution for the murderers arrived. They mocked at it; and the spy who reports the facts is told that they "would rather have a boll of wheat than all the Pope's remissions." Whatever the terms of the papal remission, they had already, before it arrived, bound themselves to England not to accept it save with English concurrence; and England, then preparing to invade Scotland, could not possibly concur. Such was the honesty of Knox's party, and we already see how far his "History" deserves to be accepted as historical.

Next, what is most surprising, Knox's account of the month of ineffectual siege by the French, while he was actually in the castle, rests on a strange error of his memory. The contemporary diary, *Diurnal of Occurrences* dates the *sending* (the arrival must be meant) of the French galleys, not on June 29, as Knox dates their arrival, but on July 24. Professor Hume Brown says that the *Diurnal* gives the date as *June* 24 (a slip of the pen), "but Knox had surely the best opportunity of knowing both facts" —that is, the number of the galleys, and the date of their coming. Despite his unrivalled opportunities of knowledge, Knox did not know. It is not quite correct to say that "Knox in his 'History' shows throughout a conscientious regard to accuracy of statement." Whatever the number of the galleys (Knox says twenty-one; the *Diurnal* says sixteen), on July 13-14, they are reported by Lord Eure, at Berwick, as passing or having just passed Eyemouth. They did not therefore suffer for three weeks at the garrison's hands, or for three weeks desert the siege, but probably reached the scene of action before the date in the *Diurnal* (July 24), as, on July 23, the French Ambassador in England heard that they were investing the castle. Allowing five or six days for transmission of news, they probably began the attack from the sea about July 16 or 17, not, as Knox says, on June 30. Perhaps he is right in saying that the French galleys only fired for two days and retreated, rather battered, to Dundee. Land forces next attacked the hold, which surrendered on July 29 (as was known in London on August 5), that is, on the first day that the *land* battery was erected.

Knox gives a much more full account of his own controversies, in April-June 1547, than of political events. He first, on arrival at the castle, drew up a catechism for his pupils, and publicly catechised them on its tenets, in the parish kirk in South Street. It is unfortunate that we do not possess this catechism. At the time when he wrote, Knox was possibly more of "Martin's" mind, as he familiarly terms Luther, both as to the Sacrament and as to the Order of Bishops, than he was after his residence in Geneva. Wishart, however, was well acquainted with Helvetic doctrine; he had, as we saw, translated a Helvetic Confession of Faith, perhaps with the view of introducing it into Scotland, and Knox may already have imbibed Calvinism from him. He was not yet—he never was—a full-blown Presbyterian, and, while thinking nothing of "orders," would not have rejected a bishop, if the bishop *preached* and was of godly and frugal life. Already sermons were the most important part of public worship in the mind of Knox.

In addition to public catechising he publicly expounded, and lectured on the Fourth Gospel, in the chapel of the castle. He doubted if he had "a lawful vocation" to *preach*. The castle pulpit was then occupied by an ex-friar named Rough. This divine, later burned in

25

England, preached a sermon declaring a doctrine accepted by Knox, namely, that any congregation could call on any man in whom they "espied the gifts of God" to be their preacher; he offered Knox the post, and all present agreed. Knox wept, and for days his gloom declared his sense of his responsibility: such was "his holy vocation." The garrison was, confessedly, brutal, licentious, and rapacious, but they "all" partook of the holy Communion.

In controversy, Knox declared the Church to be "the synagogue of Satan," and in the Pope he detected and denounced "the Man of Sin." On the following Sunday he proved, from Daniel, that the Roman Church is "that last Beast." The Church is also anti-Christ, and "the Hoore of Babylon," and Knox dilated on the personal misconduct of Popes and "all shavelings for the most part." He contrasted Justification by Faith with the customs of pardons and pilgrimages.

After these remarks, a controversy was held between Knox and the sub-prior, Wynram, the Scottish Vicar of Bray, Knox being understood to maintain that no bishop who did not preach was really a bishop; that the Mass is "abominable idolatry"; that Purgatory does not exist; and that the tithes are not necessarily the property of churchmen—a doctrine very welcome to the hungry nobles of Scotland. Knox, of course, easily overcame an ignorant opponent, a friar, who joined in the fray. His own arguments he later found time to write out fully in the French galleys, in which he was a prisoner, after the fall of the castle. If he "wrate in the galleys," as he says, they cannot have been always such floating hells as they are usually reckoned.

That Knox, and other captives from the castle, were placed in the galleys after their surrender, was an abominable stretch of French power. They were not subjects of France. The terms on which they surrendered are not exactly known. Knox avers that they were to be free to live in France, and that, if they wished to leave, they were to be conveyed, at French expense, to any country except Scotland. Buchanan declares that only the lives of the garrison and their friends were secured by the terms of surrender. Lesley supports Knox, who is probably accurate.

To account for the French severity, Knox tells us that the Pope insisted on it, appealing to both the Scottish and French Governments; and Scotland sent an envoy to France to beg "that those of the castle should be sharply handled." Men of birth were imprisoned, the rest went to the galleys. Knox's life cannot have been so bad as that of the Huguenot galley slaves under Louis XIV. He was allowed to receive letters; he read and commented on a treatise written in prison by Balnaves; and he even wrote a theological work, unless this work was his commentary on Balnaves. These things can only have been possible when the galleys were not on active service. In a very manly spirit, he never dilated on his sufferings, and merely alludes to "the torment I sustained in the galleys." He kept up his heart, always prophesying deliverance; and once (June, 1548?), when in view of St. Andrews, declared that he should preach again in the kirk where his career began. Unluckily, the person to whom he spoke, at a moment when he himself was dangerously ill, denied that he had ever been in the galleys at all! He was Sir James Balfour, a notorious scoundrel, quite untrustworthy; according to Knox, he had spoken of the prophecy, in Scotland, long before its fulfilment.

Knox's health was more or less undermined, while his spiritual temper was not mollified by nineteen months of the galleys, mitigated as they obviously were.

It is, doubtless, to his "torment" in the galleys that Knox refers when he writes: "I know how hard the battle is between the spirit and the flesh, under the heavy cross of affliction, where no worldly defence, but present death, does appear. . . . Rests only Faith, provoking us to call earnestly, and pray for assistance of God's spirit, wherein if we continue, our most desperate calamities shall turn to gladness, and to a prosperous end. . . . With experience I write this."

In February or March, 1549, Knox was released; by April he was in England, and, while Edward VI. lived, was in comparative safety.

27

CHAPTER IV.

KNOX IN ENGLAND: THE BLACK RUBRIC: EXILE: 1549-1554

Knox at once appeared in England in a character revolting to the later Presbyterian conscience, which he helped to educate. The State permitted no cleric to preach without a Royal license, and Knox was now a State licensed preacher at Berwick, one of many "State officials with a specified mission." He was an agent of the English administration, then engaged in forcing a detested religion on the majority of the English people. But he candidly took his own line, indifferent to the compromises of the rulers in that chaos of shifting opinions. For example, the Prayer Book of Edward VI. at that time took for granted kneeling as the appropriate attitude for communicants. Knox, at Berwick, on the other hand, bade his congregation sit, as he conceived that to have been the usage at the first institution of the rite. Possibly the Apostles, in fact, supped in a recumbent attitude, as Cranmer justly remarked later (John xiii. 25), but Knox supposed them to have sat. In a letter to his Berwick flock, he reminds them of his practice on this point; but he would not dissent from kneeling if "magistrates make known, as that they" (would?) "have done if ministers were willing to do their duties, that kneeling is not retained in the Lord's Supper for maintenance of any superstition," much less as "adoration of the Lord's Supper." This, "for a time," would content him: and this he obtained. Here Knox appears to make the civil authority—"the magistrates"—governors of the Church, while at the same time he does not in practice obey them unless they accept his conditions.

This letter to the Berwick flock must be prior to the autumn of 1552, in which, as we shall see, Knox obtained his terms as to kneeling. He went on, in his epistle to the Berwickians, to speak in "a tone of moderation and modesty," for which, says Dr. Lorimer, not many readers will be prepared. In this modest passage, Knox says that, as to "the chief points of religion," he, with God's help, "will give place to neither man nor angel teaching the contrary" of his preaching. Yet an angel might be supposed to be well informed on points of doctrine! "But as to ceremonies or rites, things of smaller weight, I was not minded to move contention. . . ." The one point which—"because I am but one, having in my contrary magistrates, common order, and judgments, and many learned"—he is prepared to yield, and that for a time, is the practice of kneeling, but only on three conditions. These being granted, "with patience will I bear that one thing, daily thirsting and calling unto God for reformation of that and others." But he did not bear that one thing; he would *not* kneel even after his terms were granted! This is the sum of Knox's "moderation and modesty"!

Though he is not averse from talking about himself, Knox, in his "History," spares but three lines to his five years' residence in England (1549-54). His first charge was Berwick (1549-51), where we have seen he celebrated holy Communion by the Swiss rite, all meekly sitting. The Second Prayer Book, of 1552, when Knox ministered in Newcastle, bears marks of his hand. He opposed, as has been said, the rubric bidding the communicants kneel; the attitude savoured of "idolatry."

The circumstances in which Knox carried his point on this question are most curious. Just before October 12, 1552, a foreign Protestant, Johannes Utenhovius, wrote to the Zurich Protestant, Bullinger, to the effect that a certain *vir bonus*, *Scotus natione* (a good man and a Scot), a preacher (*concionator*), of the Duke of Northumberland, had delivered a sermon before the King and Council, "in which he freely inveighed against the Anglican custom of kneeling at the Lord's Supper." Many listeners were greatly moved, and Utenhovius prayed that the sermon might be of blessed effect. Knox was certainly in London at this date, and was almost certainly the excellent Scot referred to by Utenhovius. The Second Prayer Book of Edward VI. was then in such forwardness that Parliament had appointed it to be used in churches, beginning on November 1. The book included the command to kneel at the Lord's Supper, and any agitation against the practice might seem to be too late. Cranmer, the Primate, was in favour of the rubric as it stood, and on October 7, 1552, addressed the Privy Council in a letter which, without naming Knox, clearly shows his opinion of our Reformer. The book, *as it stood*, said Cranmer, had the assent of King and Parliament—now it was to be altered, apparently, "without Parliament." The Council ought not to be thus influenced by "glorious and unquiet spirits." Cranmer calls Knox, as Throckmorton later called Queen Mary's Bothwell, "glorious" in the sense of the Latin *gloriosus*, "swaggering," or "arrogant."

Cranmer goes on to denounce the "glorious and unquiet spirits, which can like nothing but that is after their own fancy, and cease not to make trouble and disquietude when things be most quiet and in good order." Their argument (Knox's favourite), that whatever is not commanded in Scripture is unlawful and ungodly, "is a subversion of all order as well in religion as in common policy."

Cranmer ends with the amazing challenge: "I will set my foot by his to be tried in the fire, that his doctrine is untrue, and not only untrue but seditious, and perilous to be heard of any subjects, as a thing breaking the bridle of obedience and loosing them from the bond of all princes' laws."

Cranmer had a premonition of the troubled years of James VI. and of the Covenant, when this question of kneeling was the first cause of the Bishops' wars. But Knox did not accept, as far as we know, the mediæval ordeal by fire.

Other questions about practices enjoined in the Articles arose. A "Confession," in which Knox's style may be traced, was drawn up, and consequently that "Declaration on Kneeling" was intercalated into the Prayer Book, wherein it is asserted that the attitude does not imply adoration of the elements, or belief in the Real Presence, "for that were idolatry." Elizabeth dropped, and Charles II. restored, this "Black Rubric" which Anglicanism owes to the Scottish Reformer. He "once had a good opinion," he says, of the Liturgy as it now stood, but he soon found that it was full of idolatries.

The most important event in the private life of Knox, during his stay at Berwick, was his acquaintance with a devout lady of tormented conscience, Mrs. Bowes, wife of the Governor of Norham Castle on Tweed. Mrs. Bowes's tendency to the new ideas in religion was not shared by her husband and his family; the results will presently be conspicuous. In April 1550, Knox preached at Newcastle a sermon on his favourite doctrine that the Mass is "Idolatry," because it is "of man's invention," an opinion not shared by Tunstall, then Bishop of Durham. Knox used "idolatry" in a constructive sense, as when we talk of "constructive treason." But, in practice, he regarded Catholics as "idolaters," in the same sense as Elijah regarded Hebrew worshippers of alien deities, Chemosh or Moloch, and he later drew the inference that idolaters, as in the Old Testament, must be put to death. Thus his was logically a persecuting religion.

Knox was made a King's chaplain and transferred to Newcastle. He saw that the country was, by preference, Catholic; that the life of Edward VI. hung on a thread; and that with the accession of his sister, Mary Tudor, Protestant principles would be as unsafe as under "umquhile the Cardinal." Knox therefore, "from the foresight of troubles to come" (so he writes to Mrs. Bowes, February 28, 1554), declined any post, a bishopric, or a living, which would in honour oblige him to face the fire of persecution. At the same time he was even then far at odds with the Church of England that he had sound reasons for refusing benefices.

On Christmas day, 1552, he preached at Newcastle against Papists, as "thirsting nothing more than the King's death, which their iniquity would procure." In two brief years Knox was himself publicly expressing his own thirst for the Queen's death, and praying for a Jehu or a Phinehas, slayers of idolaters, such as Mary Tudor. If any fanatic had taken this hint, and the life of Mary Tudor, Catholics would have said that Knox's "iniquity procured" the murder, and they would have had fair excuse for the assertion.

Meanwhile charges were brought against the Reformer, on the ground of his Christmas sermon of peace and goodwill. Northumberland (January 9, 1552-53) sends to Cecil "a letter of poor Knox, by the which you may perceive what perplexity the poor soul remaineth in at this present." We have not Knox's interesting letter, but Northumberland pled his cause against a charge of treason. In fact, however, the Court highly approved of his sermon. He was presently again in what he believed to be imminent danger of life: "I fear that I be not yet ripe, nor able to glorify Christ by my faith," he wrote to Mrs. Bowes, "but what lacketh now, God shall perform in His own time." We do not know what peril threatened the Reformer now (probably in March 1553), but he frequently, later, seems to have doubted his own "ripeness" for martyrdom. His reluctance to suffer did not prevent him from constant attendance to the tedious self-tormentings of Mrs. Bowes, and of "three honest poor women" in London.

Knox, at all events, was not so "perplexed" that he feared to speak his mind in the pulpit. In Lent, 1553, preaching before the boy king, he denounced his ministers in trenchant historical parallels between them and Achitophel, Shebna, and Judas. Later, young Mr. Mackail, applying the same method to the ministers of Charles II., was hanged. "What wonder is it then," said Knox, "that a young and innocent king be deceived by crafty, covetous, wicked, and ungodly councillors? I am greatly afraid that Achitophel be councillor, that

Judas bear the purse, and that Shebna be scribe, comptroller, and treasurer."

This appears the extreme of audacity. Yet nothing worse came to Knox than questions, by the Council, as to his refusal of a benefice, and his declining, as he still did, to kneel at the Communion (April 14, 1553). His answers prove that he was out of harmony with the fluctuating Anglicanism of the hour. Northumberland could not then resent the audacities of pulpiteers, because the Protestants were the only party who might stand by him in his approaching effort to crown Lady Jane Grey. Now all the King's preachers, obviously by concerted action, "thundered" against Edward's Council, in the Lent or Easter of 1553. Manifestly, in the old Scots phrase, "the Kirk had a back"; had some secular support, namely that of their party, which Northumberland could not slight. Meanwhile Knox was sent on a preaching tour in Buckinghamshire, and there he was when Edward VI. died, in the first week of July 1553.

Knox's official attachment to England expired with his preaching license, on the death of Edward VI. and the accession of Mary Tudor. He did not at once leave the country, but preached both in London and on the English border, while the new queen was settling herself on the throne. While within Mary's reach, Knox did not encourage resistance against that idolatress; he did not do so till he was safe in France. Indeed, in his prayer used after the death of Edward VI., before the fires of Oxford and Smithfield were lit, Knox wrote: "Illuminate the heart of our Sovereign Lady, Queen Mary, with pregnant gifts of the Holy Ghost. . . . Repress thou the pride of those that would rebel. . . . Mitigate the hearts of those that persecute us."

In the autumn of 1553, Knox's health was very bad; he had gravel, and felt his bodily strength broken. Moreover, he was in the disagreeable position of being betrothed to a very young lady, Marjorie Bowes, with the approval of her devout mother, the wife of Richard Bowes, commander of Norham Castle, near Berwick, but to the anger and disgust of the Bowes family in general. They by no means shared Knox's ideas of religion, rather regarding him as a penniless unfrocked "Scot runagate," whose alliance was discreditable and distasteful, and might be dangerous. "Maist unpleasing words" passed, and it is no marvel that Knox, being persecuted in one city, fled to another, leaving England for Dieppe early in March 1554.

His conscience was not entirely at ease as to his flight. "Why did I flee? Assuredly I cannot tell, but of one thing I am sure, the fear of death was not the chief cause of my fleeing," he wrote to Mrs. Bowes from Dieppe. "Albeit that I have, in the beginning of this battle, appeared to play the faint-hearted and feeble soldier (the cause I remit to God), yet my prayer is that I may be restored to the battle again." Knox was, in fact, most valiant when he had armed men at his back; he had no enthusiasm for taking part in the battle when unaided by the arm of flesh. On later occasions this was very apparent, and he has confessed, as we saw, that he did not choose to face "the trouble to come" without means of retreat. His valour was rather that of the general than of the lonely martyr. The popular idea of Knox's personal courage, said to have been expressed by the Regent Morton in the words spoken at his funeral, "here lieth a man who in his life never feared the face of man," is entirely erroneous. His learned and sympathetic editor, David Laing, truly writes: "Knox cannot be said to have possessed the impetuous and heroic boldness of a Luther when surrounded with danger. . . . On more than one occasion Knox displayed a timidity or shrinking from danger, scarcely to have been expected from one who boasted of his willingness to endure the utmost torture, or suffer death in his Master's cause. Happily he was not put to the test. . . ."

Dr. Laing puts the case more strongly than I feel justified in doing, for Knox, far from "boasting of his willingness to face the utmost torture," more than once doubts his own readiness for martyrdom. We must remember that even Blessed Edmund Campion, who went gaily to torture and death, had doubts as to the necessity of that journey.

Nor was there any reason why Knox should stay in England to be burned, if he could escape—with less than ten groats in his pocket—as he did. It is not for us moderns to throw the first stone at a reluctant martyr, still less to applaud useless self-sacrifice, but we do take leave to think that, having fled early, himself, from the martyr's crown, Knox showed bad taste in his harsh invectives against

Protestants who, staying in England, conformed to the State religion under Mary Tudor.

It is not impossible that his very difficult position as the lover of Marjorie Bowes—a position of which, while he remained in England, the burden fell on the poor girl—may have been one reason for Knox's flight, while the entreaties of his friends that he would seek safety must have had their influence.

On the whole it seems more probable that when he committed himself to matrimony with a young girl, the fifth daughter of Mrs. Bowes, he was approaching his fortieth rather than his fiftieth year. Older than he are happy husbands made, sometimes, though Marjorie Bowes's choice may have been directed by her pious mother, whose soul could find no rest in the old faith, and not much in the new.

At thirty-eight the Reformer, we must remember, must have been no uncomely wooer. His conversation must have been remarkably vivid: he had adventures enough to tell, by land and sea; while such a voice as he raised withal in the pulpit, like Edward Irving, has always been potent with women, as Sir Walter Scott remarks in Irving's own case. His expression, says Young, had a certain geniality; on the whole we need not doubt that Knox could please when he chose, especially when he was looked up to as a supreme authority. He despised women in politics, but had many friends of the sex, and his letters to them display a manly tenderness of affection without sentimentality.

Writing to Mrs. Bowes from London in 1553, Knox mentions, as one of the sorrows of life, that "such as would most gladly remain together, for mutual comfort, cannot be suffered so to do. Since the first day that it pleased the providence of God to bring you and me in familiarity, I have always delighted in your company." He then wanders into religious reflections, but we see that he liked Mrs. Bowes, and Marjorie Bowes too, no doubt: he is careful to style the elderly lady "Mother." Knox's letters to Mrs. Bowes show the patience and courtesy with which the Reformer could comfort and counsel a middle-aged lady in trouble about her innocent soul. As she recited her infirmities, he reminds her, he "started back, and that is my common consuetude when anything pierces or touches my heart. Call to your mind what I did standing at the cupboard at Alnwick; in very deed I thought that no creature had been tempted as I was"—not by the charms of Mrs. Bowes, of course: he found that Satan troubled the lady with "the very same words that he troubles me with." Mrs. Bowes, in truth, with premature scepticism, was tempted to think that "the Scriptures of God are but a tale, and no credit to be given to them." The Devil, she is reminded by Knox, has induced "some philosophers to affirm that the world never had a beginning," which he refutes by showing that God predicted the pains of childbearing; and Mrs. Bowes, as the mother of twelve, knows how true *this* is.

The circular argument may or may not have satisfied Mrs. Bowes.

The young object of Knox's passion, Marjorie Bowes, is only alluded to as "she whom God hath offered unto me, and commanded me to love as my own flesh,"—after her, Mrs. Bowes is the dearest of mankind to Knox. No mortal was ever more long-suffering with a spiritual hypochondriac, who avers that "the sins that reigned in Sodom and Gomore reign in me, and I have small power or none to resist!" Knox replies, with common sense, that Mrs. Bowes is obviously ignorant of the nature of these offences.

Writing to his betrothed he says nothing personal: merely reiterates his lessons of comfort to her mother. Meanwhile the lovers were parted, Knox going abroad; and it is to be confessed that he was not eager to come back.

CHAPTER V.

EXILE: APPEALS FOR A PHINEHAS, AND A JEHU: 1554

No change of circumstances could be much more bitter than that which exile brought to Knox. He had been a decently endowed official of State, engaged in bringing a reluctant country into the ecclesiastical fold which the State, for the hour, happened to prefer. His task had been grateful, and his congregations, at least at Berwick and Newcastle, had, as a rule, been heartily with him. Wherever he preached, affectionate women had welcomed him and hung upon his words. The King and his ministers had hearkened unto him—young Edward with approval, Northumberland with such emotions as we may imagine—while the Primate of England had challenged him to a competitive ordeal by fire, and had been defeated, apparently without recourse to the fire-test.

But now all was changed; Knox was a lonely rover in a strange land, supported probably by collections made among his English friends, and by the hospitality of the learned. In his wanderings his heart burned within him many a time, and he abruptly departed from his theory of passive resistance. Now he eagerly desired to obtain, from Protestant doctors and pontiffs, support for the utterly opposite doctrine of armed resistance. Such support he did not get, or not in a satisfactory measure, so he commenced prophet on his own lines, and on his own responsibility.

When Knox's heart burned within him, he sometimes seized the pen and dashed off fiery tracts which occasionally caused inconvenience to the brethren, and trouble to himself in later years. In cooler moments, and when dubious or prosperous, he now and again displayed a calm opportunism much at odds with the inspirations of his grief and anger.

After his flight to Dieppe in March 1554, Knox was engaged, then, with a problem of difficulty, one of the central problems of his career and of the distracted age. In modern phrase, he wished to know how far, and in what fashion, persons of one religion might resist another religion, imposed upon them by the State of which they were subjects. On this point we have now no doubt, but in the sixteenth century "Authority" was held sacred, and martyrdom, according to Calvin, was to be preferred to civil war. If men were Catholics, and if the State was Protestant, they were liable, later, under Knox, to fines, exile, and death; but power was not yet given to him. If they were Protestants under a Catholic ruler, or Puritans under Anglican authority, Knox himself had laid down the rule of their conduct in his letter to his Berwick congregation. "Remembering always, beloved brethren, that due obedience be given to magistrates, rulers, and princes, without tumult, grudge, or sedition. For, howsoever wicked themselves be in life, or howsoever ungodly their precepts or commandments be, ye must obey them for conscience' sake; except in chief points of religion, and then ye ought rather to obey God than man: *not to pretend to defend God's truth or religion, ye being subjects, by violence or sword, but patiently suffering what God shall please be laid upon you for constant confession of your faith and belief.*" Man or angel who teaches contrary doctrine is corrupt of judgment, sent by God to blind the unworthy. And Knox proceeded to teach contrary doctrine!

His truly Christian ideas are of date 1552, with occasional revivals as opportunity suggested. In exile he was now asking (1554), how was a Protestant minority or majority to oppose the old faith, backed by kings and princes, fire and sword? He answered the question in direct contradiction of his Berwick programme: he was now all for active resistance. Later, in addressing Mary of Guise, and on another occasion, he recurred to his Berwick theory, and he always found biblical texts to support his contradictory messages.

At this moment resistance seemed hopeless enough. In England the Protestants of all shades were decidedly in a minority. They had no chance if they openly rose in arms; their only hope was in the death of Mary Tudor and the succession of Elizabeth—itself a poor hope in the eyes of Knox, who detested the idea of a female monarch. Might they "bow down in the House of Rimmon" by a feigned conformity? Knox, in a letter to the Faithful, printed in 1554, entirely rejected this compromise, to which Cecil stooped, thereby deserving hell, as the relentless Knox (who had fled) later assured him.

In the end of March 1554, probably, Knox left Dieppe for Geneva, where he could consult Calvin, not yet secure in his despotism, though he had recently burned Servetus. Next he went to Zurich, and laid certain questions before Bullinger, who gave answers in writing as to Knox's problems.

Could a woman rule a kingdom by divine right, and transfer the same to her husband?—Mary Tudor to Philip of Spain, is, of course, to be understood. Bullinger replied that it was a hazardous thing for the godly to resist the laws of a country. Philip the eunuch, though converted, did not drive Queen Candace out of Ethiopia. If a tyrannous and ungodly Queen reign, godly persons "have example and consolation in the case of Athaliah." The transfer of power to a husband is an affair of the laws of the country.

Again, must a ruler who enforces "idolatry" be obeyed? May true believers, in command of garrisons, repel "this ungodly violence"? Bullinger answered, in effect, that "it is very difficult to pronounce upon every particular case." He had not the details before him. In short, nothing definite was to be drawn out of Bullinger.

Dr. M'Crie observes, indeed, that Knox submitted to the learned of Switzerland "certain difficult questions, which were suggested by the present condition of affairs in England, and about which his mind had been greatly occupied. Their views with respect to these coinciding with his own, he was confirmed in the judgment which he had already formed for himself."

In fact, Knox himself merely says that he had "reasoned with" pastors and the learned; he does not say that they agreed with him, and they certainly did not. Despite the reserve of Bullinger and of Calvin, Knox was of his new opinions still. These divines never backed his views.

By May, Knox had returned to Dieppe, and published an epistle to the Faithful. The rebellion of Sir Thomas Wyatt had been put down, a blow to true religion. We have no evidence that Knox stimulated the rising, but he alludes once to his exertions in favour of the Princess Elizabeth. The details are unknown.

In July, apparently, Knox printed his "Faithful Admonition to the Professors of God's Truth in England," and two editions of the tract were published in that country. The pamphlet is full of violent language about "the bloody, butcherly brood" of persecutors, and Knox spoke of what might have occurred had the Queen "been sent to hell before these days." The piece presents nothing, perhaps, so plain spoken about the prophet's right to preach treason as a passage in the manuscript of an earlier Knoxian epistle of May 1554 to the Faithful. "The prophets of God sometimes may teach treason against kings, and yet neither he, nor such as obey the word spoken in the Lord's name by him, offends God." That sentence contains doctrine not submitted to Bullinger by Knox. He could not very well announce himself to Bullinger as a "prophet of God." But the sentence, which occurs in manuscript copies of the letter of May 1554, does not appear in the black letter printed edition. Either Knox or the publisher thought it too risky.

In the published "Admonition," however, of July 1554, we find Knox exclaiming: "God, for His great mercy's sake, stir up some Phineas, Helias, or Jehu, that the blood of abominable idolaters may pacify God's wrath, that it consume not the whole multitude. Amen." This is a direct appeal to the assassin. If anybody will play the part of Phinehas against "idolaters"—that is the Queen of England and Philip of Spain—God's anger will be pacified. "Delay not thy vengeance, O Lord, but let death devour them in haste . . . For there is no hope of their amendment, . . . He shall send Jehu to execute his just judgments against idolaters. Jezebel herself shall not escape the vengeance and plagues that are prepared for her portion." These passages are essential. Professor Hume Brown expresses our own sentiments when he remarks: "In casting such a pamphlet into England at the time he did, Knox indulged his indignation, in itself so natural under the circumstances, at no personal risk, while he seriously compromised those who had the strongest claims on his most generous consideration." This is plain truth, and when some of Knox's English brethren later behaved to him in a manner which we must wholly condemn, their conduct, they said, had for a motive the mischief done to Protestants in England by his fiery "Admonition," and their desire to separate themselves from the author of such a pamphlet.

Knox did not, it will be observed, here call all or any of the faithful to a general massacre of their Catholic fellow-subjects. He went to that length later, as we shall show. In an epistle of 1554 he only writes: "Some shall demand, 'What then, shall we go and slay all idolaters?' *That* were the office, dear brethren, of every civil magistrate within his realm. . . . The slaying of idolaters appertains not to every particular man."

This means that every Protestant king should massacre all his inconvertible Catholic subjects! This was indeed a counsel of perfection; but it could never be executed, owing to the carnal policy of worldly men.

In writing about "the office of the civil magistrate," Knox, a Border Scot of the age of the blood feud, seems to have forgotten, first, that the Old Testament prophets of the period were not unanimous in their applause of Jehu's massacre of the royal family; next, that between the sixteenth century A.D. and Jehu, had intervened the Christian revelation. Our Lord had given no word of warrant to murder or massacre! No persecuted apostle had dealt in appeals to the dagger. As for Jehu, a prophet had condemned *his* conduct. Hosea writes that the Lord said unto him, "Yet a little while, and I will avenge the blood of Jezreel upon the house of Jehu," but doubtless Knox would have argued that Hosea was temporarily uninspired, as he argued about St. Paul and St. James later.

However this delicate point may be settled, the appeal for a Phinehas is certainly unchristian. The idolaters, the unreformed, might rejoice, with the Nuncio of 1583, that the Duc de Guise had a plan for murdering Elizabeth, though it was not to be communicated to the Vicar of God, who should have no such dealings against "that wicked woman." To some Catholics, Elizabeth: to Knox, Mary was as Jezebel, and might laudably be assassinated. In idolaters nothing can surprise us; when persecuted they, in their unchristian fashion, may retort with the dagger or the bowl. But that Knox should have frequently maintained the doctrine of death to religious opponents is a strange and deplorable circumstance. In reforming the Church of Christ he omitted some elements of Christianity.

Suppose, for a moment, that in deference to the teaching of the Gospel, Knox had never called for a Jehu, but had ever denounced, by voice and pen, those murderous deeds of his own party which he celebrates as "godly facts," he would have raised Protestantism to a moral pre-eminence. Dark pages of Scottish history might never have been written: the consciences of men might have been touched, and the cruelties of the religious conflict might have been abated. Many of them sprang from the fear of assassination.

But Knox in some of his writings identified his cause with the palace revolutions of an ancient Oriental people. Not that he was a man of blood; when in France he dissuaded Kirkcaldy of Grange and others from stabbing the gaolers in making their escape from prison. Where idolaters in official position were concerned, and with a pen in his hand, he had no such scruples. He was a child of the old pre-Christian scriptures; of the earlier, not of the later prophets.

CHAPTER VI.

KNOX IN THE ENGLISH PURITAN TROUBLES AT FRANKFORT: 1554-1555

The consequences of the "Admonition" came home to Knox when English refugees in Frankfort, impeded by him and others in the use of their Liturgy, accused him of high treason against Philip and Mary, and the Emperor, whom he had compared to Nero as an enemy of Christ.

The affair of "The Troubles at Frankfort" brought into view the great gulf for ever fixed between Puritanism and the Church of England. It was made plain that Knox and the Anglican community were of incompatible temperaments, ideas, and, we may almost say, instincts. To Anglicans like Cranmer, Knox, from the first, was as antipathetic as they were to him. "We can assure you," wrote some English exiles for religion's sake to Calvin, "that that outrageous pamphlet of Knox's" (his "Admonition") "added much oil to the flame of persecution in England. For before the publication of that book not one of our brethren had suffered death; but as soon as it came forth we doubt not but you are well aware of the number of excellent men who have perished in the flames; to say nothing of how many other godly men have been exposed to the risk of all their property, and even life itself, on the sole ground of either having had this book in their possession or having read it."

Such were the charges brought against Knox by these English Protestant exiles, fleeing from the persecution that followed the "Admonition," and, they say, took fresh ferocity from that tract.

The quarrel between Knox and them definitely marks the beginning of the rupture between the fathers of the Church of England and the fathers of Puritanism, Scottish Presbyterianism, and Dissent. The representatives of Puritans and of Anglicans were now alike exiled, poor, homeless, without any abiding city. That they should instantly quarrel with each other over their prayer book (that which Knox had helped to correct) was, as Calvin told them, "extremely absurd." Each faction probably foresaw—certainly Knox's party foresaw—that, in the English congregation at Frankfort, a little flock barely tolerated, was to be settled the character of Protestantism in England, if ever England returned to Protestantism. "This evil" (the acceptance of the English Second Book of Prayer of Edward VI.) "shall in time be established . . . and never be redressed, neither shall there for ever be an end of this controversy in England," wrote Knox's party to the Senate of Frankfort. The religious disruption in England was, in fact, incurable, but so it would have been had the Knoxians prevailed in Frankfort. The difference between the Churchman and the Dissenter goes to the root of the English character; no temporary triumph of either side could have brought Peace and union. While the world stands they will not be peaceful and united.

The trouble arose thus. At the end of June 1554, some English exiles of the Puritan sort, men who objected to surplices, responses, kneeling at the Communion, and other matters of equal moment, came to Frankfort. They obtained leave to use the French Protestant Chapel, provided that they "should not dissent from the Frenchmen in doctrine or ceremonies, lest they should thereby minister occasions of offence." They had then to settle what Order of services they should use; "anything they pleased," said the magistrates of Frankfort, "as long as they and the French kept the peace." They decided to adopt the English Order, barring responses, the Litany, the surplice, "and many other things." The Litany was regarded by Knox as rather of the nature of magic than of prayer, the surplice was a Romish rag, and there was some other objection to the congregation's taking part in the prayers by responses, though they were not forbidden to mingle their voices in psalmody. *Dissidium valde absurdum*—"a very absurd quarrel," among exiled fellow-countrymen, said Calvin, was the dispute which arose on these points. The Puritans, however, decided to alter the service to their taste, and enjoyed the use of the chapel. They had obtained a service which they were not likely to have been allowed to enforce in

England had Edward VI. lived; but on this point they were of another opinion.

This success was providential. They next invited English exiles abroad to join them at Frankfort, saying nothing about their mutilations of the service book. If these brethren came in, when they were all restored to England, if ever they were restored, their example, that of sufferers, would carry the day, and their service would for ever be that of the Anglican Church. The other exiled brethren, on receiving this invitation, had enough of the wisdom of the serpent to ask, "Are we to be allowed to use our own prayer book?" The answer of the godly of Frankfort evaded the question. At last the Frankfort Puritans showed their hand: they disapproved of various things in the Prayer Book. Knox, summoned from Geneva, a reluctant visitor, was already one of their preachers. In November 1554 came Grindal, later Archbishop of Canterbury, from Zurich, ready to omit some ceremonies, so that he and his faction might have "the substance" of the Prayer Book. Negotiations went on, and it was proposed by the Puritans to use the Geneva service. But Knox declined to do that, without the knowledge of the non-Puritan exiles at Zurich and elsewhere, or to use the English book, and offered his resignation. Nothing could be more fair and above-board.

There was an inchoate plan for a new Order. That failed; and Knox, with others, consulted Calvin, giving him a sketch of the nature of the English service. They drew his attention to the surplice; the Litany, "devised by Pope Gregory," whereby "we use a certain conjuring of God"; the kneeling at the Communion; the use of the cross in baptism, and of the ring in marriage, clearly a thing of human, if not of diabolical invention, and the "imposition of hands" in confirmation. The churching of women, they said, is both Pagan and Jewish. "Other things not so much shame itself as a certain kind of pity compelleth us to keep close."

"The tone of the letter throughout was expressly calculated to prejudice Calvin on the point submitted to him," says Professor Hume Brown. Calvin replied that the quarrel might be all very well if the exiles were happy and at ease in their circumstances, though in the Liturgy, as described, there were "tolerable (endurable) follies." On the whole he sided with the Knoxian party. The English Liturgy is not pure enough; and the English exiles, not at Frankfort, merely like it because they are accustomed to it. Some are partial to "popish dregs."

To the extreme Reformers no break with the past could be too abrupt and precipitous: the framers of the English Liturgy had rather adopted the principle of evolution than of development by catastrophe, and had wedded what was noblest in old Latin forms and prayers to music of the choicest English speech. To this service, for which their fellow-religionists in England were dying at the stake, the non-Frankfortian exiles were attached. They were Englishmen; their service, they said, should bear "an English face": so Knox avers, who could as yet have no patriotic love of any religious form as exclusively and essentially Scottish.

A kind of truce was now proclaimed, to last till May 1, 1555; Knox aiding in the confection of a service without responses, "some part taken out of the English book, and other things put to," while Calvin, Bullinger, and three others were appointed as referees. The Frankfort congregation had now a brief interval of provisional peace, till, on March 13, 1555, Richard Cox, with a band of English refugees, arrived. He had been tutor to Edward VI., the young Marcellus of Protestantism, but for Frankfort he was not puritanic enough. His company would give a large majority to the anti-Knoxian congregation. He and his at once uttered the responses, and on Sunday one of them read the Litany. This was an unruly infraction of the provisional agreement. Cox and his party (April 5) represented to Calvin that they had given up surplices, crosses, and other things, "not as impure and papistical," but as indifferent, and for the sake of peace. This was after they had driven Knox from the place, as they presently did; in the beginning it was distinctly their duty to give up the Litany and responses, while the truce lasted, that is, till the end of April. In the afternoon of the Sunday Knox preached, denouncing the morning's proceedings, the "impurity" of the Prayer Book, of which "I once had a good opinion," and the absence, in England, of "discipline," that is, interference by preachers with private life. Pluralities also he denounced, and some of the exiles had been pluralists.

For all this Knox was "very sharply reproved," as soon as he left the pulpit. Two days later, at a meeting, he insisted that Cox's people should have a vote in the congregation, thus making the anti-puritans a majority; Knox's conduct was here certainly chivalrous: "I fear not your judgment," he said. He had never wished to go to Frankfort; in going he merely obeyed Calvin, and probably he had no great desire to stay. He was forbidden to preach by Cox and his majority; and a later conference with Cox led to no compromise. It seems probable that Cox and the anti-puritans already cherished a grudge against Knox for his tract, the "Admonition." He had a warning that they would use the pamphlet against him, and he avers that "some devised how to have me cast into prison." The anti-puritans, admitting in a letter to Calvin that they brought the "Admonition" before the magistrates of Frankfort as "a book which would supply their enemies with just ground for overturning the whole Church, and one which had added much oil to the flame of persecution in England," deny that they desired more than that Knox might be ordered to quit the place. The passages selected as treasonable in the "Admonition" do not include the prayer for a Jehu. They were enough, however, to secure the dismissal of Knox from Frankfort.

Cox had accepted the Order used by the French Protestant congregation, probably because it committed him and his party to nothing in England; however, Knox had no sooner departed than the anti-puritans obtained leave to use, without surplice, cross, and some other matters, the Second Prayer Book of Edward VI. In September the Puritans seceded, the anti-puritans remained, squabbling with the Lutherans and among themselves.

In the whole affair Knox acted the most open and manly part; in his "History" he declines to name the opponents who avenged themselves, in a manner so dubious, on his "Admonition." If they believed their own account of the mischief that it wrought in England, their denunciation of him to magistrates, who were not likely to do more than dismiss him, is the less inexcusable. They did not try to betray him to a body like the Inquisition, as Calvin did in the case of Servetus. But their conduct was most unworthy and unchivalrous.

CHAPTER VII.

KNOX IN SCOTLAND: LETHINGTON: MARY OF GUISE: 1555-1556

Meanwhile the Reformer returned to Geneva (April 1555), where Calvin was now supreme. From Geneva, "the den of mine own ease, the rest of quiet study," Knox was dragged, "maist contrarious to mine own judgement," by a summons from Mrs. Bowes. He did not like leaving his "den" to rejoin his betrothed; the lover was not so fervent as the evangelist was cautious. Knox had at that time probably little correspondence with Scotland. He knew that there was no refuge for him in England under Mary Tudor, "who nowise may abide the presence of God's prophets."

In Scotland, at this moment, the Government was in the hands of Mary of Guise, a sister of the Duke of Guise and of the Cardinal.

Mary was now aged forty; she was born in 1515, as Knox probably was. She was a tall and stately woman; her face was thin and refined; Henry VIII., as being himself a large man, had sought her hand, which was given to his nephew, James V. On the death of that king, Mary, with Cardinal Beaton, kept Scotland true to the French alliance, and her daughter, the fair Queen of Scots, was at this moment a child in France, betrothed to the Dauphin. As a Catholic, of the House of Lorraine, Mary could not but cleave to her faith and to the French alliance. In 1554 she had managed to oust from the Regency the Earl of Arran, the head of the all but royal Hamiltons, now gratified with the French title of Duc de Chatelherault. To crown her was as seemly a thing, says Knox, "if men had but eyes, as a saddle upon the back of *ane unrewly kow*." She practically deposed Huntly, the most treacherous of men, from the Chancellorship, substituting, with more or less reserve, a Frenchman, de Rubay; and d'Oysel, the commander of the French troops in Scotland, was her chief adviser.

Writing after the death of Mary of Guise, Knox avers that she only waited her chance "to cut the throats of all those in whom she suspected the knowledge of God to be, within the realm of Scotland." As a matter of fact, the Regent later refused a French suggestion that she should peacefully call Protestants together, and then order a massacre after the manner of the Bartholomew: itself still in the womb of the future. "Mary of Guise," says Knox's biographer, Professor Hume Brown, "had the instincts of a good ruler—the love of order and justice, and the desire to stand well with the people."

Knox, however, believed, or chose to say, that she wanted to cut all Protestant throats, just as he believed that a Protestant king should cut all Catholic throats. He attributed to her, quite erroneously and uncharitably, his own unsparing fervour. As he held this view of her character and purposes, it is not strange that a journey to Scotland was "contrairious to his judgement."

He did not understand the situation. Ferocious as had been the English invasion of Scotland in 1547, the English party in Scotland, many of them paid traitors, did not resent these "rebukes of a friend," so much as both the nobles and the people now began to detest their

French allies, and were jealous of the Queen Mother's promotion of Frenchmen.

There were not, to be sure, many Scots whom she, or any one, could trust. Some were honestly Protestant: some held pensions from England: others would sacrifice national interests to their personal revenges and clan feuds. The Rev. the Lord James Stewart, Mary's bastard brother, Prior of St. Andrews and of Pittenweem, was still very young. He had no interest in his clerical profession beyond drawing his revenues as prior of two abbeys; and his nearness to the Crown caused him to be suspected of ambition: moreover, he tended towards the new ideas in religion. He had met Knox in London, apparently in 1552. Morton was a mere wavering youth; Argyll was very old: Chatelherault was a rival of the Regent, a competitor for the Crown and quite incompetent. The Regent, in short, could scarcely have discovered a Scottish adviser worthy of employment, and when she did trust one, he was the brilliant "chamaeleon," young Maitland of Lethington, who would rather betray his master cleverly than run a straight course, and did betray the Regent. Thus Mary, a Frenchwoman and a Catholic, governing Scotland for her Catholic daughter, the Dauphiness, with the aid of a few French troops who had just saved the independence of the country, naturally employed French advisers. This made her unpopular; her attempts to bring justice into Scottish courts were odious, and she would not increase the odium by persecuting the Protestants. The Duke's bastard brother, again, the Archbishop, sharing his family ambition, was in no mood for burning heretics. The Queen Mother herself carried conciliation so far as to pardon and reinstate such trebly dyed traitors as the notorious Crichton of Brunston, and she employed Kirkcaldy of Grange, who intrigued against her while in her employment. An Edinburgh tailor, Harlaw, who seems to have been a deacon in English orders, was allowed to return to Scotland in 1554. He became a very notable preacher.

Going from Mrs. Bowes's house to Edinburgh, Knox found that "the fervency" of the godly "did ravish him." At the house of one Syme "the trumpet blew the auld sound three days thegither," he informed Mrs. Bowes, and Knox himself was the trumpeter. He found another lady, "who, by reason that she had a troubled conscience, delighted much in the company of the said John." There were pleasant sisters in Edinburgh, who later consulted Knox on the delicate subject of dress. He was more tolerant in answering them than when he denounced "the stinking pride of women" at Mary Stuart's Court; admitting that "in clothes, silks, velvets, gold, and other such, there is no uncleanness," yet "I cannot praise the common superfluity which women now use in their apparel." He was quite opposed, however, to what he pleasingly calls "correcting natural beauty" (as by dyeing the hair), and held that "farthingales cannot be justified."

On the whole, he left the sisters fairly free to dress as they pleased. His curious phrase, in a letter to a pair of sisters, "the prophets of God are often impeded to pray for such as carnally they love unfeignedly," is difficult to understand. We leave it to the learned to explain this singular limitation of the prophet, which Knox says that he had not as yet experienced. He must have heard about it from other prophets.

Knox found at this time a patron remarkable, says Dr. M'Crie, "for great respectability of character," Erskine of Dun. Born in 1508, about 1530 he slew a priest named Thomas Froster, in a curiously selected place, the belfry tower of Montrose. Nobody seems to have thought anything of it, nor should we know the fact, if the record of the blood-price paid by Mr. Erskine to the priest's father did not testify to the fervent act. Six years later, according to Knox, "God had marvellously illuminated" Erskine, and the mildness of his nature is frequently applauded. He was, for Scotland, a man of learning, and our first amateur of Greek. Why did he kill a priest in a bell tower!

In the winter or autumn of 1555, Erskine gave a supper, where Knox was to argue against crypto-protestantism. When once the Truth, whether Anglican or Presbyterian, was firmly established, Catholics were compelled, under very heavy fines, to attend services and sermons which they believed to be at least erroneous, if not blasphemous. I am not aware that, in 1555, the Catholic Church, in Scotland, thus vigorously forced people of Protestant opinions to present themselves at Mass, punishing nonconformity with ruin. I have not found any complaints to this effect, at that time. But no

51

doubt an appearance of conformity might save much trouble, even in the lenient conditions produced by the character of the Regent and by the political situation. Knox, then, discovered that "divers who had a zeal to godliness made small scruple to go to the Mass, or to communicate with the abused sacraments in the Papistical manner." He himself, therefore, "began to show the impiety of the Mass, and how dangerous a thing it was to communicate in any sort with idolatry."

Now to many of his hearers this essential article of his faith—that the Catholic doctrine of the Eucharist and form of celebration were "idolatry"—may have been quite a new idea. It was already, however, a commonplace with Anglican Protestants. Nothing of the sort was to be found in the *first* Prayer Book of Edward VI.; broken lights of various ways of regarding the Sacrament probably played, at this moment, over the ideas of Knox's Scottish disciples. Indeed, their consciences appear to have been at rest, for it was *after* Knox's declaration about the "idolatrous" character of the Mass that "the matter began to be agitated from man to man, the conscience of some being afraid."

To us it may seem that the sudden denunciation of a Christian ceremony, even what may be deemed a perverted Christian ceremony, as sheer "idolatry," equivalent to the worship of serpents, bulls, or of a foreign Baal in ancient Israel—was a step calculated to confuse the real issues and to provoke a religious war of massacre. Knox, we know, regarded extermination of idolaters as a counsel of perfection, though in the Christian scriptures not one word could be found to justify his position. He relied on texts about massacring Amalekites and about Elijah's slaughter of the prophets of Baal. The Mass was idolatry, was Baal worship; and Baal worshippers, if recalcitrant, must die.

These extreme unchristian ideas, then, were new in Scotland, even to "divers who had a zeal to godliness." For their discussion, at Erskine of Dun's party, were present, among others, Willock, a Scots preacher returned from England, and young Maitland of Lethington. We are not told what part Willock took in the conversation. The arguments turned on biblical analogies, never really coincident with the actual modern circumstances. The analogy produced in discussion by those who did not go to all extremes with Knox did not, however, lack appropriateness. Christianity, in fact, as they seem to have argued, did arise out of Judaism; retaining the same God and the same scriptures, but, in virtue of the sacrifice of its Founder, abstaining from the sacrifices and ceremonial of the law. In the same way Protestantism arose out of mediæval Catholicism, retaining the same God and the same scriptures, but rejecting the mediæval ceremonial and the mediæval theory of the sacrifice of the Mass. It did not follow that the Mass was sheer "idolatry," at which no friend of the new ideas could be present.

As a proof that such presence or participation was not unlawful, was not idolatry, in the existing state of affairs, was adduced the conduct of St. Paul and the advice given to him by St. James and the Church in Jerusalem (Acts xxi. 18-36). Paul was informed that many thousands of Jews "believed," yet remained zealous for the law, the old order. They had learned that Paul advised the Jews in Greece and elsewhere not to "walk after the customs." Paul should prove that "he also kept the law." For this purpose he, with four Christian Jews under a vow, was to purify himself, and he went into the Temple, "until that an offering should be offered for every one of them."

"Offerings," of course, is the term in our version for sacrifices, whether of animals or of "unleavened wafers anointed with oil." The argument from analogy was, I infer, that the Mass, with its wafer, was precisely such an "offering," such a survival in Catholic ritual, as in Jewish ritual St. Paul consented to, by the advice of the Church of Jerusalem; consequently Protestants in a Catholic country, under the existing circumstances, might attend the Mass. The Mass was not "idolatry." The analogy halts, like all analogies, but so, of course, and to fatal results, does Knox's analogy between the foreign worships of Israel and the Mass. "She thinks not *that* idolatry, but good religion," said Lethington to Knox once, speaking of Queen Mary's Mass. "So thought they that offered their children unto Moloch," retorted the reformer. Manifestly the Mass is, of the two, much more on a level with the "offering" of St. Paul than with human sacrifices to Moloch!

In his reply Knox, as he states his own argument, altogether overlooked the *offering* of St. Paul, which, as far as we understand, was the essence of his opponents' contention. He said that "to pay *vows* was never idolatry," but "the Mass from the original was and remained odious idolatry, therefore the facts were most unlike. Secondly, I greatly doubt whether either James's commandment or Paul's obedience proceeded from the Holy Ghost," about which Knox was, apparently, better informed than these Apostles and the Church of Jerusalem. Next, Paul was presently in danger from a mob, which had been falsely told that he took Greeks into the Temple. Hence it was manifest "that God approved not that means of reconciliation." Obviously the danger of an Apostle from a misinformed mob is no sort of evidence to divine approval or disapproval of his behaviour. We shall later find that when Knox was urging on some English nonconformists the beauty of conformity (1568), he employed the very precedent of St. Paul's conduct at Jerusalem, which he rejected when it was urged at Erskine's supper party!

We have dwelt on this example of Knox's logic, because it is crucial. The reform of the Church of Christ could not be achieved without cruel persecution on both parts, while Knox was informing Scotland that all members of the old Faith were as much idolaters as Israelites who sacrificed their children to a foreign God, while to extirpate idolaters was the duty of a Christian prince. Lethington, as he soon showed, was as clear-sighted in regard to Knox's logical methods as any man of to-day, but he "concluded, saying, I see perfectly that our shifts will serve nothing before God, seeing that they stand us in so small stead before man." But either Lethington conformed and went to Mass, or Mary of Guise expected nothing of the sort from him, for he remained high in her favour, till he betrayed her in 1559.

Knox's opinion being accepted—it obviously was a novelty to many of his hearers—the Reformers must either convert or persecute the Catholics even to extermination. Circumstances of mere worldly policy forbade the execution of this counsel of perfection, but persistent "idolaters," legally, lay after 1560 under sentence of death. There was to come a moment, we shall see, when even Knox shrank from the consequences of a theory ("a murderous syllogism," writes one of his recent biographers, Mr. Taylor Innes), which divided his countrymen into the godly, on one hand, and idolaters doomed to death by divine law, on the other. But he put his hesitation behind him as a suggestion of Satan.

Knox now associated with Lord Erskine, then Governor of Edinburgh Castle, the central strength of Scotland; with Lord Lorne, soon to be Earl of Argyll (a "Christian," but not a remarkably consistent walker), with "Lord James," the natural brother of Queen Mary (whose conscience, as we saw, permitted him to draw the benefices of the Abbacy of St. Andrews, of Pittenweem, and of an abbey in France, without doing any duties), and with many redoubtable lairds of the Lothians, Ayrshire, and Forfarshire. He also preached for ten days in the town house, at Edinburgh, of the Bishop of Dunkeld. On May 15, 1556, he was summoned to appear in the church of the Black Friars. As he was backed by Erskine of Dun, and other gentlemen, according to the Scottish custom when legal proceedings were afoot, no steps were taken against him, the clergy probably dreading Knox's defenders, as Bothwell later, in similar circumstances, dreaded the assemblage under the Earl of Moray; as Lennox shrank from facing the supporters of Bothwell, and Moray from encountering the spears of Lethington's allies. It was usual to overawe the administrators of justice by these gatherings of supporters, perhaps a survival of the old "compurgators." This, in fact, was "part of the obligation of our Scottish kyndness," and the divided ecclesiastical and civil powers shrank from a conflict.

Glencairn and the Earl Marischal, in the circumstances, advised Knox to write a letter to Mary of Guise, "something that might move her to hear the Word of God," that is, to hear Knox preach. This letter, as it then stood, was printed in a little black-letter volume, probably of 1556. Knox addresses the Regent and Queen Mother as "her humble subject." The document has an interest almost pathetic, and throws light on the whole character of the great Reformer. It appears that Knox had been reported to the Regent by some of the clergy, or by rumour, as a heretic and seducer of the people. But Knox had learned that the "dew of the heavenly grace" had quenched her displeasure, and he hoped that the Regent would be as clement to others in his case as to him. Therefore he returns to his attitude in the letter to his Berwick congregation (1552). He calls for no Jehu, he advises no armed opposition to the sovereign, but says of "God's chosen children" (the Protestants), that "their victory standeth not in resisting but in suffering," "in quietness, silence, and hope," as the Prophet Isaiah recommends. The Isaiahs (however numerous modern criticism may reckon them) were late prophets, not of the school of Elijah, whom Knox followed in 1554 and 1558-59, not in 1552 or 1555, or on one occasion in 1558-59. "The Elect of God" do not "shed blood and murder," Knox remarks, though he approves of the Elect, of the brethren at all events, when they *do* murder and shed blood.

Meanwhile Knox is more than willing to run the risks of the preacher of the truth, "partly because I would, with St. Paul, wish myself accursed from Christ, as touching earthly pleasures" (whatever that may mean), "for the salvation of my brethren and illumination of your Grace." He confesses that the Regent is probably not "so free as a public reformation perhaps would require," for that required the downcasting of altars and images, and prohibition to celebrate or attend Catholic rites. Thus Knox would, apparently, be satisfied for the moment with toleration and immunity for his fellow-religionists. Nothing of the sort really contented him, of course, but at present he asked for no more.

Yet, a few days later, he writes, the Regent handed his letter to the Archbishop of Glasgow, saying, "Please you, my Lord, to read a pasquil," an offence which Knox never forgave and bitterly avenged in his "History."

It is possible that the Regent merely glanced at his letter. She would find herself alluded to in a biblical parallel with "the Egyptian midwives," with Nebuchadnezzar, and Rahab the harlot. Her acquaintance with these amiable idolaters may have been slight, but the comparison was odious, and far from tactful. Knox also reviled the creed in which she had been bred as "a poisoned cup," and threatened her, if she did not act on his counsel, with "torment and pain everlasting." Those who drink of the cup of her Church "drink therewith damnation and death." As for her clergy, "proud prelates do Kings maintain to murder the souls for which the blood of Christ Jesus was shed."

These statements were dogmatic, and the reverse of conciliatory. One should not, in attempting to convert any person, begin by reviling his religion. Knox adopted the same method with Mary Stuart: the method is impossible. It is not to be marvelled at if the Regent did style the letter a "pasquil."

Knox took his revenge in his "History" by repeating a foolish report that Mary of Guise had designed to poison her late husband, James V. "Many whisper that of old his part was in the pot, and that the suspicion thereof caused him to be inhibited the Queen's company, while the Cardinal got his secret business sped of that gracious lady either by day or night." He styled her, as we saw, "a wanton widow"; he hinted that she was the mistress of Cardinal Beaton; he made similar insinuations about her relations with d'Oysel (who was "*a secretis mulierum*"); he said, as we have seen, that she only waited her chance to cut the throats of all suspected Protestants; he threw doubt on the legitimacy of her daughter, Mary Stuart; and he constantly accuses her of treachery, as will appear, when the charge is either doubtful, or, as far as I can ascertain, absolutely false.

These are unfortunately examples of Knox's Christianity. It is very easy for modern historians and biographers to speak with genial applause of the prophet's manly bluffness. But if we put ourselves in the position of opponents whom he was trying to convert, of the two Marys for example, we cannot but perceive that his method was hopelessly mistaken. In attempting to evangelise an Euahlayi black fellow, we should not begin by threats of damnation, and by railing accusations against his god, Baiame.

CHAPTER VIII.

KNOX'S WRITINGS FROM ABROAD: BEGINNING OF THE SCOTTISH REVOLUTION, 1556-1558

Knox was about this time summoned to be one of the preachers to the English at Geneva. He sent in advance Mrs. Bowes and his wife, visited Argyll and Glenorchy (now Breadalbane), wrote (July 7) an epistle bidding the brethren be diligent in reading and discussing the Bible, and went abroad. His effigy was presently burned by the clergy, as he had not appeared in answer to a second summons, and he was outlawed in absence.

It is not apparent that Knox took any part in the English translation of the Bible, then being executed at Geneva. Greek and Hebrew were not his forte, though he had now some knowledge of both tongues, but he preached to the men who did the work. The perfections of Genevan Church discipline delighted him. "Manners and religion so sincerely reformed I have not yet seen in any other place." The genius of Calvin had made Geneva a kind of Protestant city state κατ' ευχην; a Calvinistic Utopia—everywhere the vigilant eyes of the preachers and magistrates were upon every detail of daily life. Monthly and weekly the magistrates and ministers met to point out each other's little failings. Knox felt as if he were indeed in the City of God, and later he introduced into Scotland, and vehemently abjured England to adopt, the Genevan "discipline." England would none of it, and would not, even in the days of the Solemn League and Covenant, suffer the excommunication by preachers to pass without lay control.

It is unfortunate that the ecclesiastical polity and discipline of a small city state, like a Greek πολις, feasible in such a community as Geneva at a moment of spiritual excitement, was brought by Knox and his brethren into a nation like Scotland. The results were a hundred and twenty-nine years of unrest, civil war, and persecution.

Though happy in the affection of his wife and Mrs. Bowes, Knox, at this time, needed more of feminine society. On November 19, 1556, he wrote to his friend, Mrs. Locke, wife of a Cheapside merchant: "You write that your desire is earnest to see me. Dear sister, if I should express the thirst and languor which I have had for your presence, I should appear to pass measure. . . . Your presence is so dear to me that if the charge of this little flock . . . did not impede me, my presence should anticipate my letter." Thus Knox was ready to brave the fires of Smithfield, or, perhaps, forgot them for the moment in his affection for Mrs. Locke. He writes to no other woman in this fervid strain. On May 8, 1557, Mrs. Locke with her son and daughter (who died after her journey), joined Knox at Geneva.

He was soon to be involved in Scottish affairs. After his departure from his country, omens and prodigies had ensued. A comet appeared in November-December 1556. Next year some corn-stacks were destroyed by lightning. Worse, a calf with two heads was born, and was exhibited as a warning to Mary of Guise by Robert Ormistoun. The idolatress merely sneered, and said "it was but a common thing." Such a woman was incorrigible. Mary of Guise is always blamed for endangering Scotland in the interests of her family, the Guises of the House of Lorraine. In fact, so far as she tried to make Scotland a province of France, she was serving the ambition of Henri II. It could not be foreseen, in 1555, that Henri II. would be slain in 1559, leaving the two kingdoms in the hands of Francis II. and Mary Stuart, who were so young, that they would inevitably be ruled by the Queen's uncles of the House of Lorraine. Shortly before Knox arrived in Scotland in 1555, the Duc de Guise had advised the Regent to "use sweetness and moderation," as better than "extremity and rigour"; advice which she acted on gladly.

Unluckily the war between France and Spain, in 1557, brought English troops into collision with French forces in the Low Countries (Philip II. being king of England); this led to complications between Scotland, as ally of France, and the English on the Borders. Border raids began; d'Oysel fortified Eyemouth, as a counterpoise to

Berwick, war was declared in November, and the discontented Scots, such as Chatelherault, Huntly, Cassilis, and Argyll, mutinied and refused to cross Tweed. Thus arose a breach between the Regent and some of her nobles, who at last, in 1559, rebelled against her on the ground of religion. While the weak war languished on, in 1557-58, "the Evangel of Jesus Christ began wondrously to flourish," says Knox. Other evangelists of his pattern, Harlaw, Douglas, Willock, and a baker, Methuen (later a victim of the intolerably cruel "discipline" of the Kirk Triumphant), preached at Dundee, and Methuen started a reformed Kirk (though not without being declared rebels at the horn). When these persons preached, their hearers were apt to raise riots, wreck churches, and destroy works of sacred art. No Government could for ever wink at such lawless actions, and it was because the pulpiteers, Methuen, Willock, Douglas, and the rest, were again "put at," after being often suffered to go free, that the final crash came, and the Reformation began in the wrack and ruin of monasteries and churches.

There was drawing on another thunder-cloud. The policy of Mary of Guise certainly tended to make Scotland a mere province of France, a province infested by French forces, slender, but ill-paid and predacious. Before marrying the Dauphin, in April 1558, Mary Stuart, urged it is said by the Guises, signed away the independence of her country, to which her husband, by these deeds, was to succeed if she died without issue. Young as she was, Mary was perfectly able to understand the infamy of the transaction, and probably was not so careless as to sign the deeds unread.

Even before this secret treaty was drafted, on March 10, 1557, Glencairn, Lorne, Erskine, and the Prior of St. Andrews—best known to us in after years as James Stewart, Earl of Moray—informed Knox that no "cruelty" by way of persecution was being practised; that his presence was desired, and that they were ready to jeopard their lives and goods for the cause. The rest would be told to Knox by the bearer of the letter. Knox received the letter in May 1557, with verbal reports by the bearers, but was so far from hasty that he did not leave Geneva till the end of September, and did not reach Dieppe on his way to Scotland till October 24. Three days later he wrote to the nobles who had summoned him seven months earlier.

He had received, he said, at Dieppe two private letters of a discouraging sort; one correspondent said that the enterprise was to be reconsidered, the other that the boldness and constancy required "for such an enterprise" were lacking among the nobles. Meanwhile Knox had spent his time, or some of it, in asking the most godly and the most learned of Europe, including Calvin, for opinions of such an adventure, for the assurance of his own conscience and the consciences of the Lord James, Erskine, Lorne, and the rest. This indicates that Knox himself was not quite sure of the lawfulness of an armed rising, and perhaps explains his long delay. Knox assures us that Calvin and other godly ministers insisted on his going to Scotland. But it is quite certain that of an armed rising Calvin absolutely disapproved. On April 16, 1561, writing to Coligny, Calvin says that he was consulted several months before the tumult of Amboise (March 1560) and absolutely discouraged the appeal to arms. "Better that we all perish a hundred times than that the name of Christianity and the Gospel should come under such disgrace." If Calvin bade Knox go to Scotland, he must have supposed that no rebellion was intended. Knox tells his correspondents that they have betrayed themselves and their posterity ("in conscience I can except none that bear the name of nobility"), they have made him and their own enterprise ridiculous, and they have put him to great trouble. What is he to say when he returns to Geneva, and is asked why he did not carry out his purpose? He then encourages them to be resolute.

Knox "certainly made the most," says Professor Hume Brown, "of the two letters from correspondents unknown to us." He at once represented them as the cause of his failure to keep tryst; but, in April 1558, writing from Geneva to "the sisters," he said, "the cause of my stop to this day I do not clearly understand." He did not know why he left England before the Marian persecutions; and he did not know why he had not crossed over to Scotland in 1557. "It may be that God justly permitted Sathan to put in my mind such cogitations as these: I heard such troubles as appeared in that realm;"—troubles presently to be described.

Hearing, at Dieppe, then, in October 1557, of the troubles, and of the faint war with England, and moved, perhaps, he suggests, by

Satan, Knox "began to dispute with himself, as followeth, 'Shall Christ, the author of peace, concord, and quietness, be preached where war is proclaimed, and tumults appear to rise? What comfort canst thou have to see the one part of the people rise up against the other,'" and so forth. These truly Christian reflections, as we may think them, "yet do trouble and move my wicked heart," says Knox. He adds, hypothetically, that perhaps the letters received at Dieppe "did somewhat discourage me." He was only certain that the devil was at the bottom of the whole affair.

The "tumults that appear to arise" are probably the dissensions between the Regent and the mutinous nobles who refused to invade England at her command. D'Oysel needed a bodyguard; and he feared that the Lords would seize and carry off the Regent. Arran, in 1564, speaks of a plot to capture her in Holyrood. Here were promises of tumults. There were also signs of a renewed feud between the house of Hamilton and the Stewart Earl of Lennox, the rival claimant of the crown. There seems, moreover, to have been some tumultuary image-breaking.

Knox may have been merely timid: he is not certain, but his delay passed in consulting the learned, for the satisfaction of his conscience, and his confessed doubts as to whether Christianity should be pushed by civil war, seem to indicate that he was not always the prophet patron of modern Jehus, that he did, occasionally, consult the Gospel as well as the records of pre-Christian Israel.

The general result was that, from October 1557 to March 1558, Knox stayed in Dieppe, preaching with great success, raising up a Protestant church, and writing.

His condition of mind was unenviable. He had been brought all the way across France, leaving his wife and family; he had, it seems, been met by no letters from his noble friends, who may well have ceased to expect him, so long was his delay. He was not at ease in his conscience, for, to be plain, he was not sure that he was not afraid to risk himself in Scotland, and he was not certain that his new scruples about the justifiableness of a rising for religion were not the excuses suggested by his own timidity. Perhaps they were just that, not whisperings either of conscience or of Satan. Yet in this condition

Knox was extremely active. On December 1 and 17 he wrote, from Dieppe, a "Letter to His Brethren in Scotland," and another to "The Lords and Others Professing the Truth in Scotland." In the former he censures, as well he might, "the dissolute life of (some) such as have professed Christ's holy Evangel." That is no argument, he says, against Protestantism. Many Turks are virtuous; many orthodox Hebrews, Saints, and Patriarchs occasionally slipped; the Corinthians, though of a "trew Kirk," were notoriously profligate. Meanwhile union and virtue are especially desirable; for Satan "fiercely stirreth his terrible tail." We do not know what backslidings of the brethren prompted this letter.

The Lords, in the other letter, are reminded that they had resolved to hazard life, rank, and fortune for the delivery of the brethren: the first step must be to achieve a godly frame of mind. Knox hears rumours "that contradiction and rebellion is made by some to the Authority" in Scotland. He advises "that none do suddenly disobey or displease the established authority in things lawful," nor rebel from private motives. By "things lawful" does he mean the command of the Regent to invade England, which the nobles refused to do? They may "lawfully attempt the extremity," if Authority will not cease to persecute, and permit Protestant preaching and administration of the Sacraments (which usually ended in riot and church-wrecking). Above all, they are not to back the Hamiltons, whose chief, Chatelherault, had been a professor, had fallen back, and become a persecutor. "Flee all confederacy with that generation," the Hamiltons; with whom, after all, Knox was presently to be allied, though by no means fully believing in the "unfeigned and speedy repentance" of their chief.

All the movements of that time are not very clear. Apparently Lorne, Lord James, and the rest, in their letter of March 10, 1557, intended an armed rising: they were "ready to jeopardise lives and goods" for "the glory of God." If no more than an appeal to "the Authority" for tolerance was meant, why did Knox consult the learned so long, on the question of conscience? Yet, in December 1557, he bids his allies first of all seek the favour of "the Authority," for bare toleration of Protestantism.

From the scheme of March 10, of which the details, unknown to us, were *orally* delivered by bearer, he appears to have expected civil war.

Again, just when Knox was writing to Scotland in December 1557, his allies there, he says, made "a common Band," a confederacy and covenant such as the Scots usually drew up before a murder, as of Riccio or Darnley, or for slaying Argyll and "the bonny Earl o' Murray," under James VI. These Bands were illegal. A Band, says Knox, was now signed by Argyll, Lorne, Glencairn, Morton, and Erskine of Dun, and many others unknown, on December 3, 1557. It is alleged that "Satan cruelly doth rage." Now, how was Satan raging in December 1557? Myln, the last martyr, was not pursued till April 1558, by Knox's account.

The first godly Band being of December 1557, and drawn up, perhaps, on the impulse of Knox's severe letter from Dieppe of October 27, in that year; just after they signed the Band, what were the demands of the Banders? They asked, apparently, that the Second Prayer Book of Edward VI. should be read in all parish churches, with the Lessons: *if the curates are able to read*: if not, then by any qualified parishioner. Secondly, preaching must be permitted in private houses, "without great conventions of the people." Whether the Catholic service was to be concurrently permitted does not appear; it is not very probable, for that service is idolatrous, and the Band itself denounces the Church as "the Congregation of Satan." Dr. M'Crie thinks that the Banders, or Congregation of God, did not ask for the universal adoption of the English Prayer Book, but only requested that they themselves might bring it in "in places to which their authority and influence extended." They took that liberty, certainly, without waiting for leave, but their demand appears to apply to all parish churches. War, in fact, was denounced against Satan's Congregation; if it troubles the Lords' Congregation, there could therefore be little idea of tolerating their nefarious creed and ritual.

Probably Knox, at Dieppe in 1557 and early in 1558, did not know about the promising Band made in Scotland. He was composing his "First Blast of the Trumpet against the Monstrous Regiment of Women." In England and in Scotland were a Catholic Queen, a

Catholic Queen Mother, and the Queen of Scotland was marrying the idolatrous Dauphin. It is not worth while to study Knox's general denunciation of government by ladies: he allowed that (as Calvin suggested) miraculous exceptions to their inability might occur, as in the case of Deborah. As a rule, a Queen was an "idol," and that was enough. England deserved an idol, and an idolatrous idol, for Englishmen rejected Kirk discipline; "no man would have his life called in trial" by presbyter or preacher. A Queen regnant has, *ex officio*, committed treason against God: the Realm and Estates may have conspired with her, but her rule is unlawful. Naturally this skirl on the trumpet made Knox odious to Elizabeth, for to impeach her succession might cause a renewal of the wars of the Roses. Nothing less could have happened, if a large portion of the English people had believed in the Prophet of God, John Knox. He could predict vengeance on Mary Tudor, but could not see that, as Elizabeth would succeed, his Blast would bring inconvenience to his cause; or, seeing it, he stood to his guns.

He presently reprinted and added to his letter to Mary of Guise, arguing that civil magistrates have authority in religion, but, of course, he must mean only as far as they carry out his ideas, which are the truth. In an "Appellation" against the condemnation of himself, in absence, by the Scottish clergy, he labours the same idea. Moreover, "no idolater can be exempted from punishment by God's law." Now the Queen of Scotland happened to be an idolater, and every true believer, as a private individual, has a right to punish idolaters. That right and duty are not limited to the King, or to "the chief Nobility and Estates," whom Knox addresses. "I would your Honours should note for the first, that no idolater can be exempted from punishment by God's Law. The second is, that the punishment of such crimes as are idolatry, blasphemy, and others, that touch the Majesty of God, doth not appertain to kings and chief rulers only" (as he had argued that they do, in 1554), "but also to the whole body of that people, and to every member of the same, according to the vocation of every man, and according to that possibility and occasion which God doth minister to revenge the injury done against His glory, what time that impiety is manifestly known. . . . *Who dare be so impudent as to deny this to be most reasonable and just?*"

Knox's method of argument for his doctrine is to take, among other texts, Deuteronomy xiii. 12-18, and apply the sanguinary precepts of Hebrew fanatics to the then existing state of affairs in the Church Christian. Thus, in Deuteronomy, cities which serve "other gods," or welcome missionaries of other religions, are to be burned, and every living thing in them is to be destroyed. "To the carnal man, . . . " says Knox, "this may rather seem to be pronounced in a rage than in wisdom." God wills, however, that "all creatures stoop, cover their faces, *and desist from reasoning*, when commandment is given to execute his judgement." Knox, then, desists from reasoning so far as to preach that every Protestant, with a call that way, has a right to punish any Catholic, if he gets a good opportunity. This doctrine he publishes to his own countrymen. Thus any fanatic who believed in the prophet Knox, and was conscious of a "vocation," might, and should, avenge God's wrongs on Mary of Guise or Mary Stuart, "he had a fair opportunity, for both ladies were idolaters. This is a plain inference from the passage just cited.

Appealing to the Commonalty of Scotland, Knox next asked that he might come and justify his doctrine, and prove Popery "abominable before God." Now, could any Government admit a man who published the tidings that any member of a State might avenge God on an idolater, the Queen being, according to him, an idolater? This doctrine of the right of the Protestant individual is merely monstrous. Knox has wandered far from his counsel of "passive resistance" in his letter to his Berwick congregation; he has even passed beyond his "Admonition," which merely prayed for a Phinehas or Jehu: he has now proclaimed the right and duty of the private Protestant assassin. The "Appellation" containing these ideas was published at Geneva in 1558, with the author's, but without the printer's name on the title-page.

"The First Blast" had neither the author's nor printer's name, nor the name of the place of publication. Calvin soon found that it had given grave offence to Queen Elizabeth. He therefore wrote to Cecil that, though the work came from a press in his town, he had not been aware of its existence till a year after its publication. He now took no public steps against the book, not wishing to draw attention to its origin in Geneva, lest, "by reason of the reckless arrogance of one man" ('the ravings of others'), "the miserable crowd of exiles should have been driven away, not only from this city, but even from almost the whole world." As far as I am aware, no one approached Calvin with remonstrance about the monstrosities of the "Appellation," nor are the passages which I have cited alluded to by more than one biographer of Knox, to my knowledge. Professor Hume Brown, however, justly remarks that what the Kirk, immediately after Knox's death, called "Erastianism" (in ordinary parlance the doctrine that the Civil power may interfere in religion) could hardly "be approved in more set terms" than by Knox. He avers that "the ordering and reformation of religion . . . doth especially appertain to the Civil Magistrate . . . " "The King taketh upon him to command the Priests." The opposite doctrine, that it appertains to the Church, is an invention of Satan. To that diabolical invention, Andrew Melville and the Kirk returned in the generation following, while James VI. held to Knox's theory, as stated in the "Appellation."

The truth is that Knox contemplates a State in which the civil power shall be entirely and absolutely of his own opinions; the King, as "Christ's silly vassal," to quote Andrew Melville, being obedient to such prophets as himself. The theories of Knox regarding the duty to revenge God's feud by the private citizen, and regarding religious massacre by the civil power, ideas which would justify the Bartholomew horrors, appear to be forgotten in modern times. His address to the Commonalty, as citizens with a voice in the State, represents the progressive and permanent element in his politics. We have shown, however, that, before Knox's time, the individual Scot was a thoroughly independent character. "The man hath more words than the master, and will not be content unless he knows the master's counsel."

By March 1558, Knox had returned from Dieppe to Geneva. In Scotland, since the godly Band of December 1557, events were moving in two directions. The Church was continuing in a belated and futile attempt at reformation of manners (and wonderfully bad manners they confessedly were), and of education from within. The Congregation, the Protestants, on the other hand, were preparing openly to defend themselves and their adherents from persecution, an honest, manly, and laudable endeavour, so long as they did not persecute other Christians. Their preachers—such as Harlaw, Methuen, and Douglas—were publicly active. A moment of attempted suppression must arrive, greatly against the personal wishes of Archbishop Hamilton, who dreaded the conflict.

In March 1558, Hamilton courteously remonstrated with Argyll for harbouring Douglas. He himself was "heavily murmured against" for his slackness in the case of Argyll, by churchmen and other "well given people," and by Mary of Guise, whose daughter, by April 24, 1558, was married to the Dauphin of France. Argyll replied that he knew how the Archbishop was urged on, but declined to abandon Douglas.

"It is a far cry to Loch Awe"; Argyll, who died soon after, was too powerful to be attacked. But, sometime in April 1558 apparently, a poor priest of Forfarshire, Walter Myln, who had married and got into trouble under Cardinal Beaton, was tried for heresy, and, without sentence of a secular judge, it is said, was burned at St. Andrews, displaying serene courage, and hoping to be the last martyr in Scotland. Naturally there was much indignation; if the Lords and others were to keep their Band they must bestir themselves. They did bestir themselves in defence of their favourite preachers—Willock, Harlaw, Methuen; a *ci-devant* friar, Christison; and Douglas. Some of these men were summoned several times throughout 1558, and Methuen and Harlaw, at least, were "at the horn" (outlawed), but were protected—Harlaw at Dumfries, Methuen at Dundee—by powerful laymen. At Dundee, as we saw, by 1558, Methuen had erected a church of reformed aspect; and "reformed" means that the Kirk had already been purged of altars and images. Attempts to bring the ringleaders of Protestant riots to law were made in 1558, but the precise order of events, and of the protests of the Reformers, appears to be dislocated in Knox's narrative. He himself was not present, and he seems never to have mastered the sequence of occurrences. Fortunately there exists a fragment by a well-informed writer, apparently a contemporary, the "Historie of the Estate of Scotland" covering the events from July 1558 to 1560. There are also imperfect records of the Parliament of November-December 1558, and of the last Provincial Council of the Church, in March 1559.

For July 28 four or five of the brethren were summoned to "a day of law," in Edinburgh; their allies assembled to back them, and they were released on bail to appear, if called on, within eight days. At this time the "idol" of St. Giles, patron of the city, was stolen, and a great riot occurred at the saint's *fête*, September 3.

Knox describes the discomfiture of his foes in one of his merriest passages, frequently cited by admirers of "his vein of humour." The event, we know, was at once reported to him in Geneva, by letter.

Some time after October, if we rightly construe Knox, a petition was delivered to the Regent, from the Reformers, by Sandilands of Calder. They asserted that they should have defended the preachers, or testified with them. The wisdom of the Regent herself sees the need of reform, spiritual and temporal, and has exhorted the clergy and nobles to employ care and diligence thereon, a fact corroborated by Mary of Guise herself, in a paper, soon to be quoted, of July 1559. They ask, as they have the reading of the Scriptures in the vernacular, for common prayers in the same. They wish for freedom to interpret and discuss the Bible "in our conventions," and that Baptism and the Communion may be done in Scots, and they demand the reform of the detestable lives of the prelates.

Knox's account, in places, appears really to refer to the period of the Provincial Council of March 1559, though it does not quite fit that date either.

The Regent is said on the occasion of Calder's petition, and after the unsatisfactory replies of the clergy (apparently at the Provincial Council, March 1559), to have made certain concessions, till Parliament established uniform order. But the Parliament was of November-December 1558. Before that Parliament, at all events (which was mainly concerned with procuring the "Crown Matrimonial" for the Dauphin, husband of Mary Stuart), the brethren offered a petition, in the first place shown to the Regent, asking for (1) the suspension of persecuting laws till after a General Council has "decided all controversies in religion"—that is, till the Greek Calends. (2) That prelates shall not be judges in cases of heresy, but only accusers before secular tribunals. (3) That all lawful defences be granted to persons accused. (4) That the accused be permitted to explain "his own mind and meaning." (5) That "none be condemned for heretics unless by the manifest Word of God they be convicted to have erred from the faith which the Holy Spirit witnesses to be necessary to salvation." According to Knox this petition the Regent put in her pocket, saying that the Churchmen would oppose it, and thwart her plan for getting the "Crown Matrimonial" given to her son-in-law, Francis II., and, in short, gave good words, and drove time.

The Reformers then drew up a long Protestation, which was read in the House, but not enrolled in its records. They say that they have had to postpone a formal demand for Reformation, but protest that "it be lawful to us to use ourselves in matters of religion and conscience as we must answer to God," and they are ready to prove their case. They shall not be liable, meanwhile, to any penalties for breach of the existing Acts against heresy, "nor for violating such rites as man, without God's commandment or word, hath commanded." They disclaim all responsibility for the ensuing tumults. In fact, they aver that they will not only worship in their own way, but prevent other people from worshipping in the legal way, and that the responsibility for the riots will lie on the side of those who worship legally. And this was the chief occasion of the ensuing troubles. The Regent promised to "put good order" in controverted matters, and was praised by the brethren in a letter to Calvin, not now to be found.

Another threat had been made by the brethren, in circumstances not very obscure. As far as they are known they suggest that in January 1559 the zealots deliberately intended to provoke a conflict, and to enlist "the rascal multitude" on their side, at Easter, 1559. The obscurity is caused by a bookbinder. He has, with the fatal ingenuity of his trade, cut off the two top lines from a page in one manuscript copy of Knox's "History." The text now runs thus (in its mutilated condition): " . . . Zealous Brether . . . upon the gates and posts of all the Friars' places within this realm, in the month of January 1558 (1559), preceding that Whitsunday that they dislodged, which is this . . ."

Then follows the Proclamation.

Probably we may supply the words: ". . . Zealous Brethren caused a paper to be affixed upon the gates and posts," and so on. The paper so promulgated purported to be a warning from the poor of Scotland that, before Whitsunday, "we, the lawful proprietors," will eject the Friars and residents on the property, unlawfully withheld by the religious—"our patrimony." This feat will be performed, "with the help of God, *and assistance of his Saints on earth, of whose ready support we doubt not.*"

As the Saints, in fact, were the "Zealous Brether . . ." who affixed the written menace on "all the Friars' places," they knew what they were talking about, and could prophesy safely. To make so many copies of the document, and fix them on "all the Friars' places," implies organisation, and a deliberate plan—riots and revolution—before Whitsunday. The poor, of course, only exchanged better for worse landlords, as they soon discovered. The "Zealous Brethren"—as a rule small lairds, probably, and burgesses—were the nucleus of the Revolution. When townsfolk and yeomen in sufficient number had joined them in arms, then nobles like Argyll, Lord James, Glencairn, Ruthven, and the rest, put themselves at the head of the movement, and won the prizes which had been offered to the "blind, crooked, widows, orphans, and all other poor."

After Parliament was over, at the end of December 1558, the Archbishop of St. Andrews again summoned the preachers, Willock, Douglas, Harlaw, Methuen, and Friar John Christison to a "day of law" at St. Andrews, on February 2, 1559. (This is the statement of the "Historie.") The brethren then "caused inform the Queen Mother that the said preachers would appear with such multitude of men professing their doctrine, as was never seen before in such like cases in this country," and kept their promise. The system of overawing justice by such gatherings was usual, as we have already seen; Knox, Bothwell, Lethington, and the Lord James Stewart all profited by the practice on various occasions.

Mary of Guise, "fearing some uproar or sedition," bade the bishops put off the summons, and, in fact, the preachers never were summoned, finally, for any offences prior to this date.

On February 9, 1559, the Regent issued proclamations against eating flesh in Lent (this rule survived the Reformation by at least seventy years) and against such disturbances of religious services as the Protest just described declared to be imminent, all such deeds being denounced under "pain of death"—as pain of death was used to be threatened against poachers of deer and wild fowl.

Mary, however, had promised, as we saw, that she would summon the nobles and Estates, "to advise for some reformation in religion" (March 7, 1559), and the Archbishop called a Provincial Council to Edinburgh for March. At this, or some other juncture, for Knox's narrative is bewildering, the clergy offered free discussion, but refused to allow exiles like himself to be present, and insisted on the acceptance of the Mass, Purgatory, the invocation of saints, with security for their ecclesiastical possessions. In return they would grant prayers and baptism in English, if done privately and not in open assembly. The terms, he says, were rejected; appeal was made to Mary of Guise, and she gave toleration, except for public assemblies in Edinburgh and Leith, pending the meeting of Parliament. To the clergy, who, "some say," bribed her, she promised to "put order" to these matters. The Reformers were deceived, and forbade Douglas to preach in Leith. So writes Knox.

Now the "Historie" dates all this, bribe and all, *after the end of December* 1558. Knox, however, by some confusion, places the facts, bribe and all, *before April* 28, 1558, Myln's martyrdom! Yet he had before him as he wrote the Chronicle of Bruce of Earlshall, who states the bribe, Knox says, at £40,000; the "Historie" says "within £15,000."

In any case Knox, who never saw his book in print, has clearly dislocated the sequence of events. At this date, namely March 1559, the preaching agitators were at liberty, nor were they again put at for any of their previous proceedings. But defiances had been exchanged. The Reformers in their Protestation (December 1558) had claimed it as lawful, we know, that they should enjoy their own services, and put down those of the religion by law established, until such time as the Catholic clergy "be able to prove themselves the true ministers of Christ's Church" and guiltless of all the crimes charged against them by their adversaries. That was the challenge of the Reformers, backed by the menace affixed to the doors of all the monasteries. The Regent in turn had thrown down her glove by the proclamation of February 9, 1559, against disturbing services and "bosting" (bullying) priests. How could she possibly do less in the circumstances? If her proclamation was disobeyed, could she do less than summon the disobedient to trial? Her hand was forced.

It appears to myself, under correction, that all this part of the history of the Reformation has been misunderstood by our older historians. Almost without exception, they represent the Regent as dissembling with the Reformers till, on conclusion of the peace of Cateau Cambresis (which left France free to aid her efforts in Scotland), April 2, 1559, and on the receipt of a message from the Guises, "she threw off the mask," and initiated an organised persecution. But there is no evidence that any such message commanding her to persecute at this time came from the Guises before the Regent had issued her proclamations of February 9 and March 23, denouncing attacks on priests, disturbance of services, administering of sacraments by lay preachers, and tumults at large. Now, Sir James Melville of Halhill, the diplomatist, writing in old age, and often erroneously, makes the Cardinal of Lorraine send de Bettencourt, or Bethencourt, to the Regent with news of the peace of Cateau Cambresis and an order to punish heretics with fire and sword, and says that, though she was reluctant, she consequently published her proclamation of March 23. Dates prove part of this to be impossible.

Obviously the Regent had issued her proclamations of February-March 1559 in anticipation of the tumults threatened by the Reformers in their "Beggar's Warning" and in their Protestation of December, and arranged to occur with violence at Easter, as they did. The three or four preachers (two of them apparently "at the horn" in 1558) were to preach publicly, and riots were certain to ensue, as the Reformers had threatened. Riots were part of the evangelical programme. Of Paul Methuen, who first "reformed" the Church in Dundee, Pitscottie writes that he "ministered the sacraments of the communion at Dundee and Cupar, and caused the images thereof to be cast down, and abolished the Pope's religion so far as he passed or preached." For this sort of action he was now summoned.

The Regent, therefore, warned in her proclamations men, often challenged previously, and as often allowed, under fear of armed resistance, to escape. All that followed was but a repetition of the feeble policy of outlawing these four or five men. Finally, in May 1559, these preachers had a strong armed backing, and seized a central strategic point, so the Revolution blazed out on a question which had long been smouldering and on an occasion that had been again and again deferred. The Regent, far from having foreseen and hardened her heart to carry out an organised persecution and "cut the throats" of all Protestants in Scotland, was, in fact, intending to go to France, being in the earlier stages of her fatal malady. This appears from a letter of Sir Henry Percy, from Norham Castle, to Cecil and Parry (April 12, 1559) Percy says that the news in his latest letters (now lost) was erroneous. The Regent, in fact, "is not as yet departed." She is very ill, and her life is despaired of. She is at Stirling, where the nobles had assembled to discuss religious matters. Only her French advisers were on the side of the Regent. "The matter is pacified for the time," and in case of the Regent's death, Chatelherault, d'Oysel, and de Rubay are to be a provisional committee of Government, till the wishes of the King and Queen, Francis and Mary, are known. Again, in her letter of May 16 to Henri II. of France, she stated that she was in very bad health, and, at about the same date (May 18), the English ambassador in France mentions her intention to visit that country at once. But the Revolution of May 11, breaking out in Perth, condemned her to suffer and die in Scotland.

This, however, does not amount to proof that no plan of persecution in Scotland was intended. Throckmorton writes, on May 18, that the Marquis d'Elboeuf is to go thither. "He takes with him both men of conduct and some of war; it is thought his stay will not be long." Again (May 23, 24), Throckmorton reports that Henri II. means to persecute extremely in Poitou, Guienne, and Scotland. "Cecil may take occasion to use the matter in Scotland as may seem best to serve the turn." This was before the Perth riot had been reported (May 26) by Cecil to Throckmorton. Was d'Elboeuf intended to direct the persecution? The theory has its attractions, but Henri, just emerged with maimed forces from a ruinous war, knew that a persecution which served Cecil's "turn" did not serve *his*. To persecute in Scotland would mean renewed war with England, and could not be contemplated. If Sir James Melville can be trusted for once, the Constable, about June 1, told him, in the presence of the French King, that if the Perth revolt were only about religion, "we mon commit Scottismen's saules unto God." Melville was then despatched with promise of aid to the Regent—if the rising was political, not religious.

It is quite certain that the Regent issued her proclamations without any commands from France; and her health was inconsistent with an intention to put Protestants to fire and sword.

In the records of the Provincial Council of March 1559, the foremost place is given to "Articles" presented to the Regent by "some temporal Lords and Barons," and by her handed to the clergy. They are the proposals of conservative reformers. They ask for moral reformation of the lives of the clergy: for sermons on Sundays and holy days: for due examination of the doctrine, life, and learning of all who are permitted to preach. They demand that no vicar or curate shall be appointed unless he can read the catechism (of 1552) plainly and distinctly: that expositions of the sacraments should be clearly pronounced in the vernacular: that common prayer should be read in the vernacular: that certain exactions of gifts and dues should be abolished. Again, no one should be allowed to dishonour the sacraments, or the service of the Mass: no unqualified person should administer the sacraments: Kirk rapine, destruction of religious buildings and works of art, should not be permitted.

The Council passed thirty-four statutes on these points. The clergy were to live cleanly, and not to keep their bastards at home. They were implored, "in the bowels of Christ" to do their duty in the services of the Church. No one in future was to be admitted to a living without examination by the Ordinary. Ruined churches were to be rebuilt or repaired. Breakers of ornaments and violators or burners of churches were to be pursued. There was to be preaching as often as the Ordinary thought fit: if the Rector could not preach he must find a substitute who could. Plain expositions of the sacraments were made out, were to be read aloud to the congregations, and were published at twopence ("The Twopenny Faith"). Administration of the Eucharist except by priests was to be punished by excommunication. Knox himself desired *death* for others than true ministers who celebrated the sacrament. His "true ministers," about half-a-dozen of them at this time, of course came under the penalty of the last statute.

He says, with the usual error, that *after* peace was made between France and England, on April 2, 1559 (the treaty of Cateau Cambresis), the Regent "began to spew forth and disclose the latent venom of her double heart." She looked "frowardly" on Protestants, "commanded her household to use all abominations at Easter," she herself communicated, "and it is supposed that after that day the devil took more violent and strong possession in her than he had before . . . For incontinent she caused our preachers to be summoned."

But *why* did she summon the same set of preachers as before, for no old offence? The Regent, says the "Historie," made proclamation, during the Council (as the moderate Reformers had asked her to do), "that no manner of person should . . . preach or minister the sacraments, except they were admitted by the Ordinary or a Bishop on no less pain than death." The Council, in fact, made excommunication the penalty. Now it was for ministering the sacrament after the proclamation of March 13, for preaching heresy, and stirring up "seditions and tumults," that Methuen, Brother John Christison, William Harlaw, and John Willock were summoned to appear at Stirling on May 10, 1559.

How could any governor of Scotland abstain from summoning them in the circumstances? There seems to be no new suggestion of the devil, no outbreak of Guisian fury. The Regent was in a situation whence there was no "outgait": she must submit to the seditions and tumults threatened in the Protestation of the brethren, the disturbances of services, the probable wrecking of churches, or she must use the powers legally entrusted to her. She gave insolent answers to remonstrances from the brethren, says Knox. She would banish the preachers (not execute them), "albeit they preached as truly as ever did St. Paul." Being threatened, as before, with the consequent "inconvenients," she said "she would advise." However, summon the preachers she did, for breach of her proclamations, "tumults and seditions."

Knox himself was present at the Revolution which ensued, but we must now return to his own doings in the autumn and winter of 1558-59.

CHAPTER IX.

KNOX ON THE ANABAPTISTS: HIS APPEAL TO ENGLAND: 1558-1559

While the inevitable Revolution was impending in Scotland, Knox was living at Geneva. He may have been engaged on his "Answer" to the "blasphemous cavillations" of an Anabaptist, his treatise on Predestination. Laing thought that this work was "chiefly written" at Dieppe, in February-April 1559, but as it contains more than 450 pages it is probably a work of longer time than two months. In November 1559 the English at Geneva asked leave to print the book, which was granted, provided that the name of Geneva did not appear as the place of printing; the authorities knowing of what Knox was capable from the specimen given in his "First Blast." There seem to be several examples of the Genevan edition, published by Crispin in 1560; the next edition, less rare, is of 1591 (London).

The Anabaptist whom Knox is discussing had been personally known to him, and had lucid intervals. "Your chief Apollos," he had said, addressing the Calvinists, "be persecutors, on whom the blood of Servetus crieth a vengeance. . . . They have set forth books affirming it to be lawful to persecute and put to death such as dissent from them in controversies of religion. . . . Notwithstanding they, before they came to authority, were of another judgment, and did both say and write that no man ought to be persecuted for his conscience' sake. . . ." Knox replied that Servetus was a blasphemer, and that Moses had been a more wholesale persecutor than the Edwardian burners of Joan of Kent, and the Genevan Church which roasted Servetus (October 1553). He incidentally proves that he was better than his doctrine. In England an Anabaptist, after asking for secrecy, showed him a manuscript of his own full of blasphemies. "In me I confess there was great negligence, that neither did retain his book nor present him to the magistrate" to burn. Knox could not have done that, for the author "earnestly required of me closeness and fidelity," which, probably, Knox promised. Indeed, one fancies that his opinions and character would have been in conflict if a chance of handing an idolater over to death had been offered to him.

The death of Mary Tudor on November 17, 1558, does not appear to have been anticipated by him. The tidings reached him before January 12, 1559, when he wrote from Geneva a singular "Brief Exhortation to England for the Spedie Embrasing of Christ's Gospel heretofore by the Tyrannie of Marie Suppressed and Banished."

The gospel to be embraced by England is, of course, not nearly so much Christ's as John Knox's, in its most acute form and with its most absolute, intolerant, and intolerable pretensions. He begins by vehemently rebuking England for her "shameful defection" and by threatening God's "horrible vengeances which thy monstrous unthankfulness hath long deserved," if the country does not become much more puritan than it had ever been, or is ever likely to be. Knox "wraps you all in idolatry, all in murder, all in one and the same iniquity," except the actual Marian martyrs; those who "abstained from idolatry;" and those who "avoided the realm" or ran away. He had set one of the earliest examples of running away: to do so was easier for him than for family men and others who had "a stake in the country," for which Knox had no relish. He is hardly generous in blaming all the persons who felt no more "ripe" for martyrdom than he did, yet stayed in England, where the majority were, and continued to be, Catholics.

Having asserted his very contestable superiority and uttered pages of biblical threatenings, Knox says that the repentance of England "requireth two things," first, the expulsion of "all dregs of Popery" and the treading under foot of all "glistering beauty of vain ceremonies." Religious services must be reduced, in short, to his own bare standard. Next, the Genevan and Knoxian "kirk discipline" must be introduced. No "power or liberty (must) be permitted to any, of what estate, degree, or authority they be, either to live without the yoke of discipline by God's word commanded," or "to alter . . . one jot in religion which from God's mouth thou hast received. . . . If prince, king, or emperor would enterprise to change or disannul the same, that he be of thee reputed enemy to God," while a prince who erects idolatry . . . "must be adjudged to death."

Each bishopric is to be divided into ten. The Founder of the Church and the Apostles "all command us to preach, to preach." A brief sketch of what The Book of Discipline later set forth for the edification of Scotland is recommended to England, and is followed by more threatenings in the familiar style.

England did not follow the advice of Knox: her whole population was not puritan, many of her martyrs had died for the prayer book which Knox would have destroyed. His tract cannot have added to the affection which Elizabeth bore to the author of "The First Blast." In after years, as we shall see, Knox spoke in a tone much more moderate in addressing the early English nonconformist secessionists (1568). Indeed, it is as easy almost to prove, by isolated passages in Knox's writings, that he was a sensible, moderate man, loathing and condemning active resistance in religion, as to prove him to be a senselessly violent man. All depends on the occasion and opportunity. He speaks with two voices. He was very impetuous; in the death of Mary Tudor he suddenly saw the chance of bringing English religion up, or down, to the Genevan level, and so he wrote this letter of vehement rebuke and inopportune advice.

Knox must have given his biographers "medicines to make them love him." The learned Dr. Lorimer finds in this epistle, one of the most fierce of his writings, "a programme of what this Reformation reformed should be—a programme which was honourable alike to Knox's zeal and his moderation." The "moderation" apparently consists in not abolishing bishoprics, but substituting "ten bishops of moderate income for one lordly prelate." Despite this moderation of the epistle, "its intolerance is extreme," says Dr. Lorimer, and Knox's advice "cannot but excite astonishment." The party which agreed with him in England was the minority of a minority; the Catholics, it is usually supposed, though we have no statistics, were the majority of the English nation. Yet the only chance, according to Knox, that England has of escaping the vengeance of an irritable Deity, is for the smaller minority to alter the prayer book, resist the Queen, if she wishes to retain it unaltered, and force the English people into the "discipline" of a Swiss Protestant town.

Dr. Lorimer, a most industrious and judicious writer, adds that, in these matters of "discipline," and of intolerance, Knox "went to a tragical extreme of opinion, of which none of the other leading reformers had set an example;" also that what he demanded was substantially demanded by the Puritans all through the reign of Elizabeth. But Knox averred publicly, and in his "History," that for everything he affirmed in Scotland he had heard the judgments "of the most godly and learned that be known in Europe . . . and for my assurance I have the handwritings of many." Now he had affirmed frequently, in Scotland, the very doctrines of discipline and persecution "of which none of the other leading Reformers had set an example," according to Dr. Lorimer. Therefore, either they agreed with Knox, or what Knox told the Lords in June 1564 was not strictly accurate. In any case Knox gave to his country the most extreme of Reformations.

The death of Mary Tudor, and the course of events at home, were now to afford our Reformer the opportunity of promulgating, in Scotland, those ideas which we and his learned Presbyterian student alike regret and condemn. These persecuting ideas "were only a mistaken theory of Christian duty, and nothing worse," says Dr. Lorimer. Nothing could possibly be worse than a doctrine contrary in the highest degree to the teaching of Our Lord, whether the doctrine was proclaimed by Pope, Prelate, or Calvinist.

Here it must be observed that a most important fact in Knox's career, a most important element in his methods, has been little remarked upon by his biographers. Ever since he failed, in 1554, to obtain the adhesion of Bullinger and Calvin to his more extreme ideas, he had been his own prophet, and had launched his decrees of the right of the people, of part of the people, and of the individual, to avenge the insulted majesty of God upon idolaters, not only without warrant from the heads of the Calvinistic Church, but to their great annoyance and disgust. Of this an example will now be given.

CHAPTER X.

KNOX AND THE SCOTTISH REVOLUTION, 1559

Knox had learned from letters out of Scotland that Protestants there now ran no risks; that "without a shadow of fear they might hear prayers in the vernacular, and receive the sacraments in the right way, the impure ceremonies of Antichrist being set aside." The image of St. Giles had been broken by a mob, and thrown into a sewer; "the impure crowd of priests and monks" had fled, throwing away the shafts of the crosses they bore, and "hiding the golden heads in their robes." Now the Regent thinks of reforming religion, on a given day, at a convention of the whole realm. So William Cole wrote to Bishop Bale, then at Basle, without date. The riot was of the beginning of September 1558, and is humorously described by Knox.

This news, though regarded as "very certain," was quite erroneous except as to the riot. One may guess that it was given to Knox in letters from the nobles, penned in October 1558, which he received in November 1558; there was also a letter to Calvin from the nobles, asking for Knox's presence. It seemed that a visit to Scotland was perfectly safe; Knox left Geneva in January, he arrived in Dieppe in February, where he learned that Elizabeth would not allow him to travel through England. He had much that was private to say to Cecil, and was already desirous of procuring English aid to Scottish reformers. The tidings of the Queen's refusal to admit him to England came through Cecil, and Knox told him that he was "worthy of Hell" (for conformity with Mary Tudor); and that Turks actually granted such safe conducts as were now refused to him. Perhaps he exaggerated the amenity of the Turks. His "First Blast," if acted on, disturbed the succession in England, and might beget new wars, a matter which did not trouble the prophet. He also asked leave to visit his flock at Berwick. This too was refused.

Doubtless Knox, with his unparalleled activity, employed the period of delay in preaching the Word at Dieppe. After his arrival in Scotland, he wrote to his Dieppe congregation, upbraiding them for their Laodicean laxity in permitting idolatry to co-exist with true religion in their town. Why did they not drive out the idolatrous worship? These epistles were intercepted by the Governor of Dieppe, and their contents appear to have escaped the notice of the Reformer's biographers. A revolt followed in Dieppe. Meanwhile Knox's doings at Dieppe had greatly exasperated François Morel, the chief pastor of the Genevan congregation in Paris, and president of the first Protestant Synod held in that town. The affairs of the French Protestants were in a most precarious condition; persecution broke into fury early in June 1559. A week earlier, Morel wrote to Calvin, "Knox was for some time in Dieppe, waiting on a wind for Scotland." "He dared publicly to profess the worst and most infamous of doctrines: 'Women are unworthy to reign; Christians may protect themselves by arms against tyrants!'" The latter excellent doctrine was not then accepted by the Genevan learned. "I fear that Knox may fill Scotland with his madness. He is said to have a boon companion at Geneva, whom we hear that the people of Dieppe have called to be their minister. If he be infected with such opinions, for Christ's sake pray that he be not sent; or if he has already departed, warn the Dieppe people to beware of him." A French ex-capuchin, Jacques Trouillé, was appointed as Knox's successor at Dieppe.

Knox's ideas, even the idea that Christians may bear the sword against tyrants, were all his own, were anti-Genevan; and though Calvin (1559-60) knew all about the conspiracy of Amboise to kill the Guises, he ever maintained that he had discouraged and preached against it. We must, therefore, credit Knox with originality, both in his ideas and in his way of giving it to be understood that they had the approval of the learned of Switzerland. The reverse was true.

By May 3, Knox was in Edinburgh, "come in the brunt of the battle," as the preachers' summons to trial was for May 10. He was at once outlawed, "blown loud to the horn," but was not dismayed. On this occasion the battle would be a fair fight, the gentry, under their Band, stood by the preachers, and, given a chance in open field with the arm of the flesh to back him, Knox's courage was tenacious and indomitable. It was only for lonely martyrdom that he never thought himself ready, and few historians have a right to throw the first stone at him for his backwardness.

As for armed conflict, at this moment Mary of Guise could only reckon surely on the small French garrison of Scotland, perhaps 1500 or 2000 men. She could place no confidence in the feudal levies that gathered when the royal standard was raised. The Hamiltons merely looked to their own advancement; Lord James Stewart was bound to the Congregation; Huntly was a double dealer and was remote; the minor *noblesse* and the armed burghers, with Glencairn representing the south-west, Lollard from of old, were attached to Knox's doctrines, while the mob would flock in to destroy and plunder.

Meanwhile Mary of Guise was at Stirling, and a multitude of Protestants were at Perth, where the Reformation had just made its entry, and had secured a walled city, a thing unique in Scotland. The gentry of Angus and the people of Dundee, at Perth, were now anxious to make a "demonstration" (unarmed, says Knox) at Stirling, if the preachers obeyed the summons to go thither, on May 10. Their strategy was excellent, whether carefully premeditated or not.

The Regent, according to Knox, amused Erskine of Dun with promises of "taking some better order" till the day of May 10 arrived, when, the preachers and their backers having been deluded into remaining at Perth instead of "demonstrating" at Stirling, she outlawed the preachers and fined their sureties ("assisters"). She did not outlaw the sureties. Her treachery (alleged only by Knox and others who follow him) is examined in Appendix A. Meanwhile it is certain that the preachers were put to the horn in absence, and that the brethren, believing themselves (according to Knox) to have been disgracefully betrayed, proceeded to revolutionary extremes, such as Calvin energetically denounced.

If we ask who executed the task of wrecking the monasteries at Perth, Knox provides two different answers.

In the "History" Knox says that after the news came of the Regent's perfidy, and after a sermon "vehement against idolatry," a priest began to celebrate, and "opened a glorious tabernacle" on the high altar. "Certain godly men and a young boy" were standing near; they all, or the boy alone (the sentence may be read either way), cried that this was intolerable. The priest struck the boy, who "took up a stone" and hit the tabernacle, and "the whole multitude" wrecked the monuments of idolatry. Neither the exhortation of the preacher nor the command of the magistrate could stay them in their work of destruction. Presently "the rascal multitude" convened, *without* the gentry and "earnest professors," and broke into the Franciscan and Dominican monasteries. They wrecked as usual, and the "common people" robbed, but the godly allowed Forman, Prior of the Charter House, to bear away about as much gold and silver as he was able to carry. We learn from Mary of Guise and Lesley's "History" that the very orchards were cut down.

If, thanks to the preachers, "no honest man was enriched the value of a groat," apparently dishonest men must have sacked the gold and silver plate of the monasteries; nothing is said by Knox on this head, except as to the Charter House.

85

Writing to Mrs. Locke, on the other hand, on June 23, Knox tells her that "the brethren," after "complaint and appeal made" against the Regent, levelled with the ground the three monasteries, burned all "monuments of idolatry" accessible, "and priests were commanded under pain of death, to desist from their blasphemous mass." Nothing is said about a spontaneous and uncontrollable popular movement. The professional "brethren," earnest professors of course, reap the glory. Which is the true version?

If the version given to Mrs. Locke be accurate, Knox had sufficient reasons for producing a different account in that portion of his "History" (Book ii.) which is a tract written in autumn, 1559, and in purpose meant for contemporary foreign as well as domestic readers. The performances attributed to the brethren, in the letter to the London merchant's wife, were of a kind which Calvin severely rebuked. Similar or worse violences were perpetrated by French brethren at Lyons, on April 30, 1562. The booty of the church of St. Jean had been sold at auction. There must be no more robbery and pillage, says Calvin, writing on May 13, to the Lyons preachers. The ruffians who rob ought rather to be abandoned, than associated with to the scandal of the Gospel. "Already reckless zeal was shown in the ravages committed in the churches" (altars and images had been overthrown), "but those who fear God will not rigorously judge what was done in hot blood, from devout emotion, but what can be said in defence of looting?"

Calvin spoke even more distinctly to the "consistory" of Nîmes, who suspended a preacher named Tartas for overthrowing crosses, altars, and images in churches (July-August, 1561). The zealot was even threatened with excommunication by his fellow religionists. Calvin heard that this fanatic had not only consented to the outrages, but had incited them, and had "the insupportable obstinacy" to say that such conduct was, with him, "a matter of conscience." "But *we*" says Calvin, "know that the reverse is the case, for God never commanded any one to overthrow idols, except every man in his own house, and, in public, those whom he has armed with authority. Let that fire-brand" (the preacher) "show us by what title *he* is lord of the land where he has been burning things."

Knox must have been aware of Calvin's opinion about such outrages as those of Perth, which, in a private letter, he attributes to the brethren: in his public "History" to the mob. At St. Andrews, when similar acts were committed, he says that "the provost and bailies . . . did agree to remove all monuments of idolatry," whether this would or would not have satisfied Calvin.

Opponents of my view urge that Knox, though he knew that the brethren had nothing to do with the ruin at Perth, yet, in the enthusiasm of six weeks later, claimed this honour for them, when writing to Mrs. Locke. Still later, when cool, he told, in his "History," "the frozen truth," the mob alone was guilty, despite his exhortations and the commandment of the magistrate. Neither alternative is very creditable to the prophet.

In the "Historie of the Estate of Scotland," it is "the brethren" who break, burn, and destroy. In Knox's "History" no mention is made of the threat of death against the priests. In the letter to Mrs. Locke he says, apparently of the threat, perhaps of the whole affair, "which thing did so enrage the venom of the serpent's seed," that she decreed death against man, woman, and child in Perth, after the fashion of Knox's favourite texts in Deuteronomy and Chronicles. This was "beastlie crueltie." The "History" gives the same account of the Regent's threatening "words which might escape her in choler" (of course we have no authority for her speaking them at all), but, in the "History," Knox omits the threat by the brethren of death against the priests a threat which none of his biographers mentions!

If the menace against the priests and the ruin of monasteries were not seditious, what is sedition? But Knox's business, in Book II. of his "History" (much of it written in September-October 1559), is to prove that the movement was *not* rebellious, was purely religious, and all for "liberty of conscience"—for Protestants. Therefore, in the "History," he disclaims the destruction by the brethren of the monasteries—the mob did that; and he burkes the threat of death to priests: though he told the truth, privately, to Mrs. Locke.

Mary did not move at once. The Hamiltons joined her, and she had her French soldiers, perhaps 1500 men. On May 22 "The Faithful Congregation of Christ Jesus in Scotland," but a few gentlemen being concerned, wrote from Perth, which they were fortifying, to the Regent. If she proceeds in her "cruelty," they will take up the sword, and inform all Christian princes, and their Queen in France, that they have revolted solely because of "this cruel, unjust, and most tyrannical murder, intended against towns and multitudes." As if they had not revolted already! Their pretext seems to mean that they do not want to alter the sovereign authority, a quibble which they issued for several months, long after it was obviously false. They also wrote to the nobles, to the French officers in the Regent's service, and to the clergy.

What really occurred was that many of the brethren left Perth, after they had "made a day of it," as they had threatened earlier: that the Regent called her nobles to Council, concentrated her French forces, and summoned the levies of Clydesdale and Stirlingshire. Meanwhile the brethren flocked again into Perth, at that time, it is said, the only wall-girt town in Scotland: they strengthened the works, wrote everywhere for succour, and loudly maintained that they were not rebellious or seditious.

Of these operations Knox was the life and soul. There is no mistaking his hand in the letter to Mary of Guise, or in the epistle to the Catholic clergy. That letter is courteously addressed "To the Generation of Anti-Christ, the Pestilent Prelates and their Shavelings within Scotland, the Congregation of Jesus within the same saith."

The gentle Congregation saith that, if the clergy "proceed in their cruelty," they shall be "apprehended as murderers." "We shall begin that same war which God commanded Israel to execute against the Canaanites . . ." This they promise in the names of God, Christ, and the Gospel. Any one can recognise the style of Knox in this composition. David Hume remarks: "With these outrageous symptoms commenced in Scotland that hypocrisy and fanaticism which long infested that kingdom, and which, though now mollified by the lenity of the civil power, is still ready to break out on all occasions." Hume was wrong, there was no touch of hypocrisy in Knox; he believed as firmly in the "message" which he delivered as in the reality of the sensible universe.

A passage in the message to the nobility displays the intense ardour of the convictions that were to be potent in the later history of the Kirk. That priests, by the prescription of fifteen centuries, should have persuaded themselves of their own power to damn men's souls to hell, cut them off from the Christian community, and hand them over to the devil, is a painful circumstance. But Knox, from Perth, asserts that the same awful privilege is vested in the six or seven preachers of the nascent Kirk with the fire-new doctrine! Addressing the signers of the godly Band and other sympathisers who have not yet come in, he (if he wrote these fiery appeals) observes, that if they do *not* come in, "ye shall be *excommunicated* from our Society, and from all participation with us in the administration of the Sacraments . . . Doubt we nothing but that our church, *and the true ministers of the same*, have the power which our Master, Jesus Christ, granted to His apostles in these words, 'Whose sins ye shall forgive, shall be forgiven, and whose sins ye shall retain, shall be retained' . . . " Men were to be finally judged by Omnipotence on the faith of what Willock, Knox, Harlaw, poor Paul Methuen, and the apostate Friar Christison, "trew ministeris," thought good to decide! With such bugbears did Guthrie and his companions think, a century later, to daunt "the clear spirit of Montrose."

While reading the passages just cited, we are enabled to understand the true cause of the sorrows of Scotland for a hundred and thirty years. The situation is that analysed by Thomas Lüber, a Professor of Medicine at Heidelberg, well or ill known in Scottish ecclesiastical disputes by his Graecised name, Erastus. He argued, about 1568, that excommunication has no certain warrant in Holy Writ, under a Christian prince. Erastus writes:—

"Some men were seized on by a certain excommunicatory fever, which they did adorn with the name of 'ecclesiastical discipline.' . . . They affirmed the manner of it to be this: that certain presbyters should sit in the name of the whole Church, and should judge who were worthy or unworthy to come to the Lord's Supper. I wonder that then they consulted about these matters, when we neither had men to be excommunicated, nor fit excommunicators; for scarcely a thirtieth part of the people did understand or approve of the reformed religion."

"There was," adds Erastus, "another fruit of the same tree, that almost every one thought men had the power of opening and shutting heaven to whomsoever they would."

What men have this power in Scotland in 1559? Why, some five or six persons who, being fluent preachers, have persuaded local sets of Protestants to accept them as ministers. These preachers having a "call"—it might be from a set of perfidious and profligate murderers—are somehow gifted with the apostolic grace of binding on earth what shall be bound in heaven. Their successors, down to Mr. Cargill, who, of his own fantasy, excommunicated Charles II., were an intolerable danger to civilised society. For their edicts of "boycotting" they claimed the sanction of the civil magistrate, and while these almost incredibly fantastic pretentions lasted, there was not, and could not be, peace in Scotland.

The seed of this Upas tree was sown by Knox and his allies in May 1559. An Act of 1690 repealed civil penalties for the excommunicated.

To face the supernaturally gifted preachers the Regent had but a slender force, composed in great part of sympathisers with Knox. Croft, the English commander at Berwick, writing to the English Privy Council, on May 22, anticipated that there would be no war. The Hamiltons, numerically powerful, and strong in martial gentlemen of the name, were with the Regent. But of the Hamiltons it might always be said, as Charles I. was to remark of their chief, that "they were very active for their own preservation," and for no other cause. For centuries but one or two lives stood between them and the throne, the haven where they would be. They never produced a great statesman, but their wealth, numbers, and almost royal rank made them powerful.

At this moment the eldest son of the house, the Earl of Arran, was in France. As a boy, he had been seized by the murderers of Cardinal Beaton, and held as a hostage in the Castle of St. Andrews. Was he there converted to the Reformers' ideas by the eloquence of Knox? We know not, but, as heir to his father's French duchy of Chatelherault, he had been some years in France, commanding the Scottish Archer Guard. In France too, perhaps, he was more or less a pledge for his father's loyalty in Scotland. He was now a Protestant in earnest, had retired from the French Court, had refused to return thither when summoned, and fled from the troops who were sent to bring him; lurking in woods and living on strawberries. Cecil despatched Thomas Randolph to steer him across the frontier to Zurich. He was a piece in the game much more valuable than his father, whose portrait shows us a weak, feebly cunning, good-natured, and puzzled-looking old nobleman.

Till Arran returned to Scotland, the Hamiltons, it was certain, would be trusty allies of neither faith and of neither party. When the Perth tumult broke out, Lord James rode with the Regent, as did Argyll. But both had signed the godly Band of December 3, 1557, and could no more be trusted by the Regent than the Hamiltons.

Meanwhile, the gentry of Fife and Forfarshire, with the town of Dundee, joined Knox in the walled town of Perth, though Lord Ruthven, provost of Perth, deserted, for the moment, to the Regent. On the other hand, the courageous Glencairn, with a strong body of the zealots of Renfrewshire and Ayrshire, was moving by forced marches to join the brethren. On May 24, the Regent, instead of attacking, halted at Auchterarder, fourteen miles away, and sent Argyll and Lord James to parley. They were told that the brethren meant no rebellion (as the Regent said and doubtless thought that they did), but only desired security for their religion, and were ready to "be tried" (by whom?) "in lawful judgment." Argyll and Lord James were satisfied. On May 25, Knox harangued the two lords in his wonted way, but the Regent bade the brethren leave Perth on pain of treason. By May 28, however, she heard of Glencairn's approach with Lord Ochiltree, a Stewart (later Knox's father-in-law); Glencairn, by cross roads, had arrived within six miles of Perth, with 1200 horse and 1300 foot. The western Reformers were thus nearer Perth than her own untrustworthy levies at Auchterarder. Not being aware of this, the brethren proposed obedience, if the Regent would amnesty the Perth men, let their faith "go forward," and leave no garrison of "French soldiers." To Mrs. Locke Knox adds that no idolatry should be erected, or alteration made within the town. The Regent was now sending Lord James, Argyll, and Mr. Gawain Hamilton to treat, when Glencairn and his men marched into Perth.

Argyll and Lord James then promised to join the brethren, if the Regent broke her agreement; Knox and Willock assured their hearers that break it she would—and so the agreement was accepted (May 28).

It was thus necessary for the brethren to allege that the covenant was broken; and it was not easy for Mary to secure order in Perth without taking some step that could be seized on as a breach of her promise; Argyll and Lord James could then desert her for the party of Knox. The very Band which Argyll and Lord James signed with the Congregation provided that the godly should go on committing the disorders which it was the duty of the Regent to suppress, and they proceeded in that holy course, "breaking down the altars and idols in all places where they came." "At their whole powers" the Congregations are "to destroy and put away all that does dishonour to God's name"; that is, monasteries and works of sacred art. They are all to defend each other against "any power whatsoever" that shall trouble them in their pious work. Argyll and Lord James signed this new Band, with Glencairn, Lord Boyd, and Ochiltree. The Queen's emissaries thus deserted her cause on the last day of May 1559, or earlier, for the chronology is perplexing.

As to the terms of truce with the Regent, Knox gives no document, but says that no Perth people should be troubled for their recent destruction of idolatry "and for down casting the places of the same; that she would suffer the religion begun to go forward, and leave the town at her departing free from the garrisons of French soldiers." The "Historie" mentions no terms except that "she should leave no men of war behind her."

Thus, as it seems, the brethren by their Band were to go on wrecking the homes of the Regent's religion, while she was not to enjoy her religious privileges in the desecrated churches of Perth, for to do that was to prevent "the religion begun" from "going forward." On the Regent's entry her men "discharged their volley of hackbuts," probably to clear their pieces, a method of unloading which prevailed as late as Waterloo. But some aimed, says Knox, at the house of Patrick Murray and hit a son of his, a boy of ten or twelve, "who, being slain, was had to the Queen's presence." She mocked, and wished it had been his father, "but seeing that it so chanced, we cannot be against fortune." It is not very probable that Mary of Guise was "merry," in Knox's manner of mirth, over the death of a child (to Mrs. Locke Knox says "children"), who, for all we know, may have been the victim of accident, like the Jacobite lady who was wounded at a window as Prince Charles's men discharged their pieces when entering Edinburgh after the victory of Prestonpans. (This brave lady said that it was fortunate she was not a Whig, or the accident would have been ascribed to design.) This event at Perth was called a breach of terms, so was the attendance at Mass, celebrated on any chance table, as "the altars were not so easy to be repaired again." The soldiers were billeted on citizens, whose houses were "oppressed by" the Frenchmen, and the provost, Ruthven (who had anew deserted to the Congregation), and the bailies, were deposed.

These magistrates probably had been charged with the execution of priests who dared to do their duty; at least in the following year, on June 10, 1560, we find the provost, bailies, and town council of Edinburgh decreeing death for the third offence against idolaters who do not instantly profess their conversion. The Edinburgh municipality did this before the abolition of Catholicism by the Convention of Estates in August 1560. It does not appear that any authority in Perth except that of the provost and bailies could sentence priests to death; was their removal, then, a breach of truce? At all events it seemed necessary in the circumstances, and Mary of Guise when she departed left no *French* soldiers to protect the threatened priests, but four companies of Scots who had been in French service, under Stewart of Cardonell and Captain Cullen, the Captain of Queen Mary's guard after the murder of Riccio. The Regent is said by Knox to have remarked that she was not bound to keep faith with heretics, and that, with as fair an excuse, she would make little scruple to take the lives and goods of "all that sort." We do not know Knox's authority for these observations of the Regent.

The Scots soldiers left by Mary of Guise may have been Protestants, they certainly were not Frenchmen; and, in a town where death had just been threatened to all priests who celebrated the Mass, Mary could not abandon her clerics unprotected.

Taking advantage of what they called breach of treaty as regards the soldiers left in Perth, Lord James and Argyll, with Ruthven, had joined the brethren, accompanied by the Earl of Menteith and Murray of Tullibardine, ancestor of the ducal house of Atholl. Argyll and Lord James went to St. Andrews, summoning their allies thither for June 3. Knox meanwhile preached in Crail and Anstruther, with the usual results. On Sunday, June 11, and for three days more, despising the threats of the Archbishop, backed by a hundred spears, and referring to his own prophecy made when he was in the galleys, he thundered at St. Andrews. The poor ruins of some sacred buildings "are alive to testify" to the consequences, and a head of the Redeemer found in the latrines of the abbey is another mute witness to the destruction of that day.

It is not my purpose to dilate on the universal destruction of so much that was beautiful, and that to Scots, however godly, should have been sacred. The tomb of the Bruce in Dunfermline, for example, was wrecked by the mob, as the statue of Jeanne d'Arc on the bridge of Orleans was battered to pieces by the Huguenots. Nor need we ask what became of church treasures, perhaps of great value and antiquity. In some known cases, the magistrates held and sold those of the town churches. Some of the plate and vestments at Aberdeen were committed to the charge of Huntly, but about 1900 ounces of plate were divided among the Prebendaries, who seem to have appropriated them. The Church treasures of Glasgow were apparently carried abroad by Archbishop Beaton. If Lord James, as Prior, took possession of the gold and silver of St. Andrews, he probably used the bullion (he spent some 13,000 crowns) in his defence of the approaches to the town, against the French, in December 1559. A silver mace of St. Salvator's College escaped the robbers.

There is no sign of the possession of much specie by the Congregation in the months that followed the sack of so many treasuries of pious offerings. Lesley says that they wanted to coin the plate in Edinburgh, and for that purpose seized, as they certainly did, the dies of the mint. In France, when the brethren sacked Tours, they took twelve hundred thousand *livres d'or*; the country was enriched for the moment. Not so Scotland. In fact the plate of Aberdeen cathedral, as inventoried in the Register, is no great treasure. Monasteries and cathedrals were certain to perish sooner or later, for the lead of every such roof except Coldingham had been stripped and sold by 1585, while tombs had been desecrated for their poor spoils, and the fanes were afterwards used as quarries of hewn stone. Lord James had a peculiar aversion to idolatrous books, and is known to have ordered the burning of many manuscripts;—the loss to art was probably greater than the injury to history or literature. The fragments of things beautiful that the Reformers overlooked, were destroyed by the Covenanters. An attempt has been made to prove that the Border abbeys were not wrecked by Reformers, but by English troops in the reign of Henry VIII., who certainly ravaged them. Lesley, however, says that the abbeys of Kelso and Melrose were "by them (the Reformers) broken down and wasted." If there was nothing left to destroy on the Border, why did the brethren march against Kelso, as Cecil reports, on July 9, 1559?

After the devastation the Regent meant to attack the destroyers, intending to occupy Cupar, six miles, by Knox's reckoning, from St. Andrews. But, by June 13, the brethren had anticipated her with a large force, rapidly recruited, including three thousand men under the Lothian professors; Ruthven's horse; the levies of the Earl of Rothes (Leslie), and many burgesses. Next day the Regent's French horse found the brethren occupying a very strong post; their numbers were dissembled, their guns commanded the plains, and the Eden was in their front. A fog hung over the field; when it lifted, the French commander, d'Oysel, saw that he was outnumbered and outmanœuvred. He sent on an envoy to parley, "which gladly of us being granted, the Queen offered a free remission for all crimes past, so that they would no further proceed against friars and abbeys, and that no more preaching should be used publicly," for *that* always meant kirk-wrecking. When Wishart preached at Mauchline, long before, in 1545, it was deemed necessary to guard the church, where there was a tempting tabernacle, "beutyfull to the eie."

The Lords and the whole brethren "refused such appointment" . . . says Knox to Mrs. Locke; they would not "suffer idolatrie to be maintained in the bounds committed to their charge." To them liberty of conscience from the first meant liberty to control the

95

consciences and destroy the religion of all who differed from them. An eight days' truce was made for negotiations; during the truce neither party was to "enterprize" anything. Knox in his "History" does not mention an attack on the monastery of Lindores during the truce. He says that his party expected envoys from the Regent, as in the terms of truce, but perceived "her craft and deceit."

In fact, the brethren were the truce-breakers. Knox gives only the assurances signed by the Regent's envoys, the Duke of Chatelherault and d'Oysel. They include a promise "not to invade, trouble, or disquiet the Lords," the reforming party. But, though Knox omits the fact, the Reformers made a corresponding and equivalent promise: "That the Congregation should enterprise nothing nor make no invasion, for the space of six days following, for the Lords and principals of the Congregation read the rest on another piece of paper."

The situation is clear. The two parties exchanged assurances. Knox prints that of the Regent's party, not that, "on another piece of paper," of the Congregation. They broke their word; they "made invasion" at Lindores, during truce, as Knox tells Mrs. Locke, but does not tell the readers of his "History." It is true that Knox was probably preaching at St. Andrews on June 13, and was not present at Cupar Muir. But he could easily have ascertained what assurances the Lords of the Congregation "read from another piece of paper" on that historic waste.

CHAPTER XI.

KNOX'S INTRIGUES, AND HIS ACCOUNT OF THEM, 1559

The Reformers, and Knox as their secretary and historian, had now reached a very difficult and delicate point in their labours. Their purpose was, not by any means to secure toleration and freedom of conscience, but to extirpate the religion to which they were opposed. It was the religion by law existing, the creed of "Authority," of the Regent and of the King and Queen whom she represented. The position of the Congregation was therefore essentially that of rebels, and, in the state of opinion at the period, to be rebels was to be self-condemned. In the eyes of Calvin and the learned of the Genevan Church, kings were the Lord's appointed, and the Gospel must not be supported by the sword. "Better that we all perish a hundred times," Calvin wrote to Coligny in 1561. Protestants, therefore, if they would resist in arms, had to put themselves in order, and though Knox had no doubt that to exterminate idolaters was thoroughly in order, the leaders of his party were obliged to pay deference to European opinion.

By a singular coincidence they adopted precisely the same device as the more militant French Protestants laid before Calvin in August 1559-March 1560. The Scots and the Protestant French represented that they were illegally repressed by foreigners: in Scotland by Mary of Guise with her French troops; in France by the Cardinal and Duc de Guise, foreigners, who had possession of the persons and authority of the "native prince" of Scotland, Mary, and the "native prince" of France, Francis II., both being minors. The French idea was that, if they secured the aid of a native Protestant prince (Condé), they were in order, as against the foreign Guises, and might kill these tyrants, seize the King, and call an assembly of the Estates. Calvin was consulted by the chief of the conspiracy, La Renaudie; he disapproved; the legality lent by one native prince was insufficient; the details of the plot were "puerile," and Calvin waited to see how the country would take it. The plot failed, at Amboise, in March 1560.

In Scotland, as in France, devices about a prince of the native blood suggested themselves. The Regent, being of the house of Guise, was a foreigner, like her brothers in France. The "native princes" were Chatelherault and his eldest son, Arran. The leaders, soon after Lord James and Argyll formally joined the zealous brethren, saw that without foreign aid their enterprise was desperate. Their levies must break up and go home to work; the Regent's nucleus of French troops could not be ousted from the sea fortress of Dunbar, and would in all probability be joined by the army promised by Henri II. His death, the Huguenot risings, the consequent impotence of the Guises to aid the Regent, could not be foreseen. Scotland, it seemed, would be reduced to a French province; the religion would be overthrown.

There was thus no hope, except in aid from England. But by the recent treaty of Cateau Cambresis (April 2, 1559), Elizabeth was bound not to help the rebels of the French Dauphin, the husband of the Queen of Scots. Moreover, Elizabeth had no stronger passion than a hatred of rebels. If she was to be persuaded to help the Reformers, they must produce some show of a legitimate "Authority" with whom she could treat. This was as easy to find as it was to the Huguenots in the case of Condé. Chatelherault and Arran, native princes, next heirs to the crown while Mary was childless, could be produced as legitimate "Authority." But to do this implied a change of "Authority," an upsetting of "Authority," which was plain rebellion in the opinion of the Genevan doctors. Knox was thus obliged, in sermons and in the pamphlet (Book II. of his "History"), to maintain that nothing more than freedom of conscience and religion was contemplated, while, as a matter of fact, he was foremost in the intrigue for changing the "Authority," and even for depriving Mary Stuart of "entrance and title" to her rights. He therefore, in Book II. (much of which was written in August-October or September-October 1559, as an apologetic contemporary tract), conceals the actual facts of the case, and, while perpetually accusing the Regent of falsehood and perfidy, displays an extreme "economy of truth," and cannot hide the pettifogging prevarications of his party. His wiser plan would have been to cancel this Book, or much of it, when he set forth later to write a history of the Reformation. His party being then triumphant, he could have afforded to tell most of the truth, as in great part he does in his Book III. But he could not bring himself to throw over the narrative of his party pamphlet (Book II.), and it remains much as it was originally written, though new touches were added.

The point to be made in public and in the apologetic tract was that the Reformers contemplated no alteration of "Authority." This was untrue.

Writing later (probably in 1565-66) in his Third Book, Knox boasts of his own initiation of the appeal to England, which included a scheme for the marriage of the Earl of Arran, son of the Hamilton chief, Chatelherault, to Queen Elizabeth. Failing issue of Queen Mary, Arran was heir to the Scottish throne, and if he married the Queen of England, the rightful Queen of Scotland would not be likely to wear her crown. The contemplated match was apt to involve a change of dynasty. The lure of the crown for his descendants was likely to bring Chatelherault, and perhaps even his brother the Archbishop, over to the side of the Congregation: in short it was an excellent plot. Probably the idea occurred to the leaders of the Congregation at or shortly after the time when Argyll and Lord James threw in their lot definitely with the brethren on May 31. On June 14 Croft, from Berwick, writes to Cecil that the leaders, "from what I hear, will likely seek her Majesty's" (Elizabeth's) "assistance," and mean to bring Arran home. Some think that he is already at Geneva, and he appears to have made the acquaintance of Calvin, with whom later he corresponded. "They are likely to motion a marriage you know where"; of Arran, that is, with Elizabeth. Moreover, one Whitlaw was at this date in France, and by June 28, communicated the plan to Throckmorton, the English Ambassador. Thus the scheme was of an even earlier date than Knox claims for his own suggestion.

He tells us that at St. Andrews, after the truce of Cupar Muir (June 13), he "burstit forth," in conversation with Kirkcaldy of Grange, on the necessity of seeking support from England. Kirkcaldy long ago had watched the secret exit from St. Andrews Castle, while his friends butchered the Cardinal. He was taken in the castle when Knox was taken; he was a prisoner in France; then he entered the French service, acting, while so engaged, as an English spy. Before and during the destruction of monasteries he was in the Regent's service, but she justly suspected him of intending to desert her at this juncture. Kirkcaldy now wrote to Cecil, without date, but probably on June 21, and with the signature "Zours as ye knaw." Being in the Regent's party openly, he was secretly betraying her; he therefore accuses her of treachery. (He left her publicly, after a pension from England had been procured for him.) He says that the Regent averred that "favourers of God's word should have liberty to live after their consciences," "yet, in the conclusion of the peace" (the eight days' truce) "she has uttered her deceitful mind, having now declared that she will be enemy to all them that shall not live after her religion." *Consequently*, the Protestants are wrecking "all the friaries within their bounds." But Knox has told us that they declared their intention of thus enjoying liberty of conscience *before* "the conclusion of the peace," and wrecked Lindores Abbey during the peace! Kirkcaldy adds that the Regent already suspects him.

Kirkcaldy, having made the orthodox charge of treachery against the woman whom he was betraying, then asks Cecil whether Elizabeth will accept their "friendship," and adds, with an eye to Arran, "I wish likewise her Majesty were not too hasty in her marriage." On June 23, writing from his house, Grange, and signing his name, Kirkcaldy renews his proposals. In both letters he anticipates the march of the Reformers to turn the Regent's garrison out of Perth. On June 25 he announces that the Lords are marching thither. They had already the secret aid of Lethington, who remained, like the traitor that he was, in the Regent's service till the end of October. Knox also writes at this time to Cecil from St. Andrews.

On June 1, Henri II. of France had written to the Regent promising to send her strong reinforcements, but he was presently killed in a tourney by the broken lance shaft of Montgomery.

The Reformers now made tryst at Perth for June 25, to restore "religion" and expel the Scots in French service. The little garrison surrendered (their opponents are reckoned by Kirkcaldy at 10,000 men), idolatry was again suppressed, and Perth restored to her municipal constitution. The ancient shrines of Scone were treated in the usual way, despite the remonstrances of Knox, Lord James, and Argyll. They had threatened Hepburn, Bishop of Moray, that if he did not join them "they neither could spare nor save his place." This was on June 20, on the same day he promised to aid them and vote with them in Parliament. Knox did his best, but the Dundee people began the work of wrecking; and the Bishop, in anger, demanded and received the return of his written promise of joining the Reformers. On the following day, irritated by some show of resistance, the people of Dundee and Perth burned the palace of Scone and the abbey, "whereat no small number of us was offended." An old woman said that "filthy beasts" dwelt "in that den," to her private knowledge, "at whose words many were pacified." The old woman is an excellent authority.

The pretext of perfect loyalty was still maintained by the Reformers; their honesty we can appreciate. They did not wish, they said, to overthrow "authority"; merely to be allowed to worship in their own way (and to prevent other people from worshipping in theirs, which was the order appointed by the State). That any set of men may rebel and take their chances is now recognised, but the Reformers wanted to combine the advantages of rebellion with the reputation of loyal subjects. Persons who not only band against the sovereign, but invoke foreign aid and seek a foreign alliance, are, however noble their motives, rebels. There is no other word for them. But that they were *not* rebels Knox urged in a sermon at Edinburgh, which the Reformers, after devastating Stirling, reached by June 28-29 (?), and the Second Book of his "History" labours mainly to prove this point; no change of "authority" is intended.

What Knox wanted is very obvious. He wanted to prevent Mary Stuart from enjoying her hereditary crown. She was a woman, as such under the curse of "The First Blast of the Trumpet," and she was an idolatress. Presently, as we shall see, he shows his hand to Cecil.

Before the Reformers entered Edinburgh Mary of Guise retired to the castle of Dunbar, where she had safe access to the sea. In

Edinburgh Knox says that the poor sacked the monasteries "before our coming." The contemporary *Diurnal of Occurrents* attributes the feat to Glencairn, Ruthven, Argyll, and the Lord James.

Knox was chosen minister of Edinburgh, and as soon as they arrived the Lords, according to the "Historie of the Estate of Scotland," sent envoys to the Regent, offering obedience if she would "relax" the preachers, summoned on May 10, "from the horn" and allow them to preach. The Regent complied, but, of course, peace did not ensue, for, according to Knox, in addition to a request "that we might enjoy liberty of conscience," a demand for the withdrawal of all French forces out of Scotland was made. This could not be granted.

Presently Mary of Guise issued before July 2, in the name of the King and Queen, Francis II. and Mary Stuart, certain charges against the Reformers, which Knox in his "History" publishes. A remark that Mary Stuart lies like her mother, seems to be written later than the period (September-October 1559) when this Book II. was composed. The Regent says that the rising was only under pretence of religion, and that she has offered a Parliament for January 1560. "A manifest lie," says Knox, "for she never thought of it till we demanded it." He does not give a date to the Regent's paper, but on June 25 Kirkcaldy wrote to Percy that the Regent "is like to grant the other party" (the Reformers) "all they desire, which in part she has offered already."

Knox seizes on the word "offered" as if it necessarily meant "offered though unasked," and so styles the Regent's remark "a manifest lie." But Kirkcaldy, we see, uses the words "has in part offered already" when he means that the Regent has "offered" to grant some of the wishes of his allies.

Meanwhile the Regent will allow freedom of conscience in the country, and especially in Edinburgh. But the Reformers, her paper goes on, desire to subvert the crown. To prove this she says that they daily receive messengers from England and send their own; and they have seized the stamps in the Mint (a capital point as regards the crown) and the Palace of Holyrood, which Lesley says that they sacked. Knox replies, "there is never a sentence in the narrative true," except that his party seized the stamps merely to prevent the issue of base coin (not to coin the stolen plate of the churches and monasteries for themselves, as Lesley says they did). But Knox's own letters, and those of Kirkcaldy of Grange and Sir Henry Percy, prove that they *were* intriguing with England as early as June 23-25. Their conduct, with the complicity of Percy, was perfectly well known to the Regent's party, and was denounced by d'Oysel to the French ambassador in London in letters of July. Elizabeth, on August 7, answered the remonstrances of the Regent, promising to punish her officials if guilty. Nobody lied more frankly than "that imperial votaress."

When Knox says "there is never a sentence in the narrative true," he is very bold. It was not true that the rising was merely under pretext of religion. It may have been untrue that messengers went *daily* to England, but five letters were written between June 21 and June 28. To stand on the words of the Regent—"*every day*"—would be a babyish quibble. All the rest of her narrative was absolutely true.

Knox, on June 28, asked leave to enter England for secret discourse; he had already written to the same effect from St. Andrews. If Henri sends French reinforcement, Knox "is uncertain what will follow"; we may guess that authority would be in an ill way. Cecil temporised; he wanted a better name than Kirkcaldy's—a man in the Regent's service—to the negotiations (July 4). "Anywise kindle the fire," he writes to Croft (July 8). Croft is to let the Reformers know that Arran has escaped out of France. Such a chance will not again "come in our lives." We see what the chance is!

On July 19 Knox writes again to Cecil, enclosing what he means to be an apology for his "Blast of the Trumpet," to be given to Elizabeth. He says, while admitting Elizabeth's right to reign, as "judged godly," though a woman, that they "must be careful not to make entrance and title to many, by whom not only shall the truth be impugned, but also shall the country be brought to bondage and slavery. God give you eyes to foresee and wisdom to avoid the apparent danger."

The "many" to whom "entrance and title" are not to be given, manifestly are Mary Stuart, Queen of France and Scotland.

It is not very clear whether Knox, while thus working against a woman's "entrance and title" to the crown on the ground of her sex, is thinking of Mary Stuart's prospects of succession to the throne of England or of her Scottish rights, or of both. His phrase is cast in a vague way; "many" are spoken of, but it is not hard to understand what particular female claimant is in his mind.

Thus Knox himself was intriguing with England against his Queen at the very moment when in his "History" he denies that communications were frequent between his party and England, or that any of the Regent's charges are true. As for opposing authority and being rebellious, the manifest fundamental idea of the plot is to marry Elizabeth to Arran and deny "entrance and title" to the rightful Queen. It was an admirable scheme, and had Arran not become a lunatic, had Elizabeth not been "that imperial votaress" vowed to eternal maidenhood, their bridal, with the consequent loss of the Scottish throne by Mary, would have been the most fortunate of all possible events. The brethren had, in short, a perfect right to defend their creed in arms; a perfect right to change the dynasty; a perfect right to intrigue with England, and to resist a French landing, if they could. But for a reformer of the Church to give a dead lady the lie in his "History" when the economy of truth lay rather on his own side, as he knew, is not so well. We shall see that Knox possibly had the facts in his mind during the first interview with Mary Stuart.

The Lords, July 2, replied to the proclamation of Mary of Guise, saying that she accused them of a purpose "to invade her person." There is not a word of the kind in the Regent's proclamation as given by Knox himself. They denied what the Regent in her proclamation had not asserted, and what she had asserted about their dealings with England they did not venture to deny; "whereby," says Spottiswoode in his "History," "it seemed there was some dealing that way for expelling the Frenchmen, which they would not deny, and thought not convenient as then openly to profess." The task of giving the lie to the Regent when she spoke truth was left to the pen of Knox.

Meanwhile, at Dunbar, Mary of Guise was in evil case. She had sounded Erskine, the commander of the Castle, who, she hoped, would stand by her. But she had no money to pay her French troops, who were becoming mutinous, and d'Oysel "knew not to what Saint to vow himself." The Earl of Huntly, before he would serve the Crown, insisted on a promise of the Earldom of Moray; this desire was to be his ruin. Huntly was a double dealer; "the gay Gordons" were ever brave, loyal, and bewildered by their chiefs. By July 22, the Scots heard of the fatal wound of Henri II., to their encouragement. Both parties were in lack of money, and the forces of the Congregation were slipping home by hundreds. Mary, according to Knox, was exciting the Duke against Argyll and Lord James, by the charge that Lord James was aiming at the crown, in which if he succeeded, he would deprive not only her daughter of the sovereignty, but the Hamiltons of the succession. Young and ambitious as Lord James then was, and heavily as he was suspected, even in England, it is most improbable that he ever thought of being king.

The Congregation refused to let Argyll and Lord James hold conference with the Regent. Other discussions led to no result, except waste of time, to the Regent's advantage; and, on July 22, Mary, in council with Lord Erskine, Huntly, and the Duke, resolved to march against the Reformers at Edinburgh, who had no time to call in their scattered levies in the West, Angus, and Fife. Logan of Restalrig, lately an ally of the godly, surrendered Leith, over which he was the superior, to d'Oysel; and the Congregation decided to accept a truce (July 23-24).

At this point Knox's narrative becomes so embroiled that it reminds one of nothing so much as of Claude Nau's attempts to glide past an awkward point in the history of his employer, Mary Stuart. I have puzzled over Knox's narrative again and again, and hope that I have disentangled the knotted and slippery thread.

It is not wonderful that the brethren made terms, for the "Historie" states that their force numbered but 1500 men, whereas d'Oysel and the Duke led twice that number, horse and foot. They also heard from Erskine, in the Castle, that, if they did not accept "such appointment as they might have," he "would declare himself their enemy," as he had promised the Regent. It seems that she did not want war, for d'Oysel's French alone should have been able to rout the depleted ranks of the Congregation.

The question is, What were the terms of treaty? for it is Knox's endeavour to prove that the Regent broke them, and so justified the later proceedings of the Reformers. The terms, in French, are printed by Teulet. They run thus:—

1. The Protestants, not being inhabitants of Edinburgh, shall depart next day.

2. They shall deliver the stamps for coining to persons appointed by the Regent, hand over Holyrood, and Ruthven and Pitarro shall be pledges for performance.

3. They shall be dutiful subjects, except in matters of religion.

4. They shall not disturb the clergy in their persons or by withholding their rents, &c., before January 10, 1560.

5. They shall not attack churches or monasteries before that date.

6. The town of Edinburgh shall enjoy liberty of conscience, and shall choose its form of religion as it pleases till that date.

7. The Regent shall not molest the preachers nor suffer the clergy to molest them for cause of religion till that date.

8. Keith, Knox, and Spottiswoode, add that no garrisons, French or Scots, shall occupy Edinburgh, but soldiers may repair thither from their garrisons for lawful business.

The French soldiers are said to have swaggered in St. Giles's, but no complaint is made that they were garrisoned in Edinburgh. In fact, they abode in the Canongate and Leith.

Now, these were the terms accepted by the Congregation. This is certain, not only because historians, Knox excepted, are unanimous, but because the terms were either actually observed, or were evaded, on a stated point of construction.

1. The Congregation left Edinburgh.

2. They handed over the stamps of the Mint, Holyrood, and the two pledges.

3. 4, 5. We do not hear that they attacked any clerics or monastery before they broke off publicly from the treaty, and Knox (i. 381) admits that Article 4 was accepted.

6. They would not permit the town of Edinburgh to choose its religion by "voting of men." On July 29, when Huntly, Chatelherault, and Erskine, the neutral commander of the Castle, asked for a *plébiscite*, as provided in the treaty of July 24, the Truth, said the brethren, was not a matter of human votes, and, as the brethren held St. Giles's Church before the treaty, under Article 7 they could not be dispossessed. The Regent, to avoid shadow of offence, yielded the point as to Article 6, and was accused of breach of treaty because, occupying Holyrood, she had her Mass there. Had Edinburgh been polled, the brethren knew that they would have been outvoted.

Now, Knox's object, in that part of Book II. of his "History," which was written in September-October 1559 as a tract for contemporary reading, is to prove that the Regent was the breaker of treaty. His method is first to give "the heads drawn by us, which we desired to be granted." The heads are—

1. No member of the Congregation shall be troubled in any respect by any authority for the recent "innovation" before the Parliament of January 10, 1560, decides the controversies.

2. Idolatry shall not be restored where, on the day of treaty, it has been suppressed.

3. Preachers may preach wherever they have preached and wherever they may chance to come.

4. No soldiers shall be in garrison in Edinburgh.

5. The French shall be sent away on "a reasonable day" and no more brought in without assent of the whole Nobility and Parliament.

These articles make no provision for the safety of Catholic priests and churches, and insist on suppression of idolatry where it has been put down, and the entire withdrawal of French forces. Knox's party could not possibly denounce these terms which they demanded as "things unreasonable and ungodly," for they were the very terms which they had been asking for, ever since the Regent went to Dunbar. Yet, when the treaty was made, the preachers did say "our case is not yet so desperate that we need to grant to things unreasonable and ungodly." Manifestly, therefore, the terms actually obtained, as being "unreasonable and ungodly," were *not* those for which the Reformers asked, and which, *they publicly proclaimed*, had been conceded.

Knox writes, "These our articles were altered, and another form disposeth." And here he translates the terms as given in the French, terms which provide for the safety of Catholics, the surrender of Holyrood and the Mint, but say nothing about the withdrawal of the French troops or the non-restoration of "idolatry" where it has been suppressed.

He adds, "This alteration in words and order was made" (so it actually *was* made) "without the knowledge and consent of those whose counsel we had used in all cases before"—clearly meaning the preachers, and also implying that the consent of the noble negotiators for the Congregation *was* obtained to the French articles.

Next day the Congregation left Edinburgh, after making solemn proclamation of the conditions of truce, in which they omitted all the terms of the French version, except those in their own favour, and stated (in Knox's version) that all of their own terms, except the most important, namely, the removal of the French, and the promise to bring in no more, had been granted! It may be by accident, however, that the proclamation of the Lords, as given by Knox, omits the article securing the departure of the French. There exist two MS. copies of the proclamation, in which the Lords dare to assert "that the Frenchmen should be sent away at a reasonable date, and no more brought in except by assent of the whole nobility and Parliament."

Of the terms really settled, except as regards the immunity of their own party, the Lords told the public not one word; they suppressed what was true, and added what was false.

Against this formal, public, and impudent piece of mendacity, we might expect Knox to protest in his "History"; to denounce it as a cause of God's wrath. On the other hand he states, with no disapproval, the childish quibbles by which his party defended their action.

On reading or hearing the Lords' proclamation, the Catholics, who knew the real terms of treaty, said that the Lords "in their proclamation had made no mention of anything promised to *them*," and "had proclaimed more than was contained in the Appointment;" among other things, doubtless, the promise to dismiss the French.

The brethren replied to these "calumnies of Papists" (as Calderwood styles them), that they "proclaimed nothing that was not *finally* agreed upon, *in word and promise*, betwixt us and those with whom the Appointment was made, *whatsoever their scribes had after written*, who, in very deed, had altered, both in words and sentences, our Articles, *as they were first conceived*; and yet if their own writings were diligently examined, the self same thing shall be found *in substance*."

This is most complicated quibbling! Knox uses his ink like the cuttle-fish, to conceal the facts. The "own writings" of the Regent's party are before us, and do not contain the terms proclaimed by the Congregation. Next, in drawing up the terms which the Congregation was compelled to accept, the "scribes" of the Regent's party necessarily, and with the consent of the Protestant negotiators, altered the terms proposed by the brethren, but not granted by the Regent's negotiators. Thirdly, the Congregation now asserted that "*finally*" an arrangement in conformity with their proclamation was "agreed upon *in word and promise*"; that is, verbally, which we never find them again alleging. The game was to foist false terms on public belief, and then to accuse the Regent of perfidy in not keeping them.

These false terms were not only publicly proclaimed by the Congregation with sound of trumpets, but they were actually sent, by Knox or Kirkcaldy, or both, to Croft at Berwick, for English reading, on July 24. In a note I print the letter, signed by Kirkcaldy, but in the holograph of Knox, according to Father Stevenson. It will be remarked that the genuine articles forbidding attacks on monasteries and ensuring priests in their revenues are here omitted, while the false articles on suppression of idolatry, and expulsion of the French forces are inserted, and nothing is said about Edinburgh's special liberty to choose her religion.

The sending of this false intelligence was not the result of a misunderstanding. I have shown that the French terms were perfectly well understood, and were observed, except Article 6, on which the Regent made a concession. How then could men professionally godly venture to misreport the terms, and so make them at once seem more favourable to themselves and less discouraging to Cecil than they really were, while at the same time (as the Regent could not keep terms which she had never granted) they were used as a ground of accusation against her?

This is the point that has perplexed me, for Knox, no less than the Congregation, seems to have deliberately said good-bye to truth and honour, unless the Lords elaborately deceived their secretary and diplomatic agent. The only way in which I can suppose that Knox and his friends reconciled their consciences to their conduct is this:

Knox tells us that "when all points were communed and agreed upon by mid-persons," Chatelherault and Huntly had a private interview with Argyll, Glencairn, and others of his party. They promised that they would be enemies to the Regent if she broke any one jot of the treaty. "As much promised the duke that *he* would do, if in case that she would not remove her French at a reasonable day . . . " the duke being especially interested in their removal. But Huntly is not said to have made *this* promise—the removal of the French obviously not being part of the "Appointment."

Next, the brethren, in arguing with the Catholics about their own mendacious proclamation of the terms, said that "we proclaimed nothing which was not *finally* agreed upon, *in word and promise*, betwixt us and those with whom the Appointment was made. . . . "

I can see no explanation of Knox's conduct, except that he and his friends pacified their consciences by persuading themselves that non-official words of Huntly and Chatelherault (whatever these words may have been), spoken after "all was agreed upon," cancelled the treaty with the Regent, became the real treaty, and were binding on the Regent! Thus Knox or Kirkcaldy, or both, by letter; and Knox later, orally in conversation with Croft, could announce false terms of treaty. So great, if I am right, is a good man's power of self-persuasion! I shall welcome any more creditable theory of the Reformer's behaviour, but I can see no alternative, unless the Lords lied to Knox.

That the French should be driven out was a great point with Cecil, for he was always afraid that the Scots might slip back from the English to the old French alliance. On July 28, after the treaty of July 24, but before he heard of it, he insisted on the necessity of expelling the French, in a letter to the Reformers. He "marvels that they omit such an opportunity to help themselves." He sent a letter of vague generalities in answer to their petitions for aid. When he received, as he did, a copy of the terms of the treaty of July 24, in French, he would understand.

As further proof that Cecil was told what Knox and Kirkcaldy should have known to be untrue, we note that on August 28 the Regent, weary of the perpetual charges of perfidy anew brought against her, "ashamed not," writes Knox, to put forth a proclamation, in which she asserted that nothing, in the terms of July 23-24, forbade her to bring in more French troops, "as may clearly appear by inspection of the said Appointment, which the bearer has presently to show."

Why should the Regent have been "ashamed" to tell the truth? If the bearer showed a false and forged treaty, the Congregation must have denounced it, and produced the genuine document with the signatures. Far from that, in a reply (from internal evidence written by Knox), they admit, "neither do we *here* allege the breaking of the Appointment made at Leith (which, nevertheless, has manifestly been done), but"—and here the writer wanders into quite other questions. Moreover, Knox gives another reply to the Regent, "by some men," in which they write "we dispute not so much whether the bringing in of more Frenchmen be violating of the Appointment, which the Queen and her faction cannot deny to be manifestly broken by them in more cases than one," in no way connected with the French. One of these cases will presently be stated—it is comic enough to deserve record—but, beyond denial, the brethren could not, and did not even attempt to make out their charge as to the Regent's breach of truce by bringing in new, or retaining old, French forces.

Our historians, and the biographers of Knox, have not taken the trouble to unravel this question of the treaty of July 24. But the behaviour of the Lords and of Knox seems characteristic, and worthy of examination.

It is not argued that Mary of Guise was, or became, incapable of worse than dissimulation (a case of forgery by her in the following year is investigated in Appendix B). But her practices at this time were such as Knox could not throw the first stone at. Her French advisers were in fact "perplexed," as Throckmorton wrote to Elizabeth (August 8). They made preparations for sending large reinforcements: they advised concession in religion: they waited on events, and the Regent could only provide, at Leith (which was jealous of Edinburgh and anxious to be made a free burgh), a place whither she could fly in peril. Meantime she would vainly exert her woman's wit among many dangers.

Knox, too, was exerting his wit in his own way. Busied in preaching and in acting as secretary and diplomatic agent to the Congregation as he was, he must also have begun in or not much later than August 1559, the part of his "History" first written by him, namely Book II. That book, as he wrote to a friend named Railton on October 23, 1559 (when much of it was already penned), is meant as a defence of his party against the charge of sedition, and was clearly intended (we reiterate) for contemporary reading at home and abroad, while the strife was still unsettled. This being so, Knox continues his policy of blaming the Regent for breach of the misreported treaty of July 24: for treachery, which would justify the brethren's attack on her before the period of truce (January 10, 1559) ran out.

One clause, we know, secured the Reformers from molestation before that date. Despite this, Knox records a case of "oppressing" a brother, "which had been sufficient to prove the Appointment to be plainly violated." Lord Seton, of the Catholic party, "broke a chair on Alexander Whitelaw as he came from Preston (pans) accompanied by William Knox . . . and this he did supposing that Alexander Whitelaw had been John Knox."

So much Knox states in his Book II., writing probably in September or October 1559. But he does not here say what Alexander Whitelaw and William Knox had been doing, or inform us how he himself was concerned in the matter. He could not reveal the facts when writing in the early autumn of 1559, because the brethren were then still taking the line that they were loyal, and were suffering from the Regent's breaches of treaty, as in the matter of the broken chair.

The sole allusion here made by Knox to the English intrigues, before they were manifest to all mankind in September, is this, "Because England was of the same religion, and lay next to us, it was judged expedient first to prove them, which we did by one or two messengers, as hereafter, in its own place, more amply shall be declared." He later inserted in Book III. some account of the intrigues of July-August 1559, "in its own place," namely, in a part of his work occupied with the occurrences of January 1560.

Cecil, prior to the compact of July 24, had wished to meet Knox at Stamford. On July 30 Knox received his instructions as negotiator with England. His employers say that they hear that Huntly and Chatelherault have promised to join the Reformers if the Regent breaks a jot of the treaty of July 24, the terms of which Knox can declare. They ask money to enable them to take Stirling Castle, and "strength by sea" for the capture of Broughty Castle, on Tay. Yet they later complained of the Regent when she fortified Leith. They actually *did* take Broughty Castle, and then had the hardihood to aver that they only set about this when they heard in mid-September of the fortification of Leith by the Regent. They aimed at it six days after their treaty of July 24. They asked for soldiers to lie in garrison, for men, ships, and money for their Lords.

Bearing these instructions Knox sailed from Fife to Holy Island, near Berwick, and there met Croft, the Governor of that town. Croft kept him, not with sufficient secrecy, in Berwick, where he was well known, while Whitelaw was coming from Cecil with his answers to the petitions of the brethren. Meanwhile Croft held converse with Knox, who, as he reports, says that, as to the change of "Authority" (that is of sovereignty, temporary at least), the choice of the brethren would be subject to Elizabeth's wishes. Yet the brethren contemplated no change of Authority! Arran ought to be kept secretly in England "till wise men considered what was in him; if misliked he put Lord James second." As to what Knox told Croft about the terms of treaty of July 24, it is best to state the case in Croft's own words. "He (Knox) excusys the Protestantes, for that the French as commyng apon them at Edynbrogh when theyr popoll were departed to make new provysyon of vytaylles, forcyd them to make composycyon wyth the quene. Whereyn (sayeth he) the frenchmen ar apoynted to departe out of Scotland by the xth of thys monthe, and they truste verely by thys caus to be stronger, for that the Duke, apon breche of promys on the quene's part, wyll take playne parte withe the Protestantes."

This is quite explicit. Knox, as envoy of the Lords, declares that in the treaty it is "appointed" that the French force shall leave Scotland on August 10. (The printed calendars are not accurate.) No such matter occurred in the treaty "wyth the quene." Knox added, next day, that he himself "was unfit to treat of so great matters," and Croft appears to have agreed with him, for, by the Reformer's lack of caution, his doings in Holy Island were "well known and published." Consequently, when Whitelaw returned to Knox with Cecil's reply to the requests of the brethren, the performances of Knox and Whitelaw were no secrets, in outline at least, to the Regent's party. For this reason, Lord Seton, mistaking Whitelaw for Knox (who had set out on August 3 to join the brethren at Stirling), pursued and broke a chair on the harmless Brother Whitelaw. Such was the Regent's treacherous breach of treaty!

During this episode in his curious adventures as a diplomatist, Knox recommended Balnaves, author of a treatise on "Justification by Faith," as a better agent in these courses, and with Balnaves the new envoy of Elizabeth, Sadleir, a veteran diplomatist (wheedled in 1543 by Mary of Guise), transacted business henceforth. Sadleir was ordered to Berwick on August 6. Elizabeth infringed the treaty of Cateau Cambresis, then only four months old, by giving Sadleir

£3000 in gold, or some such sum, for the brethren. "They were tempting the Duke by all means possible," but he will only promise neutrality if it comes to the push, and they, Argyll and Lord James say (Glasgow, August 13), are not yet ready "to discharge this authority," that is, to depose the Regent. Chatelherault's promise was less vigorous than it had been reported!

Knox, who now acted as secretary for the Congregation, was not Sir Henry Wotton's ideal ambassador, "an honest man sent to lie abroad for his country." When he stooped to statements which seem scarcely candid, to put it mildly, he did violence to his nature. He forced himself to proclaim the loyalty of his party from the pulpit, when he could not do so without some economy of truth. He inserted things in his "History," and spoke things to Croft, which he should have known to be false. But he carried his point. He did advance the "union of hearts" with England, if in a blundering fashion, and we owe him eternal gratitude for his interest in the match, though "we like not the manner of the wooing." The reluctant hand of Elizabeth was now inextricably caught in the gear of that great machine which broke the ancient league of France and Scotland, and saved Scotland from some of the sorrows of France.

The papers of Sadleir, Elizabeth's secret agent with the Scots, show the godly pursuing their old plan of campaign. To make treaty with the Regent; to predict from the pulpit that she would break it; to make false statements about the terms of the treaty; to accuse her of their infringement; to profess loyalty; to aim at setting up a new sovereign power; to tell the populace that Mary of Guise's scanty French reinforcements—some 1500 men—came by virtue of a broken treaty; to tell Sadleir that they were very glad that the French *had* come, as they would excite popular hatred; to make out that the fortification of Leith was breach of treaty;—such, in brief, were the methods of the Reformers.

They now took a new method of proving the Regent's breach of treaty, that she had "set up the Mass in Holyrood, which they had before suppressed." *They* were allowed to have their sermons in St. Giles's, but *she* was not to have her rites in her own abbey. Balnaves still harped on the non-dismissal of the French as a breach of treaty!

Arran, returning from Switzerland, had an interview with Elizabeth in England, in mid-September, was smuggled across the Border with the astute and unscrupulous Thomas Randolph in his train. With Arran among them, Chatelherault might waver as he would. Meanwhile Knox and Willock preached up and down the country, doubtless repeating to the people their old charges against the Regent. Lethington, the secretary of that lady, still betrayed her, telling Sadleir "that he attended upon the Regent no longer than he might have a good occasion to revolt unto the Protestants" (September 16).

Balnaves got some two to three thousand pounds in gold (the sum is variously stated) from Sadleir. "He saith, whatever pretence they make, the principal mark they shoot at is to make an alteration of the State and authority." This at least is explicit enough. The Reformers were actually renewing the civil war on charges so stale and so false. The Duke had possibly promised to desert her if she broke the truce, and now he seized on the flimsy pretence, because the Congregation, as the leaders said, had "tempted him" sufficiently. They had come up to his price. Arran, the hoped-for Hamilton king, the hoped-for husband of the Queen of England, had arrived, and with Arran the Duke joined the Reformers. About September 20 they forbade the Regent to fortify Leith.

The brethren say that they have given no "provocation." Six weeks earlier they had requested England to help them to seize and hold Broughty Castle, though the Regent may not have known that detail.

The Regent replied as became her, and Glencairn, with Erskine of Dun, wrecked the rich abbey of Paisley. The brethren now broke the truce with a vengeance.

CHAPTER XII.

KNOX IN THE WAR OF THE CONGREGATION: THE REGENT ATTACKED: HER DEATH: CATHOLICISM ABOLISHED, 1559-1560

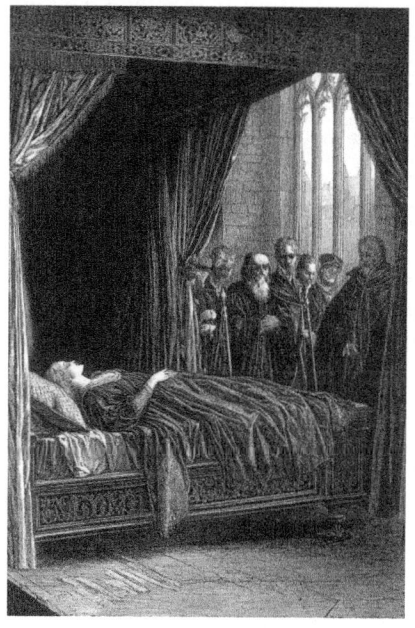

Though the Regent was now to be deposed and attacked by armed force, Knox tells us that there were dissensions among her enemies. Some held "that the Queen was heavily done to," and that the leaders "sought another end than religion." Consequently, when the Lords with their forces arrived at Edinburgh on October 16, the local brethren showed a want of enthusiasm. The Congregation nevertheless summoned the Regent to depart from Leith, and on

October 21 met at the Tolbooth to discuss her formal deposition from office. Willock moved that this might lawfully be done. Knox added, with more reserve than usual, that their hearts must not be withdrawn from their King and Queen, Mary and Francis. The Regent, too, ought to be restored when she openly repented and submitted. Willock dragged Jehu into his sermon, but Knox does not appear to have remarked that Francis and Mary were Ahab and Jezebel, idolaters. He was now in a position of less freedom and more responsibility than while he was a wandering prophet at large.

On October 24 the Congregation summoned Leith, having deposed the Regent *in the name of the King and Queen, Francis and Mary*, and of themselves as Privy Council! They did more. They caused one James Cocky, a gold worker, to forge the great seal of Francis and Mary, "wherewith they sealed their pretended laws and ordinances, tending to constrain the subjects of the kingdom to rebel and favour their usurpations." Their proclamations with the forged seal they issued at St. Andrews, Glasgow, Linlithgow, Perth, and elsewhere; using this seal in their letters to noblemen, who were ordered to obey Arran. The gold worker, whose name is variously spelled in the French record, says that the device for the coins which the Congregation meant to issue and ordered him to execute was on one side a cross with a crown of thorns, on the other the words VERBUM DEI. The artist, Cocky, was dilatory, and when the brethren were driven out of Edinburgh he gave the dies, unfinished, to John Achison, the chief official of the Mint, who often executed coins of Queen Mary. As Professor Hume Brown says of the audacious statement of the brethren, that they acted in the name of their King and Queen, their use of the forged Royal seal, "as covering their action with an appearance of law, served its purpose in their appeals to the people." Cocky and Kirkcaldy were hanged by Morton in 1573.

The idea of forging the great seal may have arisen in the fertile brain of Lethington, who about October 25 had at last deserted the Regent, and now took Knox's place as secretary of the Congregation. Henceforth their manifestoes say little about religion, and a great deal about the French design to conquer Scotland.

To the wit of Lethington we may plausibly attribute a proposal which, on October 25, Knox submitted to Croft. It was that England should lend 1000 men for the attack on the Regent in Leith. Peace with France need not be broken, for the men may come as private adventurers, and England may denounce them as rebels. Croft declined this proposal as dishonourable, and as too clearly a breach of treaty. Knox replied that he had communicated Croft's letter "to such as partly induced me before to write" (October 29). Very probably Lethington suggested the idea, leaving the burden of its proposal on Knox. Dr. M'Crie says that it is a solitary case of the Reformer's recommending dissimulation; but the proceeding was in keeping with Knox's previous statements about the nature of the terms made in July; with the protestations of loyalty; with the lie given to Mary of Guise when she spoke, on the whole, the plain truth; and generally with the entire conduct of the prophet and of the Congregation. Dr. M'Crie justly remarks that Knox "found it difficult to preserve integrity and Christian simplicity amidst the crooked wiles of political intrigue."

On the behaviour of the godly heaven did not smile—for the moment. Scaling-ladders had been constructed in St. Giles's church, "so that preaching was neglected." "The preachers spared not openly to say that they feared the success of that enterprise should not be prosperous," for this reason, "God could not suffer such contempt of His word . . . long to be unpunished." The Duke lost heart; the waged soldiers mutinied for lack of pay; Morton deserted the cause; Bothwell wounded Ormiston as he carried money from Croft, and seized the cash —behaving treacherously, if it be true that he was under promise not to act against the brethren. The French garrison of Leith made successful sorties; and despite the valour of Arran and Lord James and the counsel of Lethington, the godly fled from Edinburgh on November 5, under taunts and stones cast by the people of the town.

The fugitives never stopped till they reached Stirling, when Knox preached to them. He lectured at great length on discomfitures of the godly in the Old Testament, and about the Benjamites, and the Levite and his wife. Coming to practical politics, he reminded his audience that after the accession of the Hamiltons to their party, "there was nothing heard but This lord will bring these many hundred spears . . . if this Earl be ours, no man in such a district will trouble us." The Duke ought to be ashamed of himself. Before Knox came to Scotland we know he had warned the brethren against alliance with the Hamiltons. The Duke had been on the Regent's side, "yet without his assistance they could not have compelled us to appoint with the Queen upon such unequal conditions" in the treaty of July. So the terms *were* in favour of the Regent, after all is said and done!

God had let the brethren fall, Knox said, into their present condition because they put their trust in man—in the Duke—a noble whose repentance was very dubious.

Then Knox rose to the height of the occasion. "Yea, whatsoever becomes of us and our mortal carcases, I doubt not but that this Cause (in despite of Satan) shall prevail in the realm of Scotland. For as it is the eternal truth of the eternal God, so shall it once prevail . . ." Here we have the actual genius of Knox, his tenacity, his courage in an uphill game, his faith which might move mountains. He adjured all to amendment of life, prayer, and charity. "The minds of men began to be wonderfully erected." In Arran and Lord James too, manifestly not jealous rivals, Randolph found "more honour, stoutness, and courage than in all the rest" (November 3).

Already, before the flight, Lethington was preparing to visit England. The conduct of diplomacy with England was thus in capable hands, and Lethington was a *persona grata* to the English Queen. Meanwhile the victorious Regent behaved with her wonted moderation. "She pursueth no man that hath showed himself against her at this time." She pardoned all burgesses of Edinburgh, and was ready to receive the Congregation to her grace, if they would put away the traitor Lethington, Balnaves, and some others. Knox, however, says that she gave the houses of the most honest men to the French. The Regent was now very ill; *graviter aegrotat*, say Francis and Mary (Dec. 4, 1559).

The truth is that the Cause of Knox, far from being desperate, as for an hour it seemed to the faint-hearted, had never looked so well. Cecil and the English Council saw that they were committed; their gift of money was known, they must bestir themselves. While they had "nourished the garboil" in Scotland, fanned the flame, they professed to believe that France was aiming, through Scotland, at England. They arranged for a large levy of forces at Berwick; they promised money without stint: and Cecil drew up the paper adopted, as I conceive, by the brethren in their Latin appeal to all Christian princes. The Scots were to say that they originally took arms in defence of their native dynasty (the Hamiltons), Mary Stuart having no heirs of her body, and France intending to annex Scotland—which was true enough, but was not the cause of the rising at Perth. That England is also aimed at is proved by the fact that Mary and Francis, on the seal of Scotland, quarter the arms of England. Knox himself had seen, and had imparted the fact to Cecil, a jewel on which these fatal heraldic pretensions were made. The Queen is governed by "the new authority of the House of Guise." In short, Elizabeth must be asked to intervene for these political reasons, not in defence of the Gospel, and large preparations for armed action in Scotland were instantly made. Meanwhile Cecil's sketch of the proper manifesto for the Congregation to make, was embodied in Lethington's instructions (November 24) from the Congregation, as well as adapted in their Latin appeal to Christian princes.

We may suppose that a man of Knox's unbending honesty was glad to have thrown off his functions as secretary to the brethren. Far from disclaiming their idolatrous King and Queen (the ideal policy), they were issuing proclamations headed "Francis and Mary," and bearing the forged signet. Examples with the seal were, as late as 1652, in the possession of the Erskine of Dun of that day. In them Francis and Mary denounce the Pope as Antichrist! Keith, who wrote much later, styles these proclamations "pretty singular," and Knox must have been of the same opinion.

After Lethington took the office of secretary to the Congregation, Knox had for some time no great public part in affairs. Fife was invaded by "these bloody worms," as he calls the French; and he preached what he tells us was a "comfortable sermon" to the brethren at Cupar. But Lethington had secured the English alliance: Lord Grey was to lead 4000 foot and 2000 horse to the Border; Lord Winter with fourteen ship set sail, and was incommoded by a storm, in which vessels of d'Elboeuf, with French reinforcements for the

Regent, were, some lost, some driven back to harbour. As in Jacobite times, French aid to the loyal party was always unfortunate, and the arrival of Winter's English fleet in the Forth caused d'Oysel to retreat out of Fife back to Leith. He had nearly reached St. Andrews, where Knox dwelt in great agony of spirit. He had "great need of a good horse," probably because, as in October 1559, money was offered for his head. But private assassination had no terrors for the Reformer.

Knox, as he wrote to a friend on January 29, 1560, had forsaken all public assemblies and retired to a life of study, because "I am judged among ourselves too extreme." When the Duke of Norfolk, with the English army, was moving towards Berwick, where he was to make a league with the Protestant nobles of Scotland, Knox summoned Chatelherault, and the gentlemen of his party, then in Glasgow. They wished Norfolk to come to them by Carlisle, a thing inconvenient to Lord James. Knox chid them sharply for sloth, and want of wisdom and discretion, praising highly the conduct of Lord James. They had "unreasonable minds." "Wise men do wonder what my Lord Duke's friends do mean, that are so slack and backward in this Cause." The Duke did not, however, write to France with an offer of submission. That story, *ben trovato* but not *vero*, rests on a forgery by the Regent! The fact is that the Duke was not a true Protestant, his advisers, including his brother the Archbishop, were Catholics, and the successes of d'Oysel in winter had terrified him; but, seeing an English army at hand, he assented to the league with England at Berwick, as "second person of the realm of Scotland" (February 27, 1560). Elizabeth "accepted the realm of Scotland"— Chatelherault being recognised as heir-apparent to the throne thereof—for so long as the marriage of Queen Mary and Francis I. endured, and a year later. The Scots, however, remain dutiful subjects of Queen Mary, they say, except so far as lawless attempts to make Scotland a province of France are concerned. Chatelherault did not *sign* the league till May 10, with Arran, Huntly, Morton (at last committed to the Cause), and the usual leaders of the Congregation.

With the details of the siege of Leith, and with the attempts at negotiation, we are not here concerned. France, in fact, was powerless to aid the Regent. Since the arrival of Throckmorton in France, as ambassador of England, in the previous summer (1559), the Huguenots had been conspiring. They were in touch with Geneva, in the east; on the north, in Brittany, they appear to have been stirred up by Tremaine, a Cornish gentleman, and emissary of Cecil, who joined Throckmorton at Blois, in March 1560. Stories were put about that the young French King was a leper, and was kidnapping fair-haired children, in whose blood he meant to bathe. The Huguenots had been conspiring ever since September 1559, when they seem to have sent to Elizabeth for aid in money. More recently they had held a kind of secret convention at Nantes, and summoned bands who were to lurk in the woods, concentrate at Amboise, attack the château, slay the Guises, and probably put the King and Queen Mary under the Prince de Condé, who was by the plotters expected to take the part which Arran played in Scotland. It is far from certain that Condé had accepted the position. In all this we may detect English intrigue and the gold of Elizabeth. Calvin had been consulted; he disapproved of the method of the plot, still more of the plot itself. But he knew all about it. "All turns on killing Antonius," he wrote, "Antonius" being either the Cardinal or the Duc de Guise.

The conspiracy failed at Amboise, on March 17-19, 1560. Throckmorton was present, and describes the panic and perplexity of the Court, while he eagerly asks to be promptly and secretly recalled, as suspicion has fallen on himself. He sent Tremaine home through Brittany, where he gathered proposals for betraying French towns to Elizabeth, rather prematurely. Surrounded by treachery, and destitute of funds, the Guises could not aid the Regent, and Throckmorton kept advising Cecil to "strike while the iron was hot," and paralyse French designs. The dying Regent of Scotland never lost heart in circumstances so desperate.

Even before the outbreak at Perth, Mary of Guise had been in very bad health. When the English crossed the Border to beleaguer Leith, Lord Erskine, who had maintained neutrality in Edinburgh Castle, allowed her to come there to die (April 1, 1560).

On April 29, from the Castle of Edinburgh, she wrote a letter to d'Oysel, commanding in Leith. She told him that she was suffering from dropsy; "one of her legs begins to swell. . . . You know there are but three days for the dropsy in this country." The letter was intercepted by her enemies, and deciphered. On May 7, the English and Scots made an assault, and were beaten back with loss of 1000 men. According to Knox, the French stripped the fallen, and allowed the white carcases to lie under the wall, as also happened in 1746, after the English defeat at Falkirk. The Regent saw them, Knox says, from the Castle, and said they were "a fair tapestry." "Her words were heard of some," and carried to Knox, who, from the pulpit, predicted "that God should revenge that contumely done to his image . . . even in such as rejoiced thereat. And the very experience declared that he was not deceived, for within few days thereafter (yea, some say that same day) began her belly and loathsome legs to swell, and so continued, till that God did execute his judgments upon her."

Knox wrote thus on May 16, 1566. He was a little irritated at that time by Queen Mary's triumph over his friends, the murderers of Riccio, and his own hasty flight from Edinburgh to Kyle. This may excuse the somewhat unusual and even unbecoming nature of his language concerning the dying lady, but his memory was quite wrong about his prophecy. The symptoms of the Regent's malady had begun more than a week before the Anglo-Scottish defeat at Leith, and the nature of her complaint ought to have been known to the prophet's party, as her letter, describing her condition, had been intercepted and deciphered. But the deciphering may have been done in England, which would cause delay. We cannot, of course, prove that Knox was informed as to the Regent's malady before he prophesied; if so, he had forgotten the fact before he wrote as he did in 1566. But the circumstances fail to demonstrate that he had a supernormal premonition, or drew a correct deduction from Scripture, and make it certain that the Regent did not fall ill after his prophecy.

The Regent died on June 11, half-an-hour after the midnight of June 10. A report was written on June 13, from Edinburgh Castle, to the Cardinal of Lorraine, by Captain James Cullen, who some twelve years later was hanged by the Regent Morton. He says that since June 7, Lord James and Argyll, Marischal, and Glencairn, had assiduously attended on the dying lady. Two hours before her death she spoke apart for a whole hour with Lord James. Chatelherault had seen her twice, and Arran once. Knox mentions the visits of these lords, and says that d'Oysel was forbidden to speak with her, "belike she would have bidden him farewell, for auld familiarity was great."

According to Knox, the Regent admitted the errors of her policy, attributing it to Huntly, who had deserted her, and to "the wicked counsel of her friends," that is, her brothers. At the request of the Lords, she saw Willock, and said, as she naturally would, that "there was no salvation but in and by the death of Jesus Christ." "She was compelled . . . to approve the chief head of our religion, wherein we dissent from all papists and popery." Knox had strange ideas about the creed which he opposed. "Of any virtue that ever was espied in King James V. (*whose daughter she*," Mary Stuart, "*is called*"), "to this hour (1566) we have seen no sparkle to appear."

With this final fling at the chastity of Mary of Guise, the Reformer takes leave of the woman whom he so bitterly hated. Yet, "Knox was not given to the practice so common in his day, of assassinating reputations by vile insinuations." Posterity has not accepted, contemporary English historians did not accept, Knox's picture of Mary of Guise as the wanton widow, the spawn of the serpent, who desired to cut the throat of every Protestant in Scotland. She was placed by circumstances in a position from which there was no issue. The fatal French marriage of her daughter was a natural step, at a moment when Scottish independence could only be maintained by help of France. Had she left the Regency in the hands of Chatelherault, that is, of Archbishop Hamilton, the prelate was not the man to put down Protestantism by persecution, and so save the situation. If he had been, Mary of Guise was not the woman to abet him in drastic violence. The nobles would have revolted against the feeble Duke.

On July 6, the treaty of Edinburgh was concluded by representatives of England (Cecil was one) and of France. The Reformers carried a point of essential importance, the very point which Knox told Croft had been secured by the Appointment of July 1559. All French forces were to be dismissed the country, except one hundred and twenty men occupying Dunbar and Inchkeith, in the

Firth of Forth. A clause by which Cecil thought he had secured "the kernel" for England, and left the shell to France, a clause recognising the "rightfulness" of Elizabeth's alliance with the rebels, afforded Mary Stuart ground, or excuse, for never ratifying the treaty.

It is needless here to discuss the question—was the Convention of Estates held after the treaty, in August, a lawful Parliament? There was doubt enough, at least, to make Protestants feel uneasy about the security of the religious settlement achieved by the Convention. Randolph, the English resident, foresaw that the Acts might be rescinded.

Before the Convention of Estates met, a thanksgiving day was held by the brethren in St. Giles's, and Knox, if he was the author of the address to the Deity, said with scientific precision, "Neither in us, nor yet in our confederates was there any cause why thou shouldst have given unto us so joyful and sudden a deliverance, for neither of us both ceased to do wickedly, even in the midst of our greatest troubles." Elizabeth had lied throughout with all her natural and cultivated gift of falsehood: of the veracity of the brethren several instances have been furnished.

Ministers were next appointed to churches, Knox taking Edinburgh, while Superintendents (who were by no means Bishops) were appointed, one to each province. Erskine of Dun, a layman, was Superintendent of Angus. A new anti-Catholic Kirk was thus set up on July 20, before the Convention met and swept away Catholicism. Knox preached vigorously on "the prophet Haggeus" meanwhile, and "some" (namely Lethington, Speaker in the Convention) "said in mockage, we must now forget ourselves, and bear the barrow to build the houses of God." The unawakened Lethington, and the gentry at large, merely dilapidated the houses of God, so that they became unsafe, as well as odiously squalid. That such fervent piety should grudge repairs of church buildings (many of them in a wretched state already) is a fact creditable rather to the thrift than to the state of grace of the Reformers. After all their protestations, full of texts, the lords and lairds starved their preachers, but provided, by roofless aisles and unglazed windows, for the ventilation of the kirks. These men so bubbling over with gospel fervour were, in short, when it came to practice, traitors and hypocrites; nor did Knox spare their unseemly avarice. The cause of the poor, and of the preachers, lay near his heart, and no man was more insensible of the temptations of wealth.

Lethington did not address the Parliament as Speaker till August 9. Never had such a Parliament met in Scotland. One hundred and six barons, not of the higher order, assembled; in 1567, when Mary was a prisoner and the Regent Moray held the assembly, not nearly so many came together, nor on any later occasion at this period. The newcomers claimed to sit "as of old custom"; it was a custom long disused, and not now restored to vitality.

A supplication was presented by "the Barons, gentlemen, Burgesses, and others" to "the nobility and Estates" (of whom they do not seem to reckon themselves part, contrasting *themselves* with "yourselves"). They reminded the Estates how they had asked the Regent "for freedom and liberty of conscience with a godly reformation of abuses." They now, by way of freedom of conscience, ask that Catholic doctrine "be abolished by Act of this Parliament, and punishment appointed for the transgressors." The Man of Sin has been distributing the whole patrimony of the Church, so that "the trew ministers," the schools, and the poor are kept out of their own. The actual clergy are all thieves and murderers and "rebels to the lawful authority of Emperors, Kings, and Princes." Against these charges (murder, rebellion, profligacy) they must answer now or be so reputed. In fact, it was the nobles, rather than the Pope, who had been robbing the Kirk, education, and the poor, which they continued to do, as Knox attests. But as to doctrine, the barons and ministers were asked to lay a Confession before the House.

It will be observed that, in the petition, "Emperors, Kings, and Princes" have "lawful authority" over the clergy. But that doctrine assumes, tacitly, that such rulers are of Knox's own opinions: the Kirk later resolutely stood up against kings like James VI., Charles I., and Charles II.

The Confession was drawn up, presented, and ratified in a very few days: it was compiled in four. The Huguenots in Paris, in 1559, "established a record" by drawing up a Confession containing eighty articles in three days. Knox and his coadjutors were relatively deliberate. They aver that all points of belief necessary for salvation are contained in the canonical books of the Bible. Their interpretation pertains to no man or Church, but solely to "the spreit of God." That "spreit" must have illuminated the Kirk as it then existed in Scotland, "for we dare not receive and admit any interpretation which directly repugns to any principal point of our faith, to any other *plain* text of Scripture, or yet unto the rule of charity."

As we, the preachers of the Kirk then extant, were apostate monks or priests or artisans, about a dozen of us, in Scotland, mankind could not be expected to regard "our" interpretation, "our faith" as infallible. The framers of the Confession did not pretend that it was infallible. They request that, "if any man will note in this our Confession any article or sentence repugning to God's Holy Word," he will favour them with his criticism in writing. As Knox had announced six years earlier, that, "as touching the chief points of religion, I neither will give place to man or angel . . . teaching the contrair to that which ye have heard," a controversialist who thought it worth while to criticise the Confession must have deemed himself at least an archangel. Two years later, written criticism was offered, as we shall see, with a demand for a written reply. The critic escaped arrest by a lucky accident.

The Confession, with practically no criticism or opposition, was passed *en bloc* on August 17. The Evangel is candidly stated to be "death to the sons of perdition," but the Confession is offered hopefully to "weak and infirm brethren." Not to enter into the higher theology, we learn that the sacraments can only be administered "by lawful ministers." We learn that *they* are "such as are appointed to the preaching of the Word, or into whose mouth God has put some sermon of exhortation" and who are "lawfully chosen thereto by some Kirk." Later, we find that rather more than this, and rather more than some of the "trew ministeris" then had, is required.

As the document reaches us, it appears to have been "mitigated" by Lethington and Wynram, the Vicar of Bray of the Reformation. They altered, according to the English resident, Randolph, "many words and sentences, which sounded to proceed rather of some evil conceived opinion than of any sound judgment." As Lethington certainly was not "a lawful minister," it is surprising if Knox yielded to his criticism.

Lethington and Wynram also advised that the chapter on obedience to the sovereign power should be omitted, as "an unfit matter to be treated at this time," when it was not very obvious who the "magistrate" or authority might be. In this sense Randolph, Arran's English friend, wrote to Cecil. The chapter, however, was left standing. The sovereign, whether in empire, kingdom, duke, prince, or in free cities, was accepted as "of God's holy ordinance. To him chiefly pertains the reformation of the religion," which includes "the suppression of idolatry and superstition"; and Catholicism, we know, is idolatry. Superstition is less easily defined, but we cannot doubt that, in Knox's mind, the English liturgy was superstitious. To resist the Supreme Power, "doing that which pertains to his charge" (that is, suppressing Catholicism and superstition, among other things), is to resist God. It thus appears that the sovereign is not so supreme but that he must be disobeyed when his mandates clash with the doctrine of the Kirk. Thus the "magistrate" or "authority"—the State, in fact—is limited by the conscience of the Kirk, which may, if it pleases, detect idolatry or superstition in some act of secular policy. From this theory of the Kirk arose more than a century of unrest.

On August 24, the practical consequences of the Confession were set forth in an Act, by which all hearers or celebrants of the Mass are doomed, for the first offence, to mere confiscation of all their goods and to corporal punishment: exile rewards a repetition of the offence: the third is punished by death. "Freedom from a persecuting spirit is one of the noblest features of Knox's character," says Laing; "neither led away by enthusiasm nor party feelings nor success, to retaliate the oppressions and atrocities that disgraced the adherents of popery." This is an amazing remark! Though we do not know that Knox was ever "accessory to the death of a single individual for his religious opinions," we do know that he had not the chance; the Government, at most, and years later, put one priest to death. But Knox always insisted, vainly, that idolaters "must die the death."

To the carnal mind these rules appear to savour of harshness. The carnal mind would not gather exactly what the new penal laws were, if it confined its study to the learned Dr. M'Crie's *Life of Knox*. This erudite man, a pillar of the early Free Kirk, mildly remarks, "The Parliament . . . prohibited, under certain penalties, the celebration of the Mass." He leaves his readers to discover, in the Acts of Parliament and in Knox, what the "certain penalties" were. The Act seems, as Knox says about the decrees of massacre in Deuteronomy, "rather to be written in a rage" than in a spirit of wisdom. The majority of the human beings then in Scotland probably never had the dispute between the old and new faiths placed before them lucidly and impartially. Very many of them had never heard the ideas of Geneva stated at all. "So late as 1596," writes Dr. Hay Fleming, "there were above four hundred parishes, not reckoning Argyll and the Isles, which still lacked ministers." "The rarity of learned and godly men" of his own persuasion, is regretted by Knox in the Book of Discipline. Yet Catholics thus destitute of opportunity to know and recognise the Truth, are threatened with confiscation, exile, and death, if they cling to the only creed which they have been taught—after August 17, 1560. The death penalty was threatened often, by Scots Acts, for trifles. In this case the graduated scale of punishment shows that the threat is serious.

This Act sounds insane, but the Convention was wise in its generation. Had it merely abolished the persecuting laws of the Church, Scotland might never have been Protestant. The old faith is infinitely more attractive to mankind than the new Presbyterian verity. A thing of slow and long evolution, the Church had assimilated and hallowed the world-old festivals of the year's changing seasons. She provided for the human love of recreation. Her Sundays were holidays, not composed of gloomy hours in stuffy or draughty kirks, under the current voice of the preacher. Her confessional enabled the burdened soul to lay down its weight in sacred privacy; her music, her ceremonies, the dim religious light of her fanes, naturally awaken religious emotion. While these things, with the native tendency to resist authority of any kind, appealed to the multitude, the position of the Church, in later years, recommended itself to many educated men in Scotland as more logical than that of Knox; and convert after convert, in the noble class, slipped over to Rome. The missionaries of the counter-Reformation, but for the persecuting Act, would have arrived in a

Scotland which did not persecute, and the work of the Convention of 1560 might all have been undone, had not the stringent Act been passed.

That Act apparently did not go so far as the preachers desired. Thus Archbishop Hamilton, writing to Archbishop Beaton in Paris, the day after the passing of the Act, says, "All these new preachers openly persuade the nobility in the pulpit, to put violent hands, and slay all churchmen that will not concur and adopt their opinion. They only reproach my Lord Duke" (the Archbishop's brother), "that he will not begin first, and either cause me to do as they do, or else to use rigour on me by slaughter, sword, or, at least, perpetual prison." It is probable that the Archbishop was well informed as to what the bigots were saying, though he is not likely to have "sat under" them; moreover, he would hear of their advice from his brother, the Duke, with whom he had just held a long conference. Lesley, Bishop of Ross, in his "History," praises the humanity of the nobles, "for at this time few Catholics were banished, fewer were imprisoned, and none were executed." The nobles interfering, the threatened capital punishment was not carried out. Mob violence, oppression by Protestant landlords, Kirk censure, imprisonment, fine, and exile, did their work in suppressing idolatry and promoting hypocrisy.

No doubt this grinding ceaseless daily process of enforcing Truth, did not go far enough for the great body of the brethren, especially the godly burgesses of the towns; indeed, as early as June 10, 1560, the Provost, Bailies, and Town Council of Edinburgh proclaimed that idolaters must instantly and publicly profess their conversion before the Ministers and Elders on the penalty of the pillory for the first offence, banishment from the town for the second, and death for the third.

It must always be remembered that the threat of the death penalty often meant, in practice, very little. It was denounced, under Mary of Guise (February 9, 1559), against men who bullied priests, disturbed services, and ate meat in Lent. It was denounced against shooters of wild fowl, and against those, of either religious party, who broke the Proclamation of October 1561. Yet "nobody seemed one penny the worse" as regards their lives, though the punishments of fining and banishing were, on occasions, enforced against Catholics.

We may marvel that, in the beginning, Catholic martyrs did not present themselves in crowds to the executioner. But even under the rule of Rome it would not be easy to find thirty cases of martyrs burned at the stake by "the bloudie Bishops," between the fifteenth century and the martyrdom of Myln. By 1560 the old Church was in such a hideous decline—with ruffianly men of quality in high spiritual places; with priests who did not attend Mass, and in many cases could not read; with churches left to go to ruin; with license so notable that, in one foundation, the priest is only forbidden to keep a *constant* concubine—that faith had waxed cold, and no Catholic felt "ripe" for martyrdom. The elements of a League, as in France, did not exist. There was no fervently Catholic town population like that of Paris; no popular noble warriors, like the Ducs de Guise, to act as leaders. Thus Scotland, in this age, ran little risk of a religious civil war. No organised and armed faction existed to face the Congregation. When the counter-Reformation set in, many Catholics endured fines and exile with constancy.

The theology of the Confession of Faith is, of course, Calvinistic. No "works" are, technically, "good" which are not the work of the Spirit of our Lord, dwelling in our hearts by faith. "Idolaters," and wicked people, not having that spirit, can do no good works. The blasphemy that "men who live according to equity and justice shall be saved, what religion soever they have professed," is to be abhorred. "The Kirk is invisible," consisting of the Elect, "who are known only to God." This gave much cause of controversy to Knox's Catholic opponents. "The notes of the true Church" are those of Calvin's. As to the Sacrament, though the elements be not the *natural* body of Christ, yet "the faithful, in the right use of the Lord's Table, so do eat the body and drink the blood of the Lord Jesus that He remains in them and they in Him . . . in such conjunction with Christ Jesus as the natural man cannot comprehend."

This is a highly sacramental and confessedly mystical doctrine, not less unintelligible to "the natural man" than the Catholic theory which Knox so strongly reprobated. Alas, that men called Christian have shed seas of blood over the precise sense of that touching command of our Lord, which, though admitted to be incomprehensible, they have yet endeavoured to comprehend and define!

A serious task for Knox was to draw up, with others, a "Book of the Policy and Discipline of the Kirk," a task entrusted to them in April 1560. In politics, till January 1561, the Lords hoped that they might induce Elizabeth (then entangled with Leicester, as Knox knew) to marry Arran, but whether "Glycerium" (as Bishop Jewel calls her) had already detected in "the saucy youth" "a half crazy fool," as Mr. Froude says, or not, she firmly refused. She much preferred Lord Robert Dudley, whose wife had just then broken her neck. The unfortunate Arran had fought resolutely, Knox tells us, by the side of Lord James, in the winter of 1559, but he already, in 1560, showed strange moods, and later fell into sheer lunacy. In December died "the young King of France, husband to our Jezebel—unhappy Francis . . . he suddenly perished of a rotten ear . . . in that deaf ear that never would hear the truth of God" (December 5, 1560). We have little of Knox's poetry, but he probably composed a translation, in verse, of a Latin poem indited by one of "the godly in France," whence he borrowed his phrase "a rotten ear" (*aure putrefacta corruit*).

"Last Francis, that unhappy child,
His father's footsteps following plain,
To Christ's crying deaf ears did yield,
A rotten ear was then his bane."

The version is wonderfully close to the original Latin.

Meanwhile, Francis was hardly cold before Arran wooed his idolatrous widow, Queen Mary, "with a gay gold ring." She did not respond favourably, and "the Earl bare it heavily in his heart, and more heavily than many would have wissed," says Knox, with whom Arran was on very confidential terms. Knox does not rebuke his passion for Jezebel. He himself "was in no small heaviness by reason of the late death of his dear bedfellow, Marjorie Bowes," of whom we know very little, except that she worked hard to lighten the labours of Knox's vast correspondence. He had, as he says, "great intelligence both with the churches and some of the Court of

France," and was the first to receive news of the perilous illness of the young King. He carried the tidings to the Duke and Lord James, at the Hamilton house near Kirk o' Field, but would not name his informant. Then came the news of the King's death from Lord Grey de Wilton, at Berwick, and a Convention of the Nobles was proclaimed for January 15, 1561, to "peruse newly over again" the Book of Discipline.

CHAPTER XIII.
KNOX AND THE BOOK OF DISCIPLINE

This Book of Discipline, containing the model of the Kirk, had been seen by Randolph in August 1560, and he observed that its framers would not come into ecclesiastical conformity with England. They were "severe in that they profess, and loth to remit anything of that they have received." As the difference between the Genevan and Anglican models contributed so greatly to the Civil War under Charles I., the results may be regretted; Anglicans, by 1643, were looked on as "Baal worshippers" by the precise Scots.

In February 1561, Randolph still thought that the Book of Discipline was rather in advance of what fallen human nature could endure. Idolatry, of course, was to be removed universally; thus the

Queen, when she arrived, was constantly insulted about her religion. The Lawful Calling of Ministers was explained; we have already seen that a lawful minister is a preacher who can get a local set of men to recognise him as such. Knox, however, before his return to Scotland, had advised the brethren to be very careful in examining preachers before accepting them. The people and "every several Congregation" have a right to elect their minister, and, if they do not do so in six weeks, the Superintendent (a migratory official, in some ways superior to the clergy, but subject to periodical "trial" by the Assembly, who very soon became extinct), with his council, presents a man who is to be examined by persons of sound judgment, and next by the ministers and elders of the Kirk. Nobody is to be "violently intrused" on any congregation. Nothing is said about an university training; moral character is closely scrutinised. On the admission of a new minister, some other ministers should preach "touching the obedience which the Kirk owe to their ministers. . . . The people should be exhorted to reverence and honour their chosen ministers as the servants and ambassadors of the Lord Jesus, obeying the commandments which they speak from God's mouth and Book, even as they would obey God himself. . . ."

The practical result of this claim on the part of the preachers to implicit obedience was more than a century of turmoil, civil war, revolution, and reaction. The ministers constantly preached political sermons, and the State—the King and his advisers—was perpetually arraigned by them. To "reject" them, "and despise their ministry and exhortation" (as when Catholics were not put to death on their instance), was to "reject and despise" our Lord! If accused of libel, or treasonous libel, or "leasing making," in their sermons, they demanded to be judged by their brethren. Their brethren acquitting them, where was there any other judicature? These pretensions, with the right to inflict excommunication (in later practice to be followed by actual outlawry), were made, we saw, when there were not a dozen "true ministers" in the nascent Kirk, and, of course, the claims became more exorbitant when "true ministers" were reckoned by hundreds. No State could submit to such a clerical tyranny.

People who only know modern Presbyterianism have no idea of the despotism which the Fathers of the Kirk tried, for more than a century, to enforce. The preachers sat in the seats of the Apostles; they had the gift of the Keys, the power to bind and loose. Yet the Book of Discipline permits no other ceremony, at the induction of these mystically gifted men, than "the public approbation of the people, and declaration of the chief minister"—later there was no "*chief* minister," there was "parity" of ministers. Any other ceremony "we cannot approve"; "for albeit the Apostles used the imposition of hands, yet seeing the miracle is ceased, the using of the ceremony we judge it not necessary." The miracle had *not* ceased, if it was true that "the commandments" issued in sermons—political sermons often—really deserved to be obeyed, as men "would obey God himself." *C'est là le miracle*! There could be no more amazing miracle than the infallibility of preachers! "The imposition of hands" was, twelve years later, restored; but as far as infallible sermons were concerned, the State agreed with Knox that "the miracle had ceased."

The political sermons are sometimes justified by the analogy of modern discussion in the press. But leading articles do not pretend to be infallible, and editors do not assert a right to be obeyed by men, "even as they would obey God himself." The preachers were often right, often wrong: their sermons were good, or were silly; but what no State could endure was the claim of preachers to implicit obedience.

The difficulty in finding really qualified ministers must be met by fervent prayer, and by compulsion on the part of the Estates of Parliament.

Failing ministers, Readers, capable of reading the Common Prayers (presently it was Knox's book of these) and the Bible must be found; they may later be promoted to the ministry.

Stationary ministers are to receive less sustenance than the migratory Superintendents; the sons of the preachers must be educated, the daughters "honestly dowered." The payment is mainly in "bolls" of meal and malt. The state of the poor, "fearful and horrible" to say, is one of universal contempt. Provision must be made for the aged and weak. Superintendents, after election, are to be examined by all the ministers of the province, and by three or more Superintendents. Other ceremonies "we cannot allow." In

1581, a Scottish Catholic, Burne, averred that Willock objected to ceremonies of Ordination, because people would say, if these are necessary, what minister ordained *you*? The query was hard to answer, so ceremonies of Ordination could not be allowed. The story was told to Burne, he says, by an eyewitness, who heard Willock.

Every church must have a schoolmaster, who ought to be able to teach grammar and Latin. Education should be universal: poor children of ability must be enabled to pass on to the universities, through secondary schools. At St. Andrews the three colleges were to have separate functions, not clashing, and culminating in Divinity.

Whence are the funds to be obtained? Here the authors bid "your Honours" "have respect to your poor brethren, the labourers of the ground, who by these cruel beasts, the papists, have been so oppressed . . ." They ought only to pay "reasonable teinds, that they may feel some benefit of Christ Jesus, now preached unto them. With grief of heart we hear that some gentlemen are now as cruel over their tenants as ever were the papists, requiring of them whatsoever they paid to the Church, so that the papistical tyranny shall only be changed into the tyranny of the landlord or laird." Every man should have his own teinds, or tithes; whereas, in fact, the great lay holders of tithes took them off other men's lands, a practice leading to many blood-feuds. The attempt of Charles I. to let "every man have his own tithes," and to provide the preachers with a living wage, was one of the causes of the distrust of the King which culminated in the great Civil War. But Knox could not "recover for the Church her liberty and freedom, and that only for relief of the poor." "*We speak not for ourselves*" the Book says, "but in favour of the poor, and the labourers defrauded . . . The Church is only bound to sustain and nourish her charges . . . to wit the Ministers of the Kirk, the Poor, and the teachers of youth." The funds must be taken out of the tithes, the chantries, colleges, chaplainries, and the temporalities of Bishops, Deans, and cathedrals generally.

The ministers are to have their manses, and glebes of six acres; to this many of the Lords assented, except, oddly enough, those redoubtable leaders of the Congregation, Glencairn and Morton, with Marischal. All the part of the book which most commands our sympathy, the most Christian part of the book, regulating the disposition of the revenues of the fallen Church for the good of the poor, of education, and of the Kirk, remained a dead letter. The Duke, Arran, Lord James, and a few barons, including the ruffian Andrew Ker of Faldonside, with Glencairn and Ochiltree, signed it, in token of approval, but little came of it all. Lethington, probably, was the scoffer who styled these provisions "devout imaginations." The nobles and lairds, many of them, were converted, in matter of doctrine; in conduct they were the most avaricious, bloody, and treacherous of all the generations which had banded, revelled, robbed, and betrayed in Scotland.

There is a point in this matter of the Kirk's claim to the patrimony of the old Church which perhaps is generally misunderstood. That point is luminous as regards the absolute disinterestedness of Knox and his companions, both in respect to themselves and their fellow-preachers. The Book of Discipline contains a sentence already quoted, conceived in what we may justly style a chivalrous contempt of wealth. "Your Honours may easily understand *that we speak not now for ourselves*, but in favour of the Poor, and the labourers defrauded . . . " Not having observed a point which "their Honours" were not the men to "understand easily," Father Pollen writes, "the new preachers were loudly *claiming for themselves* the property of the rivals whom they had displaced." For themselves they were claiming a few merks, and a few bolls of meal, a decent subsistence. Mr. Taylor Innes points out that when, just before Darnley's murder, Mary offered "a considerable sum for the maintenance of the ministers," Knox and others said that, for their sustentation, they "craved of the auditors the things that were necessary, as of duty the pastors might justly crave of their flock. The General Assembly accepted the Queen's gift, but only of necessity; it was by their flock that they ought to be sustained. To take from others contrary to their will, whom they serve not, they judge it not their duty, nor yet reasonable."

Among other things the preachers, who were left with a hard struggle for bare existence, introduced a rule of honour scarcely known to the barons and nobles, except to the bold Buccleuch who rejected an English pension from Henry VIII., with a sympathetic explosion of strong language. The preachers would not take gifts from England, even when offered by the supporters of their own line of policy.

Knox's failure in his admirable attempt to secure the wealth of the old Church for national purposes was, as it happened, the secular salvation of the Kirk. Neither Catholicism nor Anglicanism could be fully introduced while the barons and nobles held the tithes and lands of the ancient Church. Possessing the wealth necessary to a Catholic or Anglican establishment, they were resolutely determined to cling to it, and oppose any Church except that which they starved. The bishops of James I., Charles I., and Charles II. were detested by the nobles. Rarely from them came any lordly gifts to learning and the Universities, while from the honourably poor ministers such gifts could not come. The Universities were founded by prelates of the old Church, doing their duty with their wealth.

The arrangements for discipline were of the drastic nature which lingered into the days of Burns and later. The results may be studied in the records of Kirk Sessions; we have no reason to suppose that sexual morality was at all improved, on the whole, by "discipline," though it was easier to enforce "Sabbath observance." A graduated scale of admonitions led up to excommunication, if the subject was refractory, and to boycotting with civil penalties. The processes had no effect, or none that is visible, in checking lawlessness, robbery, feuds, and manslayings; and, after the Reformation, witchcraft increased to monstrous proportions, at least executions of people accused of witchcraft became very numerous, in spite of provision for sermons thrice a week, and for weekly discussions of the Word.

The Book of Discipline, modelled on the Genevan scheme, and on that of A'Lasco for his London congregation, rather reminds us of the "Laws" of Plato. It was a well meant but impracticable ideal set before the country, and was least successful where it best deserved success. It certainly secured a thoroughly moral clergy, till, some twelve years later, the nobles again thrust licentious and murderous cadets into the best livings and the bastard bishoprics, before and during the Regency of Morton. Their example did not affect the genuine ministers, frugal God-fearing men.

CHAPTER XIV.

KNOX AND QUEEN MARY, 1561

In discussing the Book of Discipline, that great constructive effort towards the remaking of Scotland, we left Knox at the time of the death of his first wife. On December 20, 1560, he was one of some six ministers who, with more numerous lay representatives of districts, sat in the first General Assembly. They selected some new preachers, and decided that the church of Restalrig should be destroyed as a monument of idolatry. A fragment of it is standing yet, enclosing tombs of the wild Logans of Restalrig.

The Assembly passed an Act against lawless love, and invited the Estates and Privy Council to "use sharp punishment" against some "idolaters," including Eglintoun, Cassilis, and Quentin Kennedy,

Abbot of Crosraguel, who disputed later against Knox, the Laird of Gala (a Scott) and others.

In January 1561 a Convention of nobles and lairds at Edinburgh perused the Book of Discipline, and some signed it, platonically, while there was a dispute between the preachers and certain Catholics, including Lesley, later Bishop of Ross, an historian, but no better than a shifty and dangerous partisan of Mary Stuart. The Lord James was selected as an envoy to Mary, in France. He was bidden to refuse her even the private performance of the rites of her faith, but declined to go to that extremity; the question smouldered through five years. Randolph expected "a mad world" on Mary's return; he was not disappointed.

Meanwhile the Catholic Earls of the North, of whom Huntly was the fickle leader, with Bothwell, "come to work what mischief he can," are accused by Knox of a design to seize Edinburgh, before the Parliament in May 1561. Nothing was done, but there was a very violent Robin Hood riot; the magistrates were besieged and bullied, Knox declined to ask for the pardon of the brawlers, and, after excursions and alarms, "the whole multitude was excommunicate" until they appeased the Kirk. They may have borne the spiritual censure very unconcernedly.

The Catholic Earls now sent Lesley to get Mary's ear before the Lord James could reach her. Lesley arrived on April 14, with the offer to raise 20,000 men, if Mary would land in Huntly's region. They would restore the Mass in their bounds, and Mary would be convoyed by Captain Cullen, a kinsman of Huntly, and already mentioned as the Captain of the Guards after Riccio's murder.

It is said by Lesley that Mary had received, from the Regent, her mother, a description of the nobles of Scotland. If so, she knew Huntly for the ambitious traitor he was, a man peculiarly perfidious and self-seeking, with a son who might be thrust on her as a husband, if once she were in Huntly's hands. The Queen knew that he had forsaken her mother's cause; knew, perhaps, of his old attempt to betray Scotland to England, and she was aware that no northern Earl had raised his banner to defend the Church. She, therefore, came to no agreement with Lesley, but confided more in the Lord James, who arrived on the following day. Mary knew her brother's character fairly well, and, if Lesley says with truth that he now asked for, and was promised, the earldom of Moray, the omen was evil for Huntly, who practically held the lands. A bargain, on this showing, was initiated. Lord James was to have the earldom, and he got it; Mary was to have his support.

Much has been said about Lord James's betrayal to Throckmorton of Mary's intentions, as revealed by her to himself. But what Lord James said to Throckmorton amounts to very little. I am not certain that, both in Paris with Throckmorton, and in London with Elizabeth and Cecil, he did not moot his plan for friendship between Mary and Elizabeth, and Elizabeth's recognition of Mary's rights as her heir. Lord James proposed all this to Elizabeth in a letter of August 6, 1561. He had certainly discussed this admirable scheme with Lord Robert Dudley at Court, in May 1561, on his return from France. Nothing could be more statesmanlike and less treacherous.

Meanwhile (May 27, 1561) the brethren presented a supplication to the Parliament, with clauses, which, if conceded, would have secured the stipends of the preachers. The prayers were granted, in promise, and a great deal of church wrecking was conscientiously done; the Lord James, on his return, paid particular attention to idolatry in his hoped for earldom, but the preachers were not better paid.

Meanwhile the Protestants looked forward to the Queen's arrival with great searchings of heart. She had not ratified the treaty of Leith, but already Cardinal Guise hoped that she and Elizabeth would live in concord, and heard that Mary ceded all claims to the English throne in return for Elizabeth's promise to declare her the heir, if she herself died childless (August 21).

Knox, who had not loved Mary of Guise, was not likely to think well of her daughter. Mary, again, knew Knox as the chief agitator in the tumults that embittered her mother's last year, and shortened her life. In France she had threatened to deal with him severely, ignorant of his power and her own weakness. She could not be aware that Knox had suggested to Cecil opposition to her succession to the throne on the ground of her sex. Knox uttered his forebodings of the

Queen's future: they were as veracious as if he had really been a prophet. But he was, to an extent which can only be guessed, one of the causes of the fulfilment of his own predictions. To attack publicly, from the pulpit, the creed and conduct of a girl of spirit; to provoke cruel insults to her priests whom she could not defend; was apt to cause, at last, in great measure that wild revolt of temper which drove Mary to her doom. Her health suffered frequently from the attempt to bear with a smiling face such insults as no European princess, least of all Elizabeth, would have endured for an hour. There is a limit to patience, and before Mary passed that limit, Randolph and Lethington saw, and feebly deplored, the amenities of the preacher whom men permitted to "rule the roast." "Ten thousand swords" do not leap from their scabbards to protect either the girl Mary Stuart or the woman Marie Antoinette.

Not that natural indignation was dead, but it ended in words. People said, "The Queen's Mass and her priests will we maintain; this hand and this rapier will fight in their defence." So men bragged, as Knox reports, but when after Mary's arrival priests were beaten or pilloried, not a hand stirred to defend them, not a rapier was drawn. The Queen might be as safely as she was deeply insulted through her faith. She was not at this time devoutly ardent in her creed, though she often professed her resolution to abide in it. Gentleness might conceivably have led her even to adopt the Anglican faith, or so it was deemed by some observers, but insolence and outrage had another effect on her temper.

Mary landed at Leith in a thick fog on August 19, 1561. She was now in a country where she lay under sentence of death as an idolater. Her continued existence was illegal. With her came Mary Seton, Mary Beaton, Mary Livingstone, and Mary Fleming, the comrades of her childhood; and her uncles, the Duc d'Aumale, Francis de Lorraine, and the noisy Marquis d'Elboeuf. She was not very welcome. As late as August 9, Randolph reports that her brother, Lord James, Lethington, and Morton "wish, as you do, she might be stayed yet for a space, and if it were not for their obedience sake, some of them care not though they never see her face." None the less, on June 8 Lord James tells Mary that he had given orders for her palace to be prepared by the end of July. He informs her that "many" hope that she will never come home. Nothing is "so necessary . . . as your Majesty's own presence"; and he hopes she will arrive punctually. If she cannot come she should send her commission to some of her Protestant advisers, by no means including the Archbishop of St. Andrews (Hamilton), with whom he will never work. It is not easy to see why Lord James should have wished that Mary "might be stayed," unless he merely dreaded her arrival while Elizabeth was in a bad temper. His letter to Elizabeth of August 6 is incompatible with treachery on his part. "Mr. Knox is determined to abide the uttermost, and others will not leave him till God have taken his life and theirs together." Of what were these heroes afraid? A "familiar," a witch, of Lady Huntly's predicted that the Queen would never arrive. "If false, I would she were burned for a witch," adds honest Randolph. Lethington deemed his "own danger not least." Two galleys full of ladies are not so alarming; did these men, practically hinting that English ships should stop their Queen, think that the Catholics in Scotland were too strong for them?

Not a noble was present to meet Mary when in the fog and filth of Leith she touched Scottish soil, except her natural brother, Lord Robert. The rest soon gathered with faces of welcome. She met some Robin Hood rioters who lay under the law, and pardoned these roisterers (with their excommunication could she interfere?), because, says Knox, she was instructed that they had acted "in despite of the religion." Their festival had been forbidden under the older religion, as it happens, in 1555, and was again forbidden later by Mary herself.

All was mirth till Sunday, when the Queen's French priest celebrated Mass in her own chapel before herself, her three uncles, and Montrose. The godly called for the priest's blood, but Lord James kept the door, and his brothers protected the priest. Disappointed of blood, "the godly departed with great grief of heart," collecting in crowds round Holyrood in the afternoon. Next day the Council proclaimed that, till the Estates assembled and deliberated, no innovation should be made in the religion "publicly and universally standing." The Queen's servants and others from France must not be molested—on pain of death, the usual empty threat. They were assaulted, and nobody was punished for the offence.

Arran alone made a protest, probably written by Knox. Who but Knox could have written that the Mass is "much more abominable and odious in the sight of God" than murder! Many an honest brother was conspicuously of the opinion which Arran's protest assigned to Omnipotence. Next Sunday Knox "thundered," and later regretted that "I did not that I might have done" (caused an armed struggle?), . . . "for God had given unto me credit with many, who would have put into execution God's judgments if I would only have consented thereto." Mary might have gone the way of Jezebel and Athaliah but for the mistaken lenity of Knox, who later "asked God's mercy" for not being more vehement. In fact, he rather worked "to slokin that fervency." Let us hope that he is forgiven, especially as Randolph reports him extremely vehement in the pulpit. His repentance was publicly expressed shortly before the murder of Riccio. (In December 1565, probably, when the Kirk ordered the week's fast that, as it chanced, heralded Riccio's doom.) Privately to Cecil, on October 7, 1561, he uttered his regret that he had been so deficient in zeal. Cecil had been recommending moderation.

On August 26, Randolph, after describing the intimidation of the priest, says "John Knox thundereth out of the pulpit, so that I fear nothing so much as that one day he will mar all. He ruleth the roast, and of him all men stand in fear." In public at least he did not allay the wrath of the brethren.

On August 26, or on September 2, Knox had an interview with the Queen, and made her weep. Randolph doubted whether this was from anger or from grief. Knox gives Mary's observations in the briefest summary; his own at great length, so that it is not easy to know how their reasoning really sped. Her charges were his authorship of the "Monstrous Regiment of Women"; that he caused great sedition and slaughter in England; and that he was accused of doing what he did by necromancy. The rest is summed up in "&c."

He stood to his guns about the "Monstrous Regiment," and generally took the line that he merely preached against "the vanity of the papistical religion" and the deceit, pride, and tyranny of "that Roman Antichrist." If one wishes to convert a young princess, bred in the Catholic faith, it is not judicious to begin by abusing the Pope. This too much resembles the arbitrary and violent method of Peter in

The Tale of a Tub (by Dr. Jonathan Swift); such, however, was the method of Knox.

Mary asking if he denied her "just authority," Knox said that he was as well content to live under her as Paul under Nero. This, again, can hardly be called an agreeable historical parallel! Knox hoped that he would not hurt her or her authority "so long as ye defile not your hands with the blood of the saints of God," as if Mary was panting to distinguish herself in that way. His hope was unfulfilled. No "saints" suffered, but he ceased not to trouble.

Knox also said that if he had wanted "to trouble your estate because you are a woman, I might have chosen a time more convenient for that purpose than I can do now, when your own presence is in the realm." He *had*, in fact, chosen the convenient time in his letter to Cecil, already quoted (July 19, 1559), but he had not succeeded in his plan. He said that nobody could *prove* that the question of discarding Mary, on the ground of her sex, "was at any time moved in public or in secret." Nobody could *prove* it, for nobody could publish his letter to Cecil. Probably he had this in his mind. He did not say that the thing had not happened, only that "he was assured that neither Protestant nor papist shall be able to prove that any such question was at any time moved, either in public or in secret."

He denied that he had caused sedition in England, nor do we know what Mary meant by this charge. His appeals, from abroad, to a Phinehas or Jehu had not been answered. As to magic, he always preached against the practice.

Mary then said that Knox persuaded the people to use religion not allowed by their princes. He justified himself by biblical precedents, to which she replied that Daniel and Abraham did not resort to the sword. They had not the chance, he answered, adding that subjects might resist a prince who exceeded his bounds, as sons may confine a maniac father.

The Queen was long silent, and then said, "I perceive my subjects shall obey you and not me." Knox said that all should be subject unto God and His Church; and Mary frankly replied, "I will defend the Church of Rome, for I think that it is the true Church of God." She could not defend it! Knox answered with his wonted urbanity, that the Church of Rome was a harlot, addicted to "all kinds of fornication."

He was so accustomed to this sort of rhetoric that he did not deem it out of place on this occasion. His admirers, familiar with his style, forget its necessary effect on "a young princess unpersuaded," as Lethington put it. Mary said that her conscience was otherwise minded, but Knox knew that all consciences of "man or angel" were wrong which did not agree with his own. The Queen had to confess that in argument as to the unscriptural character of the Mass, he was "owre sair" for her. He said that he wished she would "hear the matter reasoned to the end." She may have desired that very thing: "Ye may get that sooner than ye believe," she said; but Knox expressed his disbelief that he would ever get it. Papists would never argue except when "they were both judge and party." Knox himself never answered Ninian Winzet, who, while printing his polemic, was sought for by the police of the period, and just managed to escape.

There was, however, a champion who, on November 19, challenged Knox and the other preachers to a discussion, either orally or by interchange of letters. This was Mary's own chaplain, René Benoit. Mary probably knew that he was about to offer to meet "the most learned John Knox and other most erudite men, called ministers"; it is thus that René addresses them in his "Epistle" of November 19.

He implores them not to be led into heresy by love of popularity or of wealth; neither of which advantages the preachers enjoyed, for they were detested by loose livers, and were nearly starved. Benoit's little challenge, or rather request for discussion, is a model of courtesy. Knox did not meet him in argument, as far as we are aware; but in 1562, Fergusson, minister of Dunfermline, replied in a tract full of scurrility. One quite unmentionable word occurs, and "impudent lie," "impudent and shameless shavelings," "Baal's chaplains that eat at Jezebel's table," "pestilent papistry," "abominable mass," "idol Bishops," "we Christians and you Papists," and parallels between Benoit and "an idolatrous priest of Bethel," between Mary and Jezebel are among the amenities of this meek servant of Christ in Dunfermline.

Benoit presently returned to France, and later was confessor to Henri IV. The discussion which Mary anticipated never occurred, though her champion was ready. Knox does not refer to this affair in his "History," as far as I am aware. Was René the priest whom the brethren menaced and occasionally assaulted?

Considering her chaplain's offer, it seems not unlikely that Mary was ready to listen to reasoning, but to call the Pope "Antichrist," and the Church "a harlot," is not argument. Knox ended his discourse by wishing the Queen as blessed in Scotland as Deborah was in Israel. The mere fact that Mary spoke with him "makes the Papists doubt what shall come of the world," says Randolph; and indeed nobody knows what possibly might have come, had Knox been sweetly reasonable. But he told his friends that, if he was not mistaken, she had "a proud mind, a crafty wit, and an indurate heart against God and His truth." She showed none of these qualities in the conversation as described by himself; but her part in it is mainly that of a listener who returns not railing with railing.

Knox was going about to destroy the scheme of *les politiques*, Randolph, Lethington, and the Lord James. They desired peace and amity with England, and the two Scots, at least, hoped to secure these as the Cardinal Guise did, by Mary's renouncing all present claim to the English throne, in return for recognition as heir, if Elizabeth died without issue. Elizabeth, as we know her, would never have granted these terms, but Mary's ministers, Lethington then in England, Lord James at home, tried to hope. Lord James had heard Mary's outburst to Knox about defending her own insulted Church, but he was not nervously afraid that she would take to dipping her hands in the blood of the saints. Neither he nor Lethington could revert to the old faith; they had pecuniary reasons, as well as convictions, which made that impossible.

Lethington, returned to Edinburgh (October 25), spoke his mind to Cecil. "The Queen behaves herself . . . as reasonably as we can require: if anything be amiss the fault is rather in ourselves. You know the vehemency of Mr. Knox's spirit which cannot be bridled, and yet doth utter sometimes such sentences as cannot easily be digested by a weak stomach. I would wish he should deal with her more gently, being a young princess unpersuaded. . . . Surely in her comporting with him she declares a wisdom far exceeding her age." Vituperation is not argument, and gentleness is not unchristian. St. Paul did not revile the gods of Felix and Festus.

But, prior to these utterances of October, the brethren had been baiting Mary. On her public entry (which Knox misdates by a month) her idolatry was rebuked by a pageant of Korah, Dathan, and Abiram. Huntly managed to stop a burning in effigy of a priest at the Mass. They never could cease from insulting the Queen in the tenderest point. The magistrates next coupled "mess-mongers" with notorious drunkards and adulterers, "and such filthy persons," in a proclamation, so the Provost and Bailies were "warded" (Knox says) in the Tolbooth. Knox blamed Lethington and Lord James, in a letter to Cecil; in his "History" he says, "God be merciful to some of our own."

The Queen herself, as a Papist, was clearly insulted in the proclamation. Moray and Lethington, the latter touched by her "readiness to hear," and her gentleness in the face of Protestant brutalities; the former, perhaps, lured by the hope of obtaining, as the price of his alliance, the earldom of Moray, were by the end of October still attempting to secure amity between her and Elizabeth, and to hope for the best, rather than drive the Queen wild by eternal taunts and menaces. The preachers denounced her rites at Hallowmass (All Saints), and a servant of her brother, Lord Robert, beat a priest; but men actually doubted whether subjects might interfere between the Queen and her religion. There was a discussion on this point between the preachers and the nobles, and the Church in Geneva (Calvin) was to be consulted. Knox offered to write, but Lethington said that he would write, as much stood on the "information"; that is, on the manner of stating the question. Lethington did not know, and Knox does not tell us in his "History" that he had himself, a week earlier, put the matter before Calvin in his own way. Even Lord James, he says to Calvin, though the Abdiel of godliness, "is afraid to overthrow that idol by violence"—*idolum illud missalicum*.

Knox's letter to Calvin represents the Queen as alleging that he has already answered the question, declaring that Knox's party has no right to interfere with the Royal mass. This rumour Knox disbelieves. He adds that Arran would have written, but was absent.

Apparently Arran did write to Calvin, anonymously, and dating from London, November 18, 1561. The letter, really from Scotland, is in French. The writer acknowledges the receipt, about August 20, of an encouraging epistle from Calvin. He repeats Knox's statements, in the main, and presses for a speedy reply. He says that he goes seldom to Court, both on account of "that idol," and because "sobriety and virtue" have been exiled. As Arran himself "is known to have had company of a good handsome wench, a merchant's daughter," which led to a riot with Bothwell, described by Randolph (December 27, 1561), his own "virtue and sobriety" are not conspicuous. He was in Edinburgh on November 15-19, and the London date of his anonymous letter is a blind.

It does not appear that Calvin replied to Knox, and to the anonymous correspondent, in whom I venture to detect Arran; or, if he answered, his letter was probably unfavourable to Knox, as we shall argue when the subject later presents itself.

Finally—"the votes of the Lords prevailed against the ministers"; the Queen was allowed her Mass, but Lethington, a minister of the Queen, did not consult a foreigner as to the rights of her subjects against her creed.

The lenity of Lord James was of sudden growth. At Stirling he and Argyll had gallantly caused the priests to leave the choir "with broken heads and bloody ears," the Queen weeping. So Randolph reported to Cecil (September 24).

Why her brother, foremost to insult Mary and her faith, unless Randolph errs, in September, took her part in a few weeks, we do not know. At Perth, Mary was again offended, and suffered in health by reason of the pageants; "they did too plainly condemn the errors of the world. . . . I hear she is troubled with such sudden passions after any great unkindness or grief of mind," says Randolph. She was seldom free from such godly chastisements. At Perth, however, some one gave her a cross of five diamonds with pendant pearls.

Meanwhile the statesmen did not obey the Ministers as men ought to obey God: a claim not easily granted by carnal politicians.

CHAPTER XV.

KNOX AND QUEEN MARY (continued), 1561-1564

Had Mary been a mere high-tempered and high-spirited girl, easily harmed in health by insults to herself and her creed, she might now have turned for support to Huntly, Cassilis, Montrose, and the other Earls who were Catholic or "unpersuaded." Her great-grandson, Charles II., when as young as she now was, did make the "Start"—the schoolboy attempt to run away from the Presbyterians to the loyalists of the North. But Mary had more self-control.

The artful Randolph found himself as hardly put to it now, in diplomacy, as the Cardinal's murderers had done, in war, when they met the scientific soldier, Strozzi. "The trade is now clean cut off from me," wrote Randolph (October 27); "I have to traffic now with other merchants than before. They know the value of their wares, and in all places how the market goeth. . . . Whatsoever policy is in all the chief and best practised heads of France; whatsoever craft, falsehood, or deceit is in all the subtle brains of Scotland," said the unscrupulous agent, "is either fresh in this woman's memory, or she can bring it out with a wet finger."

Mary, in fact, was in the hands of Lethington (a pensioner of Elizabeth) and of Lord James: "subtle brains" enough. *She* was the "merchandise," and Lethington and Lord James wished to make Elizabeth acknowledge the Scottish Queen as her successor, the alternative being to seek her price as a wife for an European prince. An "union of hearts" with England might conceivably mean Mary's acceptance of the Anglican faith. It is not a kind thing to say about Mary, but I suspect that, if assured of the English succession, she might have gone over to the Prayer Book. In the first months of her English captivity (July 1568) Mary again dallied with the idea of conversion, for the sake of freedom. She told the Spanish Ambassador that "she would sooner be murdered," but if she could have struck her bargain with Elizabeth, I doubt that she would have chosen the Prayer Book rather than the dagger or the bowl. Her conversion would have been bitterness as of wormwood to Knox. In his eyes Anglicanism was "a bastard religion," "a mingle-mangle now commanded in your kirks." "Peculiar services appointed for Saints' days, diverse Collects as they falsely call them in remembrance of this or that Saint . . . are in my conscience no small portion of papistical superstition." "Crossing in Baptism is a diabolical invention; kneeling at the Lord's table, mummelling," (uttering the responses, apparently), "or singing of the Litany." All these practices are "diabolical inventions," in Knox's candid opinion, "with Mr. Parson's pattering of his constrained prayers, and with the mass-munging of Mr. Vicar, and of his wicked companions . . ." (A blank in the MS.) "Your Ministers, before for the most part, were none of Christ's ministers, but mass-mumming priests." He appears to speak of the Anglican Church as it was under Edward VI. (To Mrs. Locke, Dieppe, April 6, 1559.) As Elizabeth brought in "cross and candle," her Church must have been odious to our Reformer. Calvin had regarded the "silly things" in our Prayer Book as "endurable," not so Knox. Before he came back to Scotland, the Reformers were content with the English Prayer Book. By rejecting it, Knox and his allies disunited Scotland and England.

Knox's friend Arran was threatening to stir up the Congregation for the purpose of securing him in the revenues of three abbeys, including St. Andrews, of which Lord James was Prior. The extremists raised the question, "whether the Queen, being an idolater, may be obeyed in all civil and political actions."

Knox later made Chatelherault promise this obedience; what his views were in November 1561 we know not. Lord James was already distrusted by his old godly friends; it was thought he would receive what he had long desired, the Earldom of Moray (November 11, 1561), and the precise professors meditated a fresh revolution. "It must yet come to a new day," they said. Those about Arran were discontented, and nobody was more in his confidence than Knox, but at this time Arran was absent from Edinburgh; was at St. Andrews.

Meanwhile, at Court, "the ladies are merry, dancing, lusty, and fair," wrote Randolph, who flirted with Mary Beaton (November 18); and long afterwards, in 1578, when she was Lady Boyne, spoke of her as "a very dear friend." Knox complains that the girls danced when they "got the house alone"; not a public offence! He had his intelligencers in the palace.

There was, on November 16, a panic in the unguarded palace: "the poor damsels were left alone," while men hid in fear of nobody knew what, except a rumour that Arran was coming, with his congregational friends, "to take away the Queen." The story was perhaps a fable, but Arran had been uttering threats. Mary, however, expected to be secured by an alliance with Elizabeth. "The accord between the two Queens will quite overthrow them" (the Bishops), "and they say plainly that she cannot return a true Christian woman," writes Randolph.

Lethington and Randolph both suspected that if Mary abandoned idolatry, it would be after conference with Elizabeth, and rather as being converted by that fair theologian than as compelled by her subjects. Unhappily Elizabeth never would meet Mary, who, for all that we know, might at this hour have adopted the Anglican *via media*, despite her protests to Knox and to the Pope of her fidelity to Rome. Like Henri IV., she may at this time have been capable of preferring a crown—that of England—to a dogma. Her Mass, Randolph wrote, "is rather for despite than devotion, for those that use it care not a straw for it, and jest sometimes against it."

Randolph, at this juncture, reminded Mary that advisers of the Catholic party had prevented James V. from meeting Henry VIII. She answered, "Something is reserved for us that was not then," possibly hinting at her conversion. Lord James shared the hopes of Lethington and Randolph. "The Papists storm, thinking the meeting of the queens will overthrow Mass and all."

The Ministers of Mary, *les politiques*, indulged in dreams equally distasteful to the Catholics and to the more precise of the godly; dreams that came through the Ivory Gate; with pictures of the island united, and free from the despotism of Giant Pope and Giant Presbyter. A schism between the brethren and their old leaders and advisers, Lord James and Lethington, was the result. At the General Assembly of December 1561, the split was manifest. The parties exchanged recriminations, and there was even question of the legality of such conventions as the General Assembly. Lethington asked whether the Queen "allowed" the gathering. Knox (apparently) replied, "Take from us the freedom of Assemblies, and take from us the Evangel . . ." He defended them as necessary for order among the preachers; but the objection, of course, was to their political interferences. The question was to be settled for Cromwell in his usual way, with a handful of hussars. It was now determined that the Queen might send Commissioners to the Assembly to represent her interests.

The plea of the godly that Mary should ratify the Book of Discipline was countered by the scoffs of Lethington. He and his brothers ever tormented Knox by *persiflage*. Still the preachers must be supported, and to that end, by a singular compromise, the Crown assumed dominion over the property of the old Church, a proceeding which Mary, if a good Catholic, could not have sanctioned. The higher clergy retained two-thirds of their benefices, and the other third was to be divided between the preachers and the Queen. Vested rights, those of the prelates, and the interests of the nobles to whom, in the troubles, they had feued parts of their property, were thus secured; while the preachers were put off with a humble portion. Among the abbeys, that of St. Andrews, held by the good Lord James, was one of the richest. He appears to have retained all the wealth, for, as Bishop Keith says, "the grand gulf that swallowed up the whole extent of the thirds were pensions given gratis by the Queen to those about the Court . . . of which last the Earl of Moray was always sure to obtain the thirds of his priories of St. Andrews and Pittenweem." In all, the whole reformed clergy received annually (but not in 1565-66) £24,231, 17s. 7d. Scots, while Knox and four superintendents got a few chalders of wheat and "bear." In 1568, when Mary had fallen, a gift of £333, 6s. 8d. was made to Knox from the fund, about a seventh of the money revenue of the Abbey of St. Andrews. Nobody can accuse Knox of enriching himself by the Revolution. "In the stool of Edinburgh," he declared that two parts were being given to the devil, "and the third must be divided between God and the devil," between the preachers and the

Queen, and the Earl of Moray, among others. The eminently godly Laird of Pitarro had the office of paying the preachers, in which he was so niggardly that the proverb ran, "The good Laird of Pitarro was an earnest professor of Christ, but the great devil receive the Comptroller."

It was argued that "many Lords have not so much to spend" as the preachers; and this was not denied (if the preachers were paid), but it was said the Lords had other industries whereby they might eke out their revenues. Many preachers, then or later, were driven also to other industries, such as keeping public-houses. Knox, at this period, gracefully writes of Mary, "we call her not a hoore." When she scattered his party after Riccio's murder, he went the full length of the expression, in his "History."

"Simplicity," says Thucydides, "is no small part of a noble nature," and Knox was now to show simplicity in conduct, and in his narrative of a very curious adventure.

The Hamiltons had taken little but loss by joining the Congregation. Arran could not recover his claims, on whatever they were founded, over the wealth of St. Andrews and Dunfermline. Chatelherault feared that Mary would deprive him of his place of refuge, the castle of Dumbarton, to which he confessed that his right was "none," beyond a verbal promise of a nineteen years "farm" (when given we know not), from Mary of Guise. Randolph began to believe that Arran really had contemplated a raid on Mary at Holyrood, where she had no guards. "Why," asked Arran, "was it not as easy to take her out of the Abbey, as once it had been intended to do with her mother?"

Here were elements of trouble, and Knox adds that, according to the servants of Chatelherault, Huntly and the Hamiltons devised to slay Lord James, who in January received the Earldom of Moray, but bore the title of Earl of Mar, which earldom he held for a brief space. Huntly had claims on Moray, and hence hated Lord James. Arran was openly sending messengers to France; "his councils are too patent." Randolph at the same time found Knox and the preachers "as wilfull as learned, which heartily I lament" (January 30). The rumour that Mary had been persuaded by the Cardinal to turn

Anglican "makes them run almost wild" (February 12). If the Queen were an Anglican the new Kirk would be in an ill way. Arran still sent retainers to France, and was reported to speak ill of Mary (February 21), but the Duke tried to win Randolph to a marriage between Arran and the Queen. The intended bridegroom lay abed for a week, "tormented by imaginations," but was contented, not to be reconciled with Bothwell, but to pass his misdeeds in "oblivion," as he declared to the Privy Council (February 20).

In these threatening circumstances Bothwell made Knox's friend, Barron, a rich burgess who "financed" the Earl, introduce him to our Reformer. The Earl explained that his feud with Arran was very expensive; he had for his safety to keep "a number of wicked and unprofitable men about him"—his "Lambs," the Ormistouns, young Hay of Tala, probably, and the rest. He therefore repented, and wished to be reconciled to Arran. Knox, pleased at being a reconciler where nobler men had failed, and moved, after long refusal, by the entreaties of the godly, as he tells Mrs. Locke, advised Bothwell first to be reconciled to God. So Bothwell presently was, going to sermon for that very purpose. Knox promised to approach Arran, and Bothwell, with his usual impudence, chose that moment to seize an old pupil of Knox's, the young Laird of Ormiston (Cockburn). The young laird, to be sure, had fired a pistol at his enemy. However, Bothwell repented of this lapse, and at the Hamilton's great house of Kirk-of-Field, Knox made him and Arran friends. Next day they went to sermon together; on the following day they visited Chatelherault at Kinneil, some twelve miles from Edinburgh. But on the ensuing day (March 26) came the wild end of the reconciliation.

Knox had delivered his daily sermon, and was engaged with his vast correspondence, when Arran was announced, with an advocate and the town clerk. Arran began a conference with tears, said that he was betrayed, and told his tale. Bothwell had informed him that he would seize the Queen, put her in Dumbarton, kill her misguiders, the "Earl of Moray" (Mar, Lord James), Lethington, and others, "and so shall he and I rule all."

But Arran believed Bothwell really intended to accuse him of treason, or knowledge of treason, so he meant to write to Mary and Mar. Knox asked whether he had assented to the plot, and advised him to be silent. Probably he saw that Arran was distraught, and did not credit his story. But Arran said that Bothwell (as he had once done before, in 1559) would challenge him to a judicial combat—such challenges were still common, but never led to a fight. He then walked off with his legal advisers, and wrote to Mary at Falkland. If Arran went mad, he went mad "with advice of counsel." There had come the chance of "a new day," which the extremists desired, but its dawn was inauspicious.

Arran rode to his father's house of Kinneil, where, either because he was insane, or because there really was a Bothwell-Hamilton plot, he was locked up in a room high above the ground. He let himself down from the window, reached Halyards (a place of Kirkcaldy of Grange), and was thence taken by Mar (whom Knox appears to have warned) to the Queen at Falkland. Bothwell and Gawain Hamilton were also put in ward there. Randolph gives (March 31) a similar account, but believed that there really was a plot, which Arran denied even before he arrived at Falkland. Bothwell came to purge himself, but "was found guilty on his own confession on some points."

The Queen now went to St. Andrews, where the suspects were placed in the Castle. Arran wavered, accusing Mar's mother of witchcraft. Mary was "not a little offended with Bothwell to whom she has been so good." Randolph (April 7) continued to think that Arran should be decapitated. He and Bothwell were kept in ward, and his father, the Duke, was advised to give up Dumbarton to the Crown, which he did. This was about April 23. Knox makes a grievance of the surrender; the Castle, he says, was by treaty to be in the Duke's hands till the Queen had lawful issue. Chatelherault himself, as we said, told Randolph that he had no right in the place, beyond a verbal and undated promise of the late Regent.

Knox now again illustrates his own historical methods. Mary, riding between Falkland and Lochleven, fell, was hurt, and when Randolph wrote from Edinburgh on May 11, was not expected there for two or three days. But Knox reports that, on her return from Fife to Edinburgh, she danced excessively till after midnight, because she had received letters "that persecution was begun again in France," by the Guises. Now as, according to Knox elsewhere, "Satan stirreth his terrible tail," so did one of Mary's uncles, the Duc de Guise, "stir his tail" against one of the towns appointed to pay Mary's jointure, namely Vassy, in Champagne. Here, on March 1, 1562, a massacre of Huguenots, by the Guise's retainers, began the war of religion afresh.

Now, in the first place, this could not be joyful news to set Mary dancing; as it was apt to prevent what she had most at heart, her personal interview with Elizabeth. She understood this perfectly well, and, in conversation with Randolph, after her return to Edinburgh, lamented the deeds of her uncles, as calculated "to bring them in hate and disdain of many princes," and also to chill Elizabeth's amity for herself—on which her whole policy now depended (May 29). She wept when Randolph said that, in the state of France, Elizabeth was not likely to move far from London for their interview. In this mood how could Mary give a dance to celebrate an event which threatened ruin to her hopes?

Moreover, if Knox, when he speaks of "persecution begun again," refers to the slaughter of Huguenots by Guise's retinue, at Vassy, that untoward event occurred on March 1, and Mary cannot have been celebrating it by a ball at Holyrood as late as May 14, at earliest. Knox, however, preached against her dancing, if she danced "for pleasure at the displeasure of God's people"; so he states the case. Her reward, in that case, would he "drink in hell." In his "History" he declares that Mary did dance for the evil reason attributed to her, a reason which must have been mere matter of inference on his part, and that inference wrong, judging by dates, if the reference is to the affair of Vassy. In April both French parties were committing brutalities, but these were all contrary to Mary's policy and hopes.

If Knox heard a rumour against any one, his business, according to the "Book of Discipline," was not to go and preach against that person, even by way of insinuation. Mary's offence, if any existed, was not "public," and was based on mere suspicion, or on tattle. Dr. M'Crie, indeed, says that on hearing of the affair of Vassy, the Queen "immediately after gave a splendid ball to her foreign servants." Ten weeks after the Vassy affair is not "immediately"; and Knox mentions neither foreign servants nor Vassy.

The Queen sent for Knox, and made "a long harangue," of which he does not report one word. He gives his own oration. Mary then said that she could not expect him to like her uncles, as they differed in religion. But if he heard anything of herself that he disapproved of, "come to myself and tell me, and I shall hear you." He answered that he was not bound to come "to every man in particular," but she *could* come to his sermons! If she would name a day and hour, he would give her a doctrinal lecture. At this very moment he "was absent from his book"; his studies were interrupted.

"You will not always be at your book," she said, and turned her back. To some papists in the antechamber he remarked, "Why should the pleasing face of a gentlewoman affray me? I have looked in the faces of many angry men, and yet have not been afraid above measure."

He was later to flee before that pleasing face.

Mary can hardly be said to have had the worse, as far as manners and logic went, of this encounter, at which Morton, Mar, and Lethington were present, and seem to have been silent.

Meanwhile, Randolph dates this affair, the dancing, the sermon, the interview, not in May, but about December 13-15, 1562, and connects the dancing with no event in France, nor can I find any such event in late November which might make Mary glad at heart. Knox, Randolph writes, mistrusts all that the Queen does or says, "as if he were of God's Privy Council, that knew how he had determined of her in the beginning, or that he knew the secrets of her heart so well that she neither did nor could have one good thought of God or of his true religion." His doings could not increase her respect for his religion.

The affair of Arran had been a sensible sorrow to Knox. "God hath further humbled me since that day which men call Good Friday," he wrote to Mrs. Locke (May 6), "than ever I have been in my life. . . ." He had rejoiced in his task of peace-making, in which the Privy Council had practically failed, and had shown great *naïveté* in trusting Bothwell. The best he could say to Mrs. Locke was that he felt no certainty about the fact that Bothwell had tempted Arran to conspire.

The probability is that the reckless and impoverished Bothwell did intend to bring in the desirable "new day," and to make the Hamiltons his tools. Meanwhile he was kept out of mischief and behind stone walls for a season. Knox had another source of annoyance which was put down with a high hand.

The dominie of the school at Linlithgow, Ninian Winzet by name, had lost his place for being an idolater. In February he had brought to the notice of our Reformer and of the Queen the question, "Is John Knox a lawful minister?" If he was called by God, where were his miracles? If by men, by what manner of men? On March 3, Winzet asked Knox for "your answer in writing." He kept launching letters at Knox in March; on March 24 he addressed the general public; and, on March 31, issued an appeal to the magistrates, who appear to have been molesting people who kept Easter. The practice was forbidden in a proclamation by the Queen on May 31. "The pain is death," writes Randolph. If Mary was ready to die for her faith, as she informed a nuncio who now secretly visited her, she seems to have been equally resolved that her subjects should not live in it.

Receiving no satisfactory *written* answer from Knox, Winzet began to print his tract, and then he got his reply from "soldiers and the magistrates," for the book was seized, and he himself narrowly escaped to the Continent. Knox was not to be brought to a written reply, save so far as he likened his calling to that of Amos and John the Baptist. In September he referred to his "Answer to Winzet's Questions" as forthcoming, but it never appeared. Winzet was Mary's chaplain in her Sheffield prison in 1570-72; she had him made Abbot of Ratisbon, and he is said, by Lethington's son, to have helped Lesley in writing his "History."

On June 29 the General Assembly, through Knox probably, drew up the address to the Queen, threatening her and the country with the wrath of God on her Mass, which, she is assured, is peculiarly distasteful to the Deity. The brethren are deeply disappointed that she does not attend their sermons, and ventures to prefer "your ain preconceived vain opinion." They insist that adulterers must be punished with death, and they return to their demands for the poor and the preachers. A new rising is threatened if wicked men trouble the ministers and disobey the Superintendents.

Lethington and Knox had one of their usual disputes over this manifesto; the Secretary drew up another. "Here be many fair words," said the Queen on reading it; "I cannot tell what the hearts are." She later found out the nature of Lethington's heart, a pretty black one. The excesses of the Guises in France were now the excuse or cause of the postponement of Elizabeth's meeting with Mary. The Queen therefore now undertook a northern progress, which had been arranged for in January, about the time when Lord James was made Earl of Moray.

He could not "brook" the Earldom of Moray before the Earl of Huntly was put down, Huntly being a kind of petty king in the east and north. There is every reason to suppose that Mary understood and utterly distrusted Huntly, who, though the chief Catholic in the country, had been a traitor whenever occasion served for many a year. One of his sons, John, in July, wounded an Ogilvy in Edinburgh in a quarrel over property. This affair was so managed as to drive Huntly into open rebellion, neither Mary nor her brother being sorry to take the opportunity.

The business of the ruin of Huntly has seemed more of a mystery to historians than it was, though an attack by a Catholic princess on her most powerful Catholic subject does need explanation. But Randolph was with Mary during the whole expedition, and his despatches are better evidence than the fables of Buchanan and the surmises of Knox and Mr. Froude. Huntly had been out of favour ever since Lord James obtained the coveted Earldom of Moray in January, and he was thought to be opposed to Mary's visit to Elizabeth. Since January, the Queen had been bent on a northern progress. Probably the Archbishop of St. Andrews, as reported by Knox, rightly guessed the motives. At table he said, "The Queen has gone into the north, belike to seek disobedience; she may perhaps find the thing that she seeks." She wanted a quarrel with Huntly, and a quarrel she found. Her northward expedition, says Randolph, "is rather devised by herself than greatly approved by her Council." She would not visit Huntly at Strathbogie, contrary to the advice of her Council; his son, who wounded Ogilvy, had broken prison, and refused to enter himself at Stirling Castle. Huntly then supported his sons in rebellion, while Bothwell broke prison and fortified himself in Hermitage Castle. Lord James's Earldom of Moray was now publicly announced (September 18), and Huntly was accused of a desire to murder him and Lethington, while his son John was to seize the Queen. Mary was "utterly determined to bring him to utter confusion." Huntly was put to the horn on October 18; his sons took up arms. Huntly, old and corpulent, died during a defeat at Corrichie without stroke of sword; his mischievous son John was taken and executed, Mary being pleased with her success, and declaring that Huntly thought "to have married her where he would," and to have slain her brother. John Gordon confessed to the murder plot. His eldest brother, Lord Gordon, who had tried to enlist Bothwell and the Hamiltons, lay long in prison (his sister married Bothwell just before Riccio's murder). The Queen had punished the disobedience which she "went to seek," and Moray was safe in his rich earldom, while a heavy blow was dealt at the Catholicism which Huntly had protected. Cardinal Guise reports her success to de Rennes, in Austria, with triumph, and refers to an autograph letter of hers, of which Lethington's draft has lately perished by fire, unread by historians. As the Cardinal reports that she says she is trying to win her subjects back to the Church, "in which she wishes to live and die" (January 30, 1562-63), Lethington cannot be the author of that part of her lost letter.

Knox meanwhile, much puzzled by the news from the north, was in the western counties. He induced the lairds of Ayrshire to sign a Protestant band, and he had a controversy with the Abbot of Crosraguel. In misapplication of texts the abbot was even more eccentric than Knox, though he only followed St. Jerome. In his "History" Knox "cannot certainly say whether there was any secret paction and confederacy between the Queen herself and Huntly." Knox decides that though Mary executed John Gordon and other rebels, yet "it was the destruction of others that she sought," namely, of her brother, whom she hated "for his godliness and upright plainness." His upright simplicity had won him an earldom and the destruction of his rival! He and Lethington may have exaggerated Huntly's iniquities in council with Mary, but the rumours reported against her by Knox could only be inspired by the credulity of extreme ill-will. He flattered himself that he kept the Hamiltons quiet, and, at a supper with Randolph in November, made

Chatelherault promise to be a good subject in civil matters, and a good Protestant in religion.

Knox says that preaching was done with even unusual vehemence in winter, when his sermon against the Queen's dancing for joy over some unknown Protestant misfortune was actually delivered, and the good seed fell on ground not wholly barren. The Queen's French and Scots musicians would not play or sing at the Queen's Christmas-day Mass, whether pricked in heart by conscience, or afraid for their lives. "Her poor soul is so troubled for the preservation of her silly Mass that she knoweth not where to turn for defence of it," says Randolph. These persecutions may have gone far to embitter the character of the victim.

Mr. Froude is certainly not an advocate of Mary Stuart, rather he is conspicuously the reverse. But he remarks that when she determined to marry Darnley, "divide Scotland," and trust to her Catholic party, she did so because she was "weary of the mask which she had so long worn, and unable to endure any longer these wild insults to her creed and herself." She had, in fact, given the policy of submission to "wild insults" rather more than a fair chance; she had, for a spirited girl, been almost incredibly long-suffering, when "barbarously baited," as Charles I. described his own treatment by the preachers and the Covenanters.

CHAPTER XVI.

KNOX AND QUEEN MARY (continued): 1563-1564

The new year, 1563, found Knox purging the Kirk from that fallen brother, Paul Methuen. This preacher had borne the burden and heat of the day in 1557-58, erecting, as we have seen, the first "reformed" Kirk, that of the Holy Virgin, in Dundee, and suffering some inconvenience, if no great danger, from the clergy of the religion whose sacred things he overthrew. He does not appear to have been one of the more furious of the new apostles. Contrasted with John Brabner, "a vehement man inculcating the law and pain thereof," Paul is described as "a milder man, preaching the evangel of grace and remission of sins in the blood of Christ."

Paul was at this time minister of Jedburgh. He had "an ancient matron" to wife, recommended, perhaps, by her property, and she left him for two months with a servant maid. Paul fell, but behaved not ill to the mother of his child, sending her "money and clothes at various times." Knox tried the case at Jedburgh; Paul was excommunicated, and fled the realm, sinking so low, it seems, as to take orders in the Church of England. Later he returned—probably he was now penniless—"and prostrated himself before the whole brethren with weeping and howling." He was put to such shameful and continued acts of public penance up and down the country that any spirit which he had left awoke in him, and the Kirk knew him no more. Thus "the world might see what difference there is between darkness and light."

Knox presently had to record a scandal in a higher place, the capture and execution of the French minor poet, Chastelard, who, armed with sword and dagger, hid under the Queen's bed in Holyrood; and invaded her room with great insolence at Burntisland as she was on her way to St. Andrews. There he was tried, condemned, and executed in the market-place. It seems fairly certain that Chastelard, who had joined the Queen with despatches during the expedition against Huntly, was a Huguenot. The Catholic version, and Lethington's version, of his adventure was that some intriguing Huguenot lady had set him on to sully Queen Mary's character; other tales ran that he was to assassinate her, as part of a great Protestant conspiracy.

Randolph, who knew as much as any one, thought the Queen far too familiar with the poet, but did not deem that her virtue was in fault. Knox dilates on Mary's familiarities, kisses given in a vulgar dance, dear to the French society of the period, and concludes that the fatuous poet "lacked his head, that his tongue should not utter the secrets of our Queen."

There had been a bad harvest, and a dearth, because the Queen's luxury "provoked God" (who is represented as very irritable) "to strike the staff of bread," and to "give His malediction upon the fruits of the earth. But oh, alas, who looked, or yet looks, to the very cause of all our calamities!"

Some savage peoples are said to sacrifice their kings when the weather is unpropitious. Knox's theology was of the same kind. The preachers, says Randolph (February 28), "pray daily . . . that God will either turn the Queen's heart or grant her short life. Of what charity or spirit this proceeds, I leave to be discussed by great divines." The prayers sound like encouragement to Jehus.

At this date Ruthven was placed, "by Lethington's means only," on the Privy Council. Moray especially hated Ruthven "for his sorcery"; the superstitious Moray affected the Queen with this ill opinion of one of the elect—in the affair of Riccio's murder so useful to the cause of Knox. "There is not an unworthier in Scotland" than Ruthven, writes Randolph. Meanwhile Lethington was in England to negotiate for peace in France; if he could, to keep an eye on Mary's chances for the succession, and (says Knox) to obtain leave for Lennox, the chief of the Stuarts and the deadly foe of the Hamiltons, to visit Scotland, whence, in the time of Henry VIII., he had been driven as a traitor. But Lethington was at that time confuting Lennox's argument that the Hamilton chief, Chatelherault, was illegitimate. Knox is not positive, he only reports rumours. Lethington's serious business was to negotiate a marriage for the Queen.

Despite the recent threats of death against priests who celebrated Mass, the Archbishop Hamilton and Knox's opponent, the Abbot of Crossraguel, with many others, did so at Easter. The Ayrshire brethren "determined to put to their own hands," captured some priests, and threatened others with "the punishment that God has appointed to idolaters by His law." The Queen commanded Knox to meet her at Lochleven in mid-April—Lochleven, where she was later to be a prisoner. In that state lay the priests of her religion, who had been ministering to the people, "some in secret houses, some in barns, some in woods and hills," writes Randolph, "all are in prison."

Mary, for two hours before supper, implored Knox to mediate with the western fanatics. He replied, that if princes would not use the sword against idolaters, there was the leading case of Samuel's slaughter of Agag; and he adduced another biblical instance, of a nature not usually cited before young ladies. He was on safer ground in quoting the Scots law as it stood. Judges within their bounds were to seek out and punish "mass-mongers"—that was his courteous term.

The Queen, rather hurt, went off to supper, but next morning did her best to make friends with Knox over other matters. She complained of Ruthven, who had given her a ring for some magical purpose, later explained by Ruthven, who seems to have despised the superstition of his age. The Queen, says Ruthven, was afraid of poison; he gave her the ring, saying that it acted as an antidote. Moray was at Lochleven with the Queen, and Moray believed, or pretended to believe, in Ruthven's "sossery," as Randolph spells "sorcery." She, rather putting herself at our Reformer's mercy, complained that Lethington alone placed Ruthven in the Privy Council.

"That man is absent," said Knox, "and therefore I will speak nothing on that behalf." Mary then warned him against "the man who was at time most familiar with the said John, in his house and at table," the despicable Bishop of Galloway, and Knox later found out that the warning was wise. Lastly, she asked him to reconcile the Earl and Countess of Argyll—"do this much for my sake"; and she promised to summon the offending priests who had done their duty.

Knox, with his usual tact, wrote to Argyll thus: "Your behaviour toward your wife is very offensive unto many godly." He added that, if all that was said of Argyll was true, and if he did not look out, he would be damned.

"This bill was not well accepted of the said Earl," but, like the rest of them, he went on truckling to Knox, "most familiar with the said John."

Nearly fifty priests were tried, but no one was hanged. They were put in ward; "the like of this was never heard within the realm," said pleased Protestants, not "smelling the craft." Neither the Queen nor her Council had the slightest desire to put priests to death. Six other priests "as wicked as" the Archbishop were imprisoned, and the Abbot of Crossraguel was put to the horn in his absence, just as the preachers had been. The Catholic clergy "know not where to hide their heads," says Randolph. Many fled to the more tender mercies of England; "it will be the common refuge of papists that cannot live here . . ." The tassels on the trains of the ladies, it was declared by the preachers, "would provoke God's vengeance . . . against the whole realm . . "

The state of things led to a breach between Knox and Moray, which lasted till the Earl found him likely to be useful, some eighteen months later.

The Reformer relieved his mind in the pulpit at the end of May or early in June, rebuking backsliders, and denouncing the Queen's rumoured marriage with any infidel, "and all Papists are infidels." Papists and Protestants were both offended. There was a scene with Mary, in which she wept profusely, an infirmity of hers; we constantly hear of her weeping in public. She wished the Lords of the Articles to see whether Knox's "manner of speaking" was not punishable, but nothing could be done. Elizabeth would have found out a way.

The fact that while Knox was conducting himself thus, nobody ventured to put a dirk or a bullet into him—despite the obvious strength of the temptation in many quarters—proves that he was by far the most potent human being in Scotland. Darnley, Moray, Lennox were all assassinated, when their day came, though the feeblest of the three, Darnley, had a powerful clan to take up his feud. We cannot suppose that any moral considerations prevented the many people whom Knox had offended from doing unto him as the Elect did to Riccio. Manifestly, nobody had the courage. No clan was so strong as the warlike brethren who would have avenged the Reformer, and who probably would have been backed by Elizabeth.

Again, though he was estranged from Moray, that leader was also, in some degree, estranged from Lethington, who did not allow him to know the details of his intrigues, in France and England, for the Queen's marriage. The marriage question was certain to reunite Moray and Knox. When Knox told Mary that, as "a subject of this realm," he had a right to oppose her marriage with any infidel, he spoke the modern constitutional truth. For Mary to wed a Royal Catholic would certainly have meant peril for Protestantism, war with England, and a tragic end. But what Protestant could she marry? If a Scot, he would not long have escaped the daggers of the Hamiltons; indeed, all the nobles would have borne the fiercest jealousy against such an one as, say, Glencairn, who, we learn, could say anything to Mary without offence. She admired a strong brave man, and Glencairn, though an opponent, was gallant and resolute. England chose only to offer the infamous and treacherous Leicester, whose character was ruined by the mysterious death of his wife (Amy Robsart), and who had offered to sell England and himself to idolatrous Spain. Mary's only faint chance of safety lay in perpetual widowhood, or in marrying Knox, by far the most powerful of her subjects, and the best able to protect her and himself.

This idea does not seem to have been entertained by the subtle brain of Lethington. Between February and May 1563, the Cardinal of Lorraine had reopened an old negotiation for wedding the Queen to the Archduke, and Mary had given an evasive reply; she must consult Parliament. In March, with the Spanish Ambassador in London, Lethington had proposed for Don Carlos. Philip II., as usual, wavered, consented (in August), considered, and reconsidered. Lethington, in France, had told the Queen-Mother that the Spanish plan was only intended to wring concessions from Elizabeth; and, on his return to England, had persuaded the Spanish Ambassador that Charles IX. was anxious to succeed to his brother's widow. This moved Philip to be favourable to the Don Carlos marriage, but he waited; there was no sign from France, and Philip withdrew, wavering so much that both the Austrian and Spanish matches became impossible. On October 6, Knox, who suspected more than he knew, told Cecil that out of twelve Privy Councillors, nine would consent to a Catholic marriage. The only hope was in Moray, and Knox "daily thirsted" for death. He appealed to Leicester (about whose relations with Elizabeth he was, of course, informed) as to a man who "may greatly advance the purity of religion."

These letters to Cecil and Leicester are deeply pious in tone, and reveal a cruel anxiety. On June 20, three weeks after Knox's famous sermon, Lethington told de Quadra, the Spanish Ambassador, that Elizabeth threatened to be Mary's enemy if she married Don Carlos or any of the house of Austria. On August 26, 1563, Randolph received instructions from Elizabeth, in which the tone of menace was unconcealed. Elizabeth would offer an English noble: "we and our country cannot think any mighty prince a meet husband for her."

Knox was now engaged in a contest wherein he was triumphant; an affair which, in later years, was to have sequels of high importance. During the summer vacation of 1563, while Mary was moving about the country, Catholics in Edinburgh habitually attended at Mass in her chapel. This was contrary to the arrangement which permitted no Mass in the whole realm, except that of the Queen, when her priests were not terrorised. The godly brawled in the Chapel Royal, and two of them were arrested, two very dear brethren, named Cranstoun and Armstrong; they were to be tried on October 24. Knox had a kind of Dictator's commission from the Congregation, "to see that the Kirk took no harm," and to the Congregation he appealed by letter. The accused brethren had only "noted what persons repaired to the Mass," but they were charged with divers crimes, especially invading her Majesty's palace. Knox therefore convoked the Congregation to meet in Edinburgh on the day of trial, in the good old way of overawing justice. Of course we do not know to what lengths the dear brethren went in their pious indignation. The legal record mentions that they were armed with pistols, in the town and Court suburb; and it was no very unusual thing, later, for people to practise pistol shooting at each other even in their own Kirk of St. Giles's.

Still, pistols, if worn in the palace chapel have not a pacific air. The brethren are also charged with assaulting some of the Queen's domestic servants.

Archbishop Spottiswoode, son of one of the Knoxian Superintendents, says that the brethren "forced the gates, and that some of the worshippers were taken and carried to prison. . . . " Knox admits in his "History" that "some of the brethren *burst in*" to the chapel. In his letter to stir up the godly, he says that the brethren "passed" (in), "and that *in most quiet manner.*"

On receiving Knox's summons the Congregation prepared its levies in every town and province. The Privy Council received a copy of Knox's circular, and concluded that it "imported treason."

To ourselves it does seem that for a preacher to call levies out of every town and province, to meet in the capital on a day when a trial was to be held, is a thing that no Government can tolerate. The administration of justice is impossible in the circumstances. But it was the usual course in Scotland, and any member of the Privy Council might, at any time, find it desirable to call a similar convocation of his allies. Mary herself, fretted by the perfidies of Elizabeth, had just been consoled by that symbolic jewel, a diamond shaped like a rock, and by promises in which she fondly trusted when she at last sought an asylum in England, and found a prison. For two months she had often been in deep melancholy, weeping for no known cause, and she was afflicted by the "pain in her side" which ever haunted her (December 13-21).

Accused by the Master of Maxwell of unbecoming conduct, Knox said that such things had been done before, and he had the warrant "of God, speaking plainly in his Word." The Master (later Lord Herries), not taking this view of the case, was never friendly with

Knox again; the Reformer added this comment as late as December 1571.

Lethington and Moray, like Maxwell, remonstrated vainly with our Reformer. Randolph (December 21) reports that the Lords assembled "to take order with Knox and his faction, who intended by a mutinous assembly made by his letter before, to have rescued two of their brethren from course of law. . . . " Knox was accompanied to Holyrood by a force of brethren who crowded "the inner close and all the stairs, even to the chamber door where the Queen and Council sat." Probably these "slashing communicants" had their effect on the minds of the councillors. Not till after Riccio's murder was Mary permitted to have a strong guard.

According to Knox, Mary laughed a horse laugh when he entered, saying, "Yon man gart me greit, and grat never tear himself. I will see gif I can gar him greit." Her Scots, textually reported, was certainly idiomatic.

Knox acknowledged his letter to the Congregation, and Lethington suggested that he might apologise. Ruthven said that Knox made convocation of people daily to hear him preach; what harm was there in his letter merely calling people to convocation. This was characteristic pettifogging. Knox said that he convened the people to meet on the day of trial according to the order "that the brethren has appointed . . . at the commandment of the general Kirk of the Realm."

Mary seems, strangely enough, to have thought that this was a valid reply. Perhaps it was, and the Kirk's action in that sense, directed against the State, finally enabled Cromwell to conquer the Kirk-ridden country. Mary appears to have admitted the Kirk's *imperium in imperio*, for she diverted the discussion from the momentous point really at issue—the right of the Kirk to call up an armed multitude to thwart justice. She now fell on Knox's employment of the word "cruelty." He instantly started on a harangue about "pestilent Papists," when the Queen once more introduced a personal question; he had caused her to weep, and he recounted all their interview after he attacked her marriage from the pulpit.

He was allowed to go home—it might not have been safe to arrest him, and the Lords, unanimously, voted that he had done no offence.

They repeated their votes in the Queen's presence, and thus a precedent for "mutinous convocation" by Kirkmen was established, till James VI. took order in 1596. We have no full narrative of this affair except that of Knox. It is to be guessed that the nobles wished to maintain the old habit of mutinous convocation which, probably, saved the life of Lethington, and helped to secure Bothwell's acquittal from the guilt of Darnley's murder. Perhaps, too, the brethren who filled the whole inner Court and overflowed up the stairs of the palace, may have had their influence.

This was a notable triumph of our Reformer, and of the Kirk; to which, on his showing, the Queen contributed, by feebly wandering from the real point at issue. She was no dialectician. Knox's conduct was, of course, approved of and sanctioned by the General Assembly. He had, in his circular, averred that Cranstoun and Armstrong were summoned "that a door may be opened to execute cruelty upon a greater multitude." To put it mildly, the General Assembly sanctioned contempt of Court. Unluckily for Scotland contempt of Court was, and long remained, universal, the country being desperately lawless, and reeking with blood shed in public and private quarrels. When a Prophet followed the secular example of summoning crowds to overawe justice, the secular sinners had warrant for thwarting the course of law.

As to the brethren and the idolaters who caused these troubles, we know not what befell them. The penalty, both for the attendants at Mass and for the disturbers thereof, should have been death! The dear brethren, if they attacked the Queen's servants, came under the Proclamation of October 1561; so did the Catholics, for *they* "openly made alteration and innovation of the state of religion. . . . " They ought "to be punished to the death with all rigour." Three were outlawed, and their sureties "unlawed." Twenty-one others were probably not hanged; the records are lost. For the same reason we know not what became of the brethren Armstrong, Cranstoun, and George Rynd, summoned with the other malefactors for November 13.

CHAPTER XVII.

KNOX AND QUEEN MARY (continued), 1564-1567

During the session of the General Assembly in December 1563, Knox was compelled to chronicle domestic enormities. The Lord Treasurer, Richardson, having, like Captain Booth, "offended the law of Dian," had to do penance before the whole congregation, and the sermon (unfortunately it is lost, probably it never was written out) was preached by Knox. A French apothecary of the Queen's, and his mistress, were hanged on a charge of murdering their child. On January 9, 1564-65, Randolph noted that one of the Queen's Maries, Mary Livingstone, is to marry John Sempill, son of Robert, third Lord Sempill, by an English wife. Knox assures us that "it is well known that shame hastened marriage between John Sempill, called 'the Dancer,' and Mary Livingstone, surnamed 'the Lusty.'" The young people appear, however, to have been in no pressing hurry, as Randolph, on January 9, did not expect their marriage till the very end of February; they wished the Earl of Bedford, who was coming on a diplomatic mission, to be present. Mary, on March 9, 1565, made them a grant of lands, since "it has pleased God to move their hearts to join together in the state of matrimony." She had ever since January been making the bride presents of feminine finery.

These proceedings indicating no precipitate haste, we may think that Mary Livingstone, like Mary of Guise, is only a victim of the Reformer's taste for "society journalism." Randolph, though an egregious gossip, says of the Four Maries, "they are all good," but Knox writes that "the ballads of that age" did witness to the "bruit" or reputation of these maidens. As is well known the old ballad of "Mary Hamilton," which exists in more than a dozen very diverse variants, in some specimens confuses one of the Maries, an imaginary "Mary Hamilton," with the French maid who was hanged at the end of 1563. The balladist is thus responsible for a scandal against the fair sisterhood; there was no "Mary Hamilton," and no "Mary Carmichael," in their number—Beaton, Seton, Fleming, and Livingstone.

An offended Deity now sent frost in January 1564, and an aurora borealis in February, Knox tells us, and "the threatenings of the preachers were fearful," in face of these unusual meteorological phenomena.

Vice rose to such a pitch that men doubted if the Mass really was idolatry! Knox said, from the pulpit, that if the sceptics were right, *he* was "miserably deceived." "Believe me, brethren, in the bowels of Christ, it is possible that you may be mistaken," Cromwell was to tell the Commissioners of the General Assembly, on a day that still was in the womb of the future; the dawn of common sense rose in the south.

On March 20, much to the indignation of the Queen, the banns were read twice between Knox and a lady of the Royal blood and name, Margaret Stewart, daughter of Lord Ochiltree, a girl not above sixteen, in January 1563, when Randolph first speaks of the wooing. The good Dr. M'Crie does not mention the age of the bride! The lady was a very near kinswoman of Chatelherault. She had plenty of time for reflection, and as nobody says that she was coerced into the marriage, while Nicol Burne attributes her passion to sorcery, we may suppose that she was in love with our Reformer. She bore him several daughters, and it is to be presumed that the marriage, though in every way *bizarre*, was happy. Burne says that Knox wished to marry a Lady Fleming, akin to Chatelherault, but was declined; if so, he soon consoled himself.

At this time Riccio—a *valet de chambre* of the Queen in 1561-62—"began to grow great in Court," becoming French Secretary at the end of the year. By June 3, 1565, Randolph is found styling Riccio "only governor" to Darnley. His career might have rivalled that of the equally low-born Cardinal Alberoni, but for the daggers of Moray's party.

In the General Assembly of June 1564, Moray, Morton, Glencairn, Pitarro, Lethington, and other Lords of the Congregation held aloof from the brethren, but met the Superintendents and others to discuss the recent conduct of our Reformer, who was present. He was invited, by Lethington, to "moderate himself" in his references to the Queen, as others might imitate him, "albeit not with the same modesty and foresight," for Lethington could not help bantering Knox. Knox, of course, rushed to his doctrine of "idolatry" as provocative of the wrath of God—we have heard of the bad harvest, and the frost in January. It is not worth while to pursue in detail the discourses, in which Knox said that the Queen rebelled against God "in all the actions of her life." Ahab and Jezebel were again brought on the scene. It profited not Lethington to say that all these old biblical "vengeances" were "singular motions of the Spirit of God, and appertain nothing to our age." If Knox could have understood *that*, he would not have been Knox. The point was intelligible; Lethington perceived it, but Knox never chose to do so. He went on with his isolated texts, Lethington vainly replying "the cases are nothing alike." Knox came to his old stand, "the idolater must die the death," and the executioners must be "the people of God." Lethington quoted many opinions against Knox's, to no purpose, opinions of Luther, Melanchthon, Bucer, Musculus, and Calvin, but our Reformer brought out the case of "Amasiath, King of Judah," and "The Apology of Magdeburg." As to the opinion of Calvin and the rest he drew a distinction. They had only spoken of the godly who were suffering under oppression, not of the godly triumphant in a commonwealth. He forgot, or did not choose to remember, a previous decision of his own, as we shall see.

When the rest of the party were discussing the question, Makgill, Clerk Register, reminded them of their previous debate in November 1561, when Knox, after secretly writing to Calvin, had proposed to write to him for his opinion about the Queen's Mass, and Lethington had promised to do so himself. But Lethington now said that, on later reflection, as Secretary of the Queen, he had scrupled, without her consent, to ask a foreigner whether her subjects might prevent her from enjoying the rites of her own religion—for that was what the "controversies" between her Highness and her subjects really and confessedly meant.

Knox was now requested to consult Calvin, "and the learned in other Kirks, to know their judgment in that question." The question, judging from Makgill's interpellation, was "whether subjects might lawfully take her Mass from the Queen." As we know, Knox had already put the question to Calvin by a letter of October 24, 1561, and so had the anonymous writer of November 18, 1561, whom I identify with Arran. Knox now refused to write to "Mr. Calvin, and the learned of other Kirks," saying (I must quote him textually, or be accused of misrepresentation), "I myself am not only fully resolved in conscience, but also I have heard the judgments in this, and all other things that I have affirmed in this Realm, of the most godly and most learned that be known in Europe. I come not to this Realm without their resolution; and for my assurance I have the handwritings of many; and therefore if I should move the same question again, what else should I do but either show my own ignorance and forgetfulness, or else inconstancy?" He therefore said that his opponents might themselves "write and complain upon him," and so learn "the plain minds" of the learned—but nobody took the trouble. Knox's defence was worded with the skill of a notary. He said that he had "heard the judgments" of "the learned and godly";

he did not say what these judgments were. Calvin, Morel, Bullinger, and such men, we know, entirely differed from his extreme ideas. He "came not without their resolution," or approval, to Scotland, but that was not the question at issue.

If Knox had received from Calvin favourable replies to his own letter, and Arran's, of October 24, November 18, 1561, can any one doubt that he would now have produced them, unless he did not wish the brethren to find out that he himself had written without their knowledge? We know what manner of answers he received, in 1554, orally from Calvin, in writing from Bullinger, to his questions about resistance to the civil power. I am sceptical enough to suppose that, if Knox had now possessed letters from Calvin, justifying the propositions which he was maintaining, such as that "the people, yea, *or ane pairt of the people*, may execute God's jugementis against their King, being ane offender," he would have exhibited them. I do not believe that he had any such letters from such men as Bullinger and Calvin. Indeed, we may ask whether the question of the Queen's Mass had arisen in any realm of Europe except Scotland. Where was there a Catholic prince ruling over a Calvinistic state? If nowhere, then the question would not be raised, except by Knox in his letter to Calvin of October 24, 1561. And where was Calvin's answer, and to what effect?

Knox may have forgotten, and Lethington did not know, that, about 1558-59, in a tract, already noticed (pp. 101-103 *supra*), of 450 pages against the Anabaptists, Knox had expressed the reverse of his present opinion about religious Regicide. He is addressing the persecuting Catholic princes of Europe: " . . . Ye shall perish, both temporally and for ever. And by whom doth it most appear that temporally ye shall be punished? By *us*, whom ye banish, whom ye spoil and rob, whom cruelly ye persecute, and whose blood ye daily shed? There is no doubt, but as the victory which overcometh the world is our faith, so it behoveth us to possess our souls in our patience. We neither privily nor openly deny the power of the Civil Magistrate. . . . "

The chosen saints and people of God, even when under oppression, lift not the hand, but possess their souls in patience, says Knox, in 1558-59. But the idolatrous shall be temporally punished—

by other hands. "And what instruments can God find in this life more apt to punish you than those" (the Anabaptists), "that hate and detest all lawful powers? . . . God will not use his saints and chosen people to punish you. *For with them there is always mercy*, yea, even although God have pronounced a curse and malediction, as in the history of Joshua is plain."

In this passage Knox is speaking for the English exiles in Geneva. He asserts that we "neither publicly nor privately deny the power of the Civil Magistrate," in face of his own published tracts of appeal to a Jehu or a Phinehas, and of his own claim that the Prophet may preach treason, and that his instruments may commit treason. To be sure all the English in Geneva were not necessarily of Knox's mind.

It is altogether a curious passage. God's people are more merciful than God! Israel was bidden to exterminate all idolaters in the Promised Land, but, as the Book of Joshua shows, they did not always do it: "for with them is always mercy"; despite the massacres, such as that of Agag, which Knox was wont to cite as examples to the backward brethren! Yet, relying on another set of texts, not in *Joshua*, Knox now informed Lethington that the executors of death on idolatrous princes were "the people of God"—"the people, or a part of the people."

Mercy! Happily the policy of carnal men never allowed Knox's "people of God" to show whether, given a chance to destroy idolaters, they would display the mercy on which he insists in his reply to the Anabaptist.

It was always useless to argue with Knox; for whatever opinion happened to suit him at the moment (and at different moments contradictory opinions happened to suit him), he had ever a Bible text to back him. On this occasion, if Lethington had been able to quote Knox's own statement, that with the people of God "there is always mercy" (as in the case of Cardinal Beaton), he could hardly have escaped by saying that there was always mercy, *when the people of God had not the upper hand in the State*, when unto them God has *not* "given sufficient force." For in the chosen people of God "there is *always* mercy, yea even although God have pronounced a curse and malediction."

In writing against Anabaptists (1558-59), Knox wanted to make *them*, not merciful Calvinists, the objects of the fear and revenge of Catholic rulers. He even hazarded one of his unfulfilled prophecies: Anabaptists, wicked men, will execute those divine judgments for which Protestants of his species are too tender-hearted; though, somehow, they make exceptions in the cases of Beaton and Riccio, and ought to do so in the case of Mary Stuart!

Lethington did not use this passage of our Reformer's works against him, though it was published in 1560. Probably the secretary had not worked his way through the long essay on Predestination. But we have, in the book against the Anabaptists and in the controversy with Lethington, an example of Knox's fatal intellectual faults. As an individual man, he would not have hurt a fly. As a prophet, he deliberately tried to restore, by a pestilent anachronism, in a Christian age and country, the ferocities attributed to ancient Israel. This he did not even do consistently, and when he is inconsistent with his prevailing mood, his biographers applaud his "moderation"! If he saw a chance against an Anabaptist, or if he wanted to conciliate Mary of Guise, he took up a Christian line, backing it by texts appropriate to the occasion.

His influence lasted, and the massacre of Dunavertie (1647), and the slaying of women in cold blood, months after the battle of Philiphaugh, and the "rouping" of covenanted "ravens" for the blood of cavaliers taken under quarter, are the direct result of Knox's intellectual error, of his appeals to Jehu, Phinehas, and so forth.

At this point the Fourth Book of Knox's "History" ends with a remark on the total estrangement between himself and Moray. The Reformer continued to revise and interpolate his work, up to 1571, the year before his death, and made collections of materials, and notes for the continuation. An uncertain hand has put these together in Book V. But we now miss the frequent references to "John Knox," and his doings, which must have been vigorous during the troubles of 1565, after the arrival in Scotland of Darnley (February 1565), and his courtship and marriage of the Queen. These events brought together Moray, Chatelherault, and many of the Lords in the armed party of the Congregation. They rebelled; they were driven by Mary into England, by October 1565, and Bothwell came at her call from

France. The Queen had new advisers—Riccio, Balfour, Bothwell, the eldest son of the late Huntly, and Lennox, till the wretched Darnley in a few weeks proved his incapacity. Lethington, rather neglected, hung about the Court, as he remained with Mary of Guise long after he had intended to desert her.

Mary, whose only chance lay in outstaying Elizabeth in the policy of celibacy, had been driven, or led, by her rival Queen into a marriage which would have been the best possible, had Darnley been a man of character and a Protestant. He was the typical "young fool," indolent, incapable, fierce, cowardly, and profligate. His religion was dubious. After his arrival (on February 26, 1565) he went with Moray to hear Knox preach, but he had been bred by a Catholic mother, and, on occasion, posed as an ardent Catholic. It is unfortunate that Randolph is silent about Knox during all the period of the broils which preceded and followed Mary's marriage.

On August 19, 1565, Darnley, now Mary's husband, went to hear Knox preach in St. Giles's, on the text, "O Lord our God, other lords than Thou have ruled over us." "God," he said, "sets in that room (for the offences and ingratitude of the people) boys and women." Ahab also appeared, as usual. Ahab "had not taken order with that harlot, Jezebel." So Book V. says, and "harlot" would be a hit at Mary's alleged misconduct with Riccio. A hint in a letter of Randolph's of August 24, may point to nascent scandal about the pair. But the printed sermon, from Knox's written copy, reads, not "harlot" but "idolatrous wife." At all events, Darnley was so moved by this sermon that he would not dine. Knox was called "from his bed" to the Council chamber, where were Atholl, Ruthven, Lethington, the Justice Clerk, and the Queen's Advocate. He was attended by a great crowd of notable citizens, but Lethington forbade him to preach for a fortnight or three weeks. He said that, "If the Church would command him to preach or abstain he would obey, so far as the Word of God would permit him."

It seems that he would only obey even the Church as far as he chose.

The Town Council protested against the deprivation, and we do not know how long Knox desisted from preaching. Laing thinks that, till Mary fell, he preached only "at occasional intervals." But we shall see that he did presently go on preaching, with Lethington for a listener. He published his sermon, without name of place or printer. The preacher informs his audience that "in the Hebrew there is no conjunction copulative" in a certain sentence; probably he knew more Hebrew than most of our pastors.

The sermon is very long, and, wanting the voice and gesture of the preacher, is no great proof of eloquence; in fact, is tedious. Probably Darnley was mainly vexed by the length, though he may have had intelligence enough to see that he and Mary were subjects of allusions. Knox wrote the piece from memory, on the last of August, in "the terrible roaring of guns, and the noise of armour." The banded Lords, Moray and the rest, had entered Edinburgh, looking for supporters, and finding none. Erskine, commanding the Castle, fired six or seven shots as a protest, and the noise of these disturbed the prophet at his task. As a marginal note says, "The Castle of Edinburgh was shooting against the exiled for Christ Jesus' sake" — namely, at Moray and his company. Knox prayed for them in public, and was accused of so doing, but Lethington testified that he had heard "the sermons," and found in them no ground of offence.

Moray, Ochiltree, Pitarro, and many others being now exiles in England, whose Queen had subsidised and repudiated them and their revolution, things went hard with the preachers. For a whole year at least (December 1565-66) their stipends were not paid, the treasury being exhausted by military and other expenses, and Pitarro being absent. At the end of December, Knox and his colleague, Craig, were ordered by the General Assembly to draw up and print a service for a general Fast, to endure from the last Sunday in February to the first in March, 1566. One cause alleged is that the Queen's conversion had been hoped for, but now she said that she would "maintain and defend" her own faith. She had said no less to Knox at their first interview, but now she had really written, when invited to abolish her Mass, that her subjects may worship as they will, but that she will not desert her religion. It was also alleged that the godly were to be destroyed all over Europe, in accordance with decrees of the Council of Trent. Moreover, vice, manslaughter, and oppression of the poor continued, prices of commodities rose, and work was scamped. The date of the Fast was fixed, not to coincide with Lent, but because it preceded an intended meeting of Parliament, a Parliament interrupted by the murder of Riccio, and the capture of the Queen. No games were to be played during the two Sundays of the Fast, which looks as if they were still permitted on other Sundays. The appointed lessons were from Judges, Esther, Chronicles, Isaiah, and Esdras; the New Testament, apparently, supplied nothing appropriate. It seldom did. The lay attendants of the Assembly of Christmas Day which decreed the Fast, were Morton, Mar, Lindsay, Lethington, with some lairds.

The Protestants must have been alarmed, in February 1566, by a report, to which Randolph gave circulation, that Mary had joined a Catholic League, with the Pope, the Emperor, the King of Spain, the Duke of Savoy, and others. Lethington may have believed this; at all events he saw no hope of pardon for Moray and his abettors—"no certain way, unless we chop at the very root, you know where it lieth" (February 9). Probably he means the murder of Riccio, not of the Queen. Bedford said that Mary had not yet signed the League. We are aware of no proof that there was any League to sign, and though Mary was begging money both from Spain and the Pope, she probably did not expect to procure more than tolerance for her own religion. The rumours, however, must have had their effect in causing apprehension. Moreover, Darnley, from personal jealousy; Morton, from fear of losing the Seals; the Douglases, kinsmen of Morton and Darnley; and the friends of the exiled nobles, seeing that they were likely to be forfeited, conspired with Moray in England to be Darnley's men, to slay Riccio, and to make the Queen subordinate to Darnley, and "to fortify and maintain" the Protestant faith. Mary, indeed, had meant to reintroduce the Spiritual Estate into Parliament, as a means of assisting her Church; so she writes to Archbishop Beaton in Paris.

Twelve wooden altars, to be erected in St. Giles's, are said by Knox's continuator to have been found in Holyrood.

Mary's schemes, whatever they extended to, were broken by the murder of Riccio in the evening of March 9. He was seized in her presence, and dirked by fifty daggers outside of her room. Ruthven, who in June 1564 had come into Mary's good graces, and Morton were, with Darnley, the leaders of the Douglas feud, and of the brethren.

The nobles might easily have taken, tried, and hanged Riccio, but they yielded to Darnley and to their own excited passions, when once they had torn him from the Queen. The personal pleasure of dirking the wretch could not be resisted, and the danger of causing the Queen's miscarriage and death may have entered into the plans of Darnley. Knox does not tell the story himself; his "History" ends in June 1564. But "in plain terms" he "lets the world understand what we mean," namely, that Riccio "was justly punished," and that "the act" (of the murderers) was "most just and most worthy of *all* praise." This Knox wrote just after the event, while the murderers were still in exile in England, where Ruthven died—seeing a vision of angels! Knox makes no drawback to the entirely and absolutely laudable character of the deed. He goes out of his way to tell us "in plain terms what we mean," in a digression from his account of affairs sixteen years earlier. Thus one fails to understand the remark, that "of the manner in which the deed was done we may be certain that Knox would disapprove as vehemently as any of his contemporaries." The words may be ironical, for vehement disapproval was not conspicuous among Protestant contemporaries. Knox himself, after Mary scattered the party of the murderers and recovered power, prayed that heaven would "put it into the heart of a multitude" to treat Mary like Athaliah.

Mary made her escape from Holyrood to Dunbar, to safety, in the night of March 11. March 12 found Knox on his knees; the game was up, the blood had been shed in vain. The Queen had not died, but was well, and surrounded by friends; and the country was rather for her than against her. The Reformer composed a prayer, repenting that "in quiet I am negligent, in trouble impatient, tending to desperation," which shows insight. He speaks of his pride and ambition, also of his covetousness and malice. That he was really covetous we cannot believe, nor does he show malice except against idolaters. He "does not doubt himself to be elected to eternal salvation," of which he has "assured signs." He has "knowledge above the common sort of my brethren" (pride has crept in again!), and has been compelled to "forespeak," or prophesy. He implores mercy for his "desolate bedfellow," for her children, and for his sons by his first wife. "Now, Lord, put end to my misery!" (Edinburgh, March 12, 1566). Knox fled from Edinburgh, "with a great mourning of the godly of religion," says a Diarist, on the same day as the chief murderers took flight, March 17; his place of refuge was Kyle in Ayrshire (March 21, 1566).

In Randolph's letter, recording the flight of these nobles, he mentions eight of their accomplices, and another list is pinned to the letter, giving names of men "all at the death of Davy and privy thereunto." This applies to about a dozen men, being a marginal note opposite their names. A line lower is added, "John Knox, John Craig, preachers." There is no other evidence that Knox, who fled, or Craig, who stood to his pulpit, were made privy to the plot. When idolaters thought it best not to let the Pope into a scheme for slaying Elizabeth, it is hardly probable that Protestants would apprise their leading preachers. On the other hand, Calvin was consulted by the would-be assassins of the Duc de Guise, in 1559-60, and he prevented the deed, as he assures the Duchesse de Ferrare, the mother-in-law of the Duc, after that noble was murdered in good earnest. Calvin, we have shown, knew beforehand of the conspiracy of Amboise, which aimed at the death of "Antonius," obviously Guise. He disapproved of but did not reveal the plot. Knox, whether privy to the murder or not, did not, when he ran away, take the best means of disarming suspicion. Neither his name nor that of Craig occurs in two lists containing those of between seventy and eighty persons "delated," and it is to be presumed that he fled because he did not feel sure of protection against Mary's frequently expressed dislike.

In earlier days, with a strong backing, he had not feared "the pleasing face of a gentlewoman," as he said, but now he did fear it. Kyle suited him well, because the Earl of Cassilis, who had been an idolater, was converted by a faithful bride, in August. Dr. M'Crie says that Mary "wrote to a nobleman in the west country with whom Knox resided, to banish him from his house." The evidence for this is a letter of Parkhurst to Bullinger, in December 1567. Parkhurst tells Bullinger, among other novelties, that Riccio was a necromancer, who happened to be dirked; by whom he does not say.

He adds that Mary commanded "a certain pious earl" not to keep Knox in his house.

In Kyle Knox worked at his "History." On September 4 he signed a letter sent from the General Assembly at St. Andrews to Beza, approving of a Swiss confession of faith, except so far as the keeping of Christmas, Easter, and other Christian festivals is concerned. Knox himself wrote to Beza, about this time, an account of the condition of Scotland. It would be invaluable, as the career of Mary was rushing to the falls, but it is lost.

On December 24, Mary pardoned all the murderers of Riccio; and Knox appears to have been present, though it is not certain, at the Christmas General Assembly in Edinburgh. He received permission to visit his sons in England, and he wrote two letters: one to the Protestant nobles on Mary's attempt to revive the consistorial jurisdiction of the Primate; the other to the brethren. To England he carried a remonstrance from the Kirk against the treatment of Puritans who had conscientious objections to the apparel—"Romish rags"—of the Church Anglican. Men ought to oppose themselves boldly to Authority; that is, to Queen Elizabeth, if urged further than their consciences can bear.

Being in England, Knox, of course, did not witness the events associated with the Catholic baptism of the baby prince (James VI.); the murder of Darnley, in February 1567; the abduction of Mary by Bothwell, and her disgraceful marriage to her husband's murderer, in May 1567. If Knox excommunicated the Queen, it was probably about this date. Long afterwards, on April 25, 1584, Mary was discussing the various churches with Waad, an envoy of Cecil. Waad said that the Pope stirred up peoples not to obey their sovereigns. "Yet," said the Queen, "a Pope shall excommunicate *you*, but *I* was excommunicated by a pore minister, Knokes. In fayth I feare nothinge else but that they will use my sonne as they have done the mother."

CHAPTER XVIII.

THE LAST YEARS OF KNOX: 1567-1572

The Royal quarry, so long in the toils of Fate, was dragged down at last, and the doom forespoken by the prophet was fulfilled. A multitude had their opportunity with this fair Athaliah; and Mary had ridden from Carberry Hill, a draggled prisoner, into her own town, among the yells of "burn the harlot." But one out of all her friends was faithful to her. Mary Seton, to her immortal honour, rode close by the side of her fallen mistress and friend.

For six years insulted and thwarted; her smiles and her tears alike wasted on greedy, faithless courtiers and iron fanatics; perplexed and driven desperate by the wiles of Cecil and Elizabeth; in bodily pain and constant sorrow—the sorrow wrought by the miscreant whom she had married; without one honest friend; Mary had wildly turned to the man who, it is to be supposed, she thought could protect her, and her passion had dragged her into unplumbed deeps of crime and shame.

The fall of Mary, the triumph of Protestantism, appear to have, in some degree, rather diminished the prominence of Knox. He would never make Mary weep again. He had lost the protagonist against whom, for a while, he had stood almost alone, and soon we find him complaining of neglect. He appeared at the General Assembly of June 25, 1567—a scanty gathering. George Buchanan, a layman, was Moderator: the Assembly was adjourned to July 21, and the brethren met in arms; wherefore Argyll, who had signed the band for Darnley's murder, declined to come. The few nobles, the barons, and others present, vowed to punish the murder of Darnley and to defend the child prince; and it was decided that henceforth all Scottish princes should swear to "set forward the true religion of Jesus Christ, as at present professed and established in this realm"—as they are bound to do—"by Deuteronomy and the second chapter of the Book of Kings," which, in fact, do not speak of establishing Calvinism.

Among those who sign are Morton, who had guilty foreknowledge of the murder; while his kinsman, Archibald Douglas, was present at the doing; Sir James Balfour, who was equally involved; Lethington, who signed the murder covenant; and Douglas of Whittingham, and Ker of Faldonside, two of Riccio's assassins. Most of the nobles stood aloof.

Presently Throckmorton arrived, sent by Elizabeth with the pretence, at least, of desiring to save Mary's life, which, but for his exertions, he thought would have been taken. He "feared Knox's austerity as much as any man's" (July 14).

On July 17 Knox arrived from the west, where he had been trying to unite the Protestants. Throckmorton found Craig and Knox "very austere," well provided with arguments from the Bible, history, the laws of Scotland, and the Coronation Oath. Knox in his sermons "threatened the great plague of God to this whole nation and country if the Queen be spared from her condign punishment."

Murderers were in the habit of being lightly let off, in Scotland, and, as to Mary, she could easily have been burned for husband-murder, but not so easily convicted thereof with any show of justice. The only direct evidence of her complicity lay in the Casket Letters, and several of her lordly accusers were (if she were guilty) her accomplices. Her prayer to be heard in self-defence at the ensuing Parliament of December was refused, for excellent reasons; and her opponents had the same good reasons for not bringing her to trial. Knox was perfectly justified if he desired her to be tried, but several lay members of the General Assembly could not have faced that ordeal, and Randolph later accused Lethington, in a letter to him, of advising her assassination.

On July 29 Knox preached at the Coronation of James VI. at Stirling, protesting against the rite of anointing. True, it was Jewish, but it had passed through the impure hands of Rome, as, by the way, had Baptism. Knox also preached at the opening of Parliament, on December 15. We know little of him at this time. He had sent his sons to Cambridge, into danger of acquiring Anglican opinions, which they did; but now he seems to have taken a less truculent view of Anglicanism than in 1559-60. He had been drawing a prophetic historical parallel between Chatelherault (more or less of the Queen's party) and Judas Iscariot, and was not loved by the Hamiltons. The Duke was returning from France, "to restore Satan to his kingdom," with the assistance of the Guises. Knox mentions an attempt to assassinate Moray, now Regent, which is obscure. "I live as a man already dead from all civil things." Thus he wrote to Wood, Moray's agent, then in England on the affair of the Casket Letters (September 10, 1568).

He had already (February 14) declined to gratify Wood by publishing his "History." He would not permit it to appear during his life, as "it will rather hurt me than profit them" (his readers). He was, very naturally, grieved that the conduct of men was not conformable to "the truth of God, now of some years manifest." He was not concerned to revenge his own injuries "by word or writ," and he foresaw schism in England over questions of dress and rites.

He was neglected. "Have not thine oldest and stoutest acquaintance" (Moray, or Kirkcaldy of Grange?) "buried thee in present oblivion, and art thou not in that estate, by age, that nature itself calleth thee from the pleasure of things temporal?" (August 19, 1569).

"*In trouble impatient, tending to desperation,*" Knox had said of himself. He was still unhappy. "Foolish Scotland" had "disobeyed God by sparing the Queen's life," and now the proposed Norfolk marriage of Mary and her intended restoration were needlessly dreaded. A month later, Lethington, thrown back on Mary by his own peril for his share in Darnley's murder, writes to the Queen that some ministers are reconcilable, "but Nox I think be inflexible."

A year before Knox wrote his melancholy letter, just cited, he had some curious dealings with the English Puritans. In 1566 many of them had been ejected from their livings, and, like the Scottish Catholics, they "assembled in woods and private houses to worship God." The edifying controversies between these precisians and Grindal, the Bishop of London, are recorded by Strype. The bishop was no zealot for surplices and the other momentous trifles which agitate the human conscience, but Elizabeth insisted on them; and "Her Majesty's Government must be carried on." The precisians had deserted the English Liturgy for the Genevan Book of Common Order; both sides were appealing to Beza, in Geneva, and were wrangling about the interpretation of that Pontiff's words.

Calvin had died in 1564, but the Genevan Church and Beza were still umpires, whose decision was eagerly sought, quibbled over, and disputed. The French Puritans, in fact, extremely detested the Anglican Book of Common Prayer. Thus, in 1562, De la Vigne, a preacher at St. Lô, consulted Calvin about the excesses of certain Flemish brethren, who adhered to "a certain bobulary (*bobulaire*) of prayers, compiled, or brewed, in the days of Edward VI." The Calvinists of St. Lô decided that these Flemings must not approach their holy table, and called our communion service "a disguised Mass." The Synod (Calvinistic) of Poictiers decided that our Liturgy contains "impieties," and that Satan was the real author of the work! There are saints' days, "with epistles, lessons, or gospels, as under the papacy." They have heard that the Prayer Book has been condemned by Geneva.

The English sufferers from our Satanic Prayer Book appealed to Geneva, and were answered by Beza (October 24, 1567). He observed, "Who are we to give any judgment of these things, which, as it seems to us, can be healed only by prayers and patience." Geneva has not heard both sides, and does not pretend to judge. The English brethren complain that ministers are appointed "without any lawful consent of the Presbytery," the English Church not being Presbyterian, and not intending to be. Beza hopes that it will become Presbyterian. He most dreads that any should "execute their ministry contrary to the will of her Majesty and the Bishops," which is exactly what the seceders did. Beza then speaks out about the question of costume, which ought not to be forced on the ministers. But he does not think that the vestments justify schism. In other points the brethren should, in the long run, "give way to manifest violence," and "live as private men." "Other defilements" (kneeling, &c.) Beza hopes that the Queen and Bishops will remove. Men must "patiently bear with one another, and heartily obey the Queen's Majesty and all their Bishops."

As far as this epistle goes, Beza and his colleagues certainly do not advise the Puritan seceders to secede.

Bullinger and Gualterus in particular were outworn by the pertinacious English Puritans who visited them. One Sampson had, when in exile, made the life of Peter Martyr a burden to him by his "clamours," doubts, and restless dissatisfaction. "England," wrote Bullinger to Beza (March 15, 1567), "has many characters of this sort, who cannot be at rest, who can never be satisfied, and who have always something or other to complain about." Bullinger and Gualterus "were unwilling to contend with these men like fencing-masters," tired of their argufying; unable to "withdraw our entire confidence from the Bishops." "If any others think of coming hither, let them know that they will come to no purpose."

Knox may have been less unsympathetic, but his advice agreed with the advice of the Genevans. Some of the seceders were imprisoned; Cecil and the Queen's commissioners encouraged others "to go and preach the Gospel in Scotland," sending with them, as it seems, letters commendatory to the ruling men there. They went, but they were not long away. "They liked not that northern climate, but in May returned again," and fell to their old practices. One of them reported that, at Dunbar, "he saw men going to the church, on Good Friday, barefooted and bare-kneed, and creeping to the cross!" "If this be so," said Grindal, "the Church of Scotland will not be pure enough for our men."

These English brethren, when in Scotland, consulted Knox on the dispute which they made a ground of schism. One brother, who was uncertain in his mind, visited Knox in Scotland at this time. The result appears in a letter to Knox from a seceder, written just after Queen Mary escaped from Lochleven in May 1568. The dubiously seceding brother "told the Bishop" (Grindal) "that you are flat against and condemn all our doings . . . whereupon the Church" (the seceders) "did excommunicate him"! He had reviled "the Church," and they at once caught "the excommunicatory fever." Meanwhile the earnestly seceding brother thought that he had won Knox to *his* side. But a letter from our Reformer proved his error, and the letter, as the brother writes, "is not in all points liked." They would not "go back again to the wafer-cake and kneelings" (the Knoxian Black Rubric had been deleted from Elizabeth's prayer book), "and to other knackles of Popery."

In fact they obeyed Knox's epistle to England of January 1559. "Mingle-mangle ministry, Popish order, and Popish apparel," they will not bear. Knox's arguments in favour of their conforming, for the time at all events, are quoted and refuted: "And also concerning Paul his purifying at Jerusalem." The analogy of Paul's conformity had been rejected by Knox, at the supper party with Lethington in 1556. He had "doubted whether either James's commandment or Paul's obedience proceeded from the Holy Ghost." Yet now Knox had used the very same argument from Paul's conformity which, in 1556, he had scouted! The Mass was not in question in 1568; still, if Paul was wrong (and he did get into peril from a mob!), how could Knox now bid the English brethren follow his example? (See pp. 65-67 *supra*.)

To be sure Mary was probably at large, when Knox wrote, with 4000 spears at her back. The Reformer may have rightly thought it an ill moment to irritate Elizabeth, or he may have grown milder than he was in 1559, and come into harmony with Bullinger. In February of the year of this correspondence he had written, "God comfort that dispersed little flock," apparently the Puritans of his old Genevan congregation, now in England, and in trouble, "amongst whom I would be content to end my days...."

In January 1570, Knox, "with his one foot in the grave," as he says, did not despair of seeing his desire upon his enemy. Moray was asking Elizabeth to hand over to him Queen Mary, giving hostages for the safety of her life. Moray sent his messenger to Cecil, on January 2, 1570, and Knox added a brief note. "If ye strike not at the root," he said, "the branches that appear to be broken will bud again. . . . More days than one would not suffice to express what I think." What he thought is obvious; "stone dead hath no fellow." But Mary's day of doom had not yet come; Moray was not to receive her as a prisoner, for the Regent was shot dead, in Linlithgow, on January 23, by Hamilton of Bothwellhaugh, to the unconcealed delight of his sister, for whom his death was opportune.

The assassin, Bothwellhaugh, in May 1568, had been pardoned for his partisanship of Mary, at Knox's intercession. "Thy image, O Lord, did so clearly shine on that personage" (Moray)—he said in his public prayer at the Regent's funeral —"that the devil, and the people to whom he is Prince, could not abide it." We know too much of Moray to acquiesce, without reserve, in this eulogium.

Knox was sorely disturbed, at this time, by the publication of a *jeu d'esprit*, in which the author professed to have been hidden in a bed, in the cabinet of a room, while the late Regent held a council of his friends. The tone and manner of Lindsay, Wood, Knox and others were admirably imitated; in their various ways, and with appropriate arguments, some of them urged Moray to take the crown for his life. By no people but the Scots, perhaps, could this jape have been taken seriously, but, with a gravity that would have delighted Charles Lamb, Knox denounced the skit from the pulpit as a fabrication by the Father of Lies. The author, the human penman, he said (according to Calderwood), was fated to die friendless in a strange land. The galling shaft came out of the Lethington quiver; it may have been composed by several of the family, but Thomas Maitland, who later died in Italy, was regarded as the author, perhaps because he did die alone in a strange country.

At this time the Castle of Edinburgh was held in the Queen's interest by Kirkcaldy of Grange, who seems to have been won over by the guile of Lethington. That politician needed a shelter from the danger of the Lennox feud, and the charge of having been guilty of Darnley's murder. To take the place was beyond the power of the Protestant party, and it did not fall under the guns of their English allies during the life of the Reformer.

He had a tedious quarrel with Kirkcaldy in December 1570- January 1571. A retainer of Kirkcaldy's had helped to kill a man whom his master only wanted to be beaten. The retainer was put into the Tolbooth; Kirkcaldy set him free, and Knox preached against Kirkcaldy. Hearing that Knox had styled him a murderer, Kirkcaldy bade Craig read from the pulpit a note in which he denied the charge. He prayed God to decide whether he or Knox "has been most desirous of innocent blood." Craig would not read the note: Kirkcaldy appealed in a letter to the kirk-session. He explained the origin of the trouble: the slain man had beaten his brother; he bade his agents beat the insulter, who drew his sword, and got a stab. On this Knox preached against him, he was told, as a cut-throat.

Next Sunday Knox reminded his hearers that he had not called Kirkcaldy a murderer (though in the case of the Cardinal, he was), but had said that the lawless proceedings shocked him more than if they had been done by common cut-throats. Knox then wrote a letter to the kirk-session, saying that Kirkcaldy's defence proved him "to be a murderer at heart," for St. John says that "whoso loveth not his brother is a man-slayer"; and Kirkcaldy did not love the man who was killed. All this was apart from the question: had Knox called Kirkcaldy a common cut-throat? Kirkcaldy then asked that Knox's explanation of what he said in the pulpit might be given in writing, as his words had been misreported, and Knox, "creeping upon his club," went personally to the kirk-session, and requested the Superintendent to admonish Kirkcaldy of his offences. Next Sunday he preached about his eternal Ahab, and Kirkcaldy was offended by the historical parallel. When he next was in church Knox went at him again; it was believed that Kirkcaldy would avenge himself, but the western brethren wrote to remind him of their "great care" for Knox's person. So the quarrel, which made sermons lively, died out.

There was little goodwill to Knox in the Queen's party, and as the conflict was plainly to be decided by the sword, Robert Melville, from the Castle, advised that the prophet should leave the town, in May 1571. The "Castilian" chiefs wished him no harm, they would even shelter him in their hold, but they could not be responsible for his "safety from the multitude and rascal," in the town, for the craftsmen preferred the party of Kirkcaldy. Knox had a curious interview in the Castle with Lethington, now stricken by a mortal malady. The two old foes met courteously, and parted even in merriment; Lethington did not mock, and Knox did not threaten. They were never again to see each other's faces, though the dying Knox was still to threaten, and the dying Lethington was still to mock.

July found Knox and his family at St. Andrews, in the New Hospice, a pre-Reformation ecclesiastical building, west of the Cathedral, and adjoining the gardens of St. Leonard's College. At this time James Melville, brother of the more celebrated scholar and divine, Andrew Melville, was a golf-playing young student of St. Leonard's College. He tells us how Knox would walk about the College gardens, exhorting the St. Leonard's lads to be staunch Protestants; for St. Salvator's and St. Mary's were not devoted to the Reformer and his party. The smitten preacher (he had suffered a touch of apoplexy) walked slowly, a fur tippet round his neck in summer, leaning on his staff, and on the shoulder of his secretary, Bannatyne. He returned, at St. Andrews, in his sermons, to the Book of Daniel with which, nearly a quarter of a century ago, he began his pulpit career. In preaching he was moderate—for half-an-hour; and then, warming to his work, he made young Melville shudder and tremble, till he could not hold his pen to write. No doubt the prophet was denouncing "that last Beast," the Pope, and his allies in Scotland, as he had done these many years ago. Ere he had finished his sermon "he was like to ding the pulpit to blads and fly out of it." He attended a play, written by Davidson, later a famous preacher, on the siege and fall of the Castle, exhibiting the hanging of his old ally, Kirkcaldy, "according to Mr. Knox's doctrine," says Melville. This cheerful entertainment was presented at the marriage of John Colville, destined to be a traitor, a double spy, and a renegade from the Kirk to "the Synagogue of Satan."

Knox now collected historical materials from Alexander Hay, Clerk of the Privy Council, and heard of the publication of Buchanan's scurrilous "Detection" of Queen Mary, in December 1571.

Knox had denounced the Hamiltons as murderers, so one of that name accused our Reformer of having signed a band for the murder of Darnley—not the murder at Kirk o' Field, but a sketch for an attempt at Perth! He had an interview with Knox, not of the most satisfactory, and there was a quarrel with another Hamilton, who later became a Catholic and published scurrilous falsehoods about Knox, in Latin. In fact our Reformer had quarrels enough on his hands at St. Andrews, and to one adversary he writes about what he would do, if he had his old strength of body.

Not in the Regency, but mainly under the influence of Morton, bishops were reintroduced, at a meeting of the Kirk held at Leith, in January 1572. The idea was that each bishop should hand over most of his revenues to Morton, or some other person in power. Knox, of course, objected; he preached at St. Andrews before Morton inducted a primate of his clan, but he refused to "inaugurate" the new prelate. The Superintendent of Fife did what was to be done, and a bishop (he of Caithness) was among the men who imposed their hands on the head of the new Archbishop of St. Andrews. Thus the imposition of hands, which Knox had abolished in the Book of Discipline, crept back again, and remains in Presbyterian usage.

Had Knox been in vigour he might have summoned the brethren in arms to resist; but he was weak of body, and Morton was an ill man to deal with. Knox did draw up articles intended to minimise the mischief of these bastard and simoniacal bishoprics and abused patronages (August 1572). On May 26, 1572, he describes himself as "lying in St. Andrews, half dead." He was able, however, to preach at a witch, who was probably none the better for his distinguished attentions.

On August 17, during a truce between the hostile parties, Knox left St. Andrews for Edinburgh, "not without dolour and displeasure of the few godly that were in the town, but to the great joy and pleasure of the rest;" for, "half dead" as he was, Knox had preached a political sermon every Sunday, and he was in the pulpit at St. Giles's on the last Sunday of August. As his colleague, Craig, had disgusted the brethren by his moderation and pacific temper, a minister named Lawson was appointed as Knox's coadjutor.

Late in August came the news of the St. Bartholomew massacre (August 24). Knox rose to the occasion, and, preaching in the presence of du Croc, the French ambassador, bade him tell his King that he was a murderer, and that God's vengeance should never depart from him or his house. The prophecy was amply fulfilled. Du Croc remonstrated, "but the Lords answered they could not stop the mouths of ministers to speak against themselves."

There was a convention of Protestants in Edinburgh on October 20, but lords did not attend, and few lairds were present. The preachers and other brethren in the Assembly proposed that all Catholics in the realm should be compelled to recant publicly, to lose their whole property and be banished if they were recalcitrant, and, if they remained in the country, that all subjects should be permitted, lawfully, to put them to death. ("To invade them, and every one of them, to the death.") This was the ideal, embodied in law, of the brethren in 1560. Happily they were not permitted to disgrace Scotland by a Bartholomew massacre of her own.

Mr. Hume Brown thinks that these detestable proposals "if not actually penned by Knox, must have been directly inspired by him." He does not, however, mention the demand for massacre, except as "pains and penalties for those who *preached* the old religion." "Without exception of persons, great or small," *all* were to be obliged to recant, or to be ruined and exiled, or to be massacred. Dr. M'Crie does not hint at the existence of these articles, "to be given to the Regent and Council." They included a very proper demand for the reformation of vice at home. Certainly Knox did not pen or dictate the Articles, for none of his favourite adjectives occurs in the document.

At this time Elizabeth, Leicester, and Cecil desired to hand over Queen Mary to Mar, the Regent, "to proceed with her by way of justice," a performance not to be deferred, "either for Parliament or a great Session." Very Petty Sessions indeed, if any, were to suffice for the trial of the Queen. There are to be no "temporising solemnities," all are to be "stout and resolute *in execution*," Leicester thus writes to an unknown correspondent on October 10. Killigrew, who was to arrange the business with Mar, was in Scotland by September 19. On October 6, Killigrew writes that Knox is very feeble but still preaching, and that he says, if he is not a bishop, it is by no fault of Cecil's. "I trust to satisfy Morton," says Killigrew, "and as for John Knox, that thing, as you may see by my letter to Mr. Secretary, is done and doing daily; the people in general well bent to England, abhorring the fact in France, and fearing their tyranny."

"That thing" is *not* the plan for murdering Mary without trial; if Killigrew meant that he had obtained Knox's assent to *that*, he would not write "that thing is doing daily." Even Morton, more scrupulous than Elizabeth and Cecil, said that "there must be some kind of process" (trial, *procès*), attended secretly by the nobles and the ministers. The trial would be in Mary's absence, or would be brief indeed, for the prisoner was not to live three hours after crossing the Border! Others, unnamed, insisted on a trial; the Queen had never been found guilty. Killigrew speaks of "two ministers" as eager for the action, but nothing proves that Knox was one of them. While Morton and Mar were haggling for the price of Mary's blood, Mar died, on October 28, and the whole plot fell through. Anxious as Knox had declared himself to be to "strike at the root," he could not, surely, be less scrupulous about a trial than Morton, though the decision of the Court was foredoomed. Sandys, the Bishop of London, advised that Mary's head should be chopped off!

On November 9, 1572, Knox inducted Mr. Lawson into his place as minister at St. Giles's. On the 13th he could not read the Bible aloud, he paid his servants, and gave his man a present, the last, in addition to his wages. On the 15th two friends came to see Knox at noon, dinner time. He made an effort, and for the last time sat at meat with them, ordering a fresh hogshead of wine to be drawn. "He willed Archibald Stewart to send for the wine so long as it lasted, for he would never tarry until it were drunken." On the 16th the Kirk came to him, by his desire; and he protested that he had never hated any man personally, but only their errors, nor had he made merchandise of the Word. He sent a message to Kirkcaldy bidding him repent, or the threatenings should fall on him and the Castle. His exertions increased his illness. There had been a final quarrel with the dying Lethington, who complained that Knox, in sermons and otherwise, charged him with saying there is "neither heaven nor hell," an atheistic position of which (see his eloquent prayer before Corrichie fight, wherein Huntly died) he was incapable. On the 16th he told "the Kirk" that Lethington's conduct proved that he really did disbelieve in God, and a future of rewards and punishments. That was not the question. The question was—Did Knox, publicly and privately, as Lethington complained, attribute to him words which he denied having spoken, asking that the witnesses should be produced. We wish that Knox had either produced good evidences, or explained why he could not produce them, or had apologised, or had denied that he spoke in the terms reported to Lethington.

James Melville says that the Rev. Mr. Lindsay, of Leith, told him that Knox bade him carry a message to Kirkcaldy in the Castle. After compliments, it ran: "He shall be disgracefully dragged from his nest to punishment, and hung on a gallows before the face of the sun, unless he speedily amend his life, and flee to the mercy of God." Knox added: "That man's soul is dear to me, and I would not have it perish, if I could save it." Kirkcaldy consulted Maitland, and returned with a reply which contained Lethington's last scoff at the prophet. However, Morton, when he had the chance, did hang Kirkcaldy, as in the play acted before Knox at St. Andrews, "according to Mr. Knox's doctrine." "The preachers clamoured for blood to cleanse blood."

As to a secret conference with Morton on the 17th, the Earl, before his execution, confessed that the dying man asked him, "if he knew anything of the King's (Darnley's) murder?" "I answered, indeed, I knew nothing of it"—perhaps a pardonable falsehood in the circumstances. Morton said that the people who had suffered from Kirkcaldy and the preachers daily demanded the soldier's death.

Other sayings of the Reformer are reported. He repressed a lady who, he thought, wished to flatter him: "Lady, lady, the black ox has never trodden yet upon your foot!" "I have been in heaven and have possession, and I have tasted of these heavenly joys where presently I am," he said, after long meditation, beholding, as in Bunyan's allegory, the hills of Beulah. He said the Creed, which soon vanished from Scottish services; and in saying "Our Father," broke off to murmur, "Who can pronounce so holy words?" On November 24 he rose and dressed, but soon returned to bed. His wife read to him the text, "where I cast my first anchor," St. John's Gospel, chapter xvii. About half-past ten he said, "Now it is come!" and being asked for a sign of his steadfast faith, he lifted up one hand, "and so slept away without any pain."

Knox was buried on November 26 in the churchyard south of St. Giles. A flat stone, inscribed J. K., beside the equestrian statue of Charles II., is reported to mark his earthly resting-place. He died as he had lived, a poor man; a little money was owed to him; all his debts were paid. His widow, two years later, married Andrew Ker of Faldonside, so notorious for levelling a pistol at the Queen on the occasion of Riccio's murder. Ker appears to have been intimate with the Reformer. Bannatyne speaks of a story of Lady Atholl's witchcraft, told by a Mr. Lundie to Knox, at dinner, "at Falsyde." This was a way of spelling Faldonside, the name of Ker's place, hard by the Tweed, within a mile of Abbotsford. Probably Ker and his wife sleep in the family burying-ground, the disused kirkyard of Lindean, near a little burn that murmurs under the broad burdock leaves on its way to join the Ettrick.

APPENDIX A.

ALLEGED PERFIDY OF MARY OF GUISE

The Regent has usually been accused of precipitating, or causing the Revolution of 1559, by breaking a pledge given to the Protestants assembled at Perth (May 10-11, 1559). Knox's "History" and a letter of his are the sources of this charge, and it is difficult to determine the amount of truth which it may contain.

Our earliest evidence on the matter is found in a letter to the English Privy Council, from Sir James Croft, commanding at Berwick. The letter, of May 19, is eight days later than the riots at Perth. It is not always accurately informed; Croft corrects one or two statements in later despatches, but the points corrected are not those with which we are here concerned. Neither in this nor in other English advices do I note any charge of ill faith brought against the Regent on this occasion. Croft says that, on Knox's arrival, many nobles and a multitude of others repaired to Dundee to hear him and others preach. The Regent then summoned these preachers before her to Stirling, but as they had a "train" of 5000 or 6000, she "dismissed the appearance," putting the preachers to the horn, and commanding the nobility to appear before her in Edinburgh. The "companies" then retired and wrecked monasteries at Perth. The Lords and they had *previously* sent Erskine of Dun to the Regent, offering to appear before her with only their household servants, to hear the preachers dispute with the clergy, if she would permit. The Regent, "taking displeasure with" Erskine of Dun, bade him begone out of her sight. He rode off (to Perth), and she had him put to the horn (as a fact, he was only fined in his recognisances as bail for one of the preachers). The riots followed his arrival in Perth.

Such is our earliest account; there is no mention of a promise broken by the Regent.

Knox himself wrote two separate and not always reconcilable accounts of the first revolutionary explosion; one in a letter of June 23 to Mrs. Locke, the other in a part of Book II. of his "History," composed at some date before October 23, 1559. That portion of his "History" is an *apologia* for the proceedings of his party, and was apparently intended for contemporary publication.

This part of the "History," therefore, as the work of an advocate, needs to be checked, when possible, by other authorities. We first examine Knox's letter of June 23, 1559, to Mrs. Locke. He says that he arrived in Edinburgh on May 2, and, after resting for a day, went (on May 4) to the brethren assembled at Dundee. They all marched to Perth, meaning thence to accompany the preachers to their day of law at Stirling, May 10. But, lest the proceeding should seem rebellious, they sent a baron (Erskine of Dun, in fact) to the Regent, "with declaration of our minds." The Regent *and Council* in reply, bade the multitude "stay, and not come to Stirling . . . and so should no extremity be used, but the summons should be continued" (deferred) "till further advisement. Which, being gladly granted of us, some of the brethren returned to their dwelling-places. But the Queen *and her Council*, nothing mindful of her and their promise, incontinent did call" (summon) "the preachers, and for lack of their appearance, did exile and put them and their assistants to the horn. . . ."

It would be interesting to know who the Regent's Council were on this occasion. The Reformer errs when he tells Mrs. Locke that the Regent outlawed "the assisters" of the preachers. Dr. M'Crie publishes an extract from the "Justiciary Records" of May 10, in which Methuen, Christison, Harlaw, and Willock, and no others, are put to the horn, or outlawed, in absence, for breach of the Regent's proclamations, and for causing "tumults and seditions." No one else is put to the horn, but the sureties for the preachers' appearance are fined.

In his "History," Knox says that the Regent, when Erskine of Dun arrived at Stirling as an emissary of the brethren, "began to craft with him, soliciting him to stay the multitude, and the preachers also, with promise that she would take some better order." Erskine wrote to the brethren, "to stay and not to come forward, showing what promise

202

and *hope* he had of the Queen's Grace's favours." Some urged that they should go forward till the summons was actually "discharged," otherwise the preachers and their companions would be put to the horn. Others said that the Regent's promises were "not to be suspected . . . and so did the whole multitude with their preachers stay. . . . The Queen, perceiving that the preachers did not appear, began to utter her malice, and notwithstanding any request made on the contrary, gave command to put them to the horn. . . ." Erskine then prudently withdrew, rode to Perth, and "did conceal nothing of the Queen's craft and falsehood."

In this version the Regent bears all the blame, nothing is said of the Council. "The whole multitude stay"—at Perth, or it may perhaps be meant that they do not come forward towards Stirling. The Regent's promise is merely that she would "take some better order." She does not here promise to *postpone* the summons, and refuses "any request made" to abstain from putting them to the horn. The account, therefore, is somewhat more vague than that in the letter to Mrs. Locke. Prof. Hume Brown puts it that the Regent "in her understanding with Erskine of Dun *had publicly cancelled* the summons of the preachers for the 10th of May," which rather overstates the case perhaps. That she should "publicly cancel" or "discharge" the summons was what a part of the brethren desired, and did not get.

We now turn to a fragmentary and anonymous "Historie of the Estate of Scotland," concerning which Prof. Hume Brown says, "Whoever the author may have been, he writes as a contemporary, or from information supplied by a contemporary . . . what inspires confidence in him is that certain of his facts not recorded by other contemporary Scottish historians are corroborated by the despatches of d'Oysel and others in Teulet."

I elsewhere give reasons for thinking that this "Historie" is perhaps the chronicle of Bruce of Earl's Hall, a contemporary gentleman of Fife. I also try to show that he writes, on one occasion, as an eye-witness.

This author, who is a strong partisan of the Reformers, says nothing of the broken promise of the Regent and Council. He mentions the intention to march to Stirling, and then writes: "And although the Queen Regent was most earnestly requested and persuaded to continue"—that is to defer the summons—"nevertheless she remained wilful and obstinate, so that the counsel of God must needs take effect. Shortly, the day being come, because they appeared not, their sureties were outlawed, and the preachers ordered to be put to the horn. The Laird of Dun, who was sent from Perth by the brethren, perceiving her obstinacy, they" (who?) "turned from Stirling, and coming to Perth, declared to the brethren the obstinacy they found in the Queen. . . . "

This sturdy Protestant's version, which does not accuse the Regent of breaking troth, is corroborated by a Catholic contemporary, Lesley, Bishop of Ross. He says that Erskine of Dun was sent to beg the Regent not to impose a penalty on the preachers in their absence. But as soon as Dun returned and Knox learned from him that the Regent would not grant their request, he preached the sermon which provoked the devastation of the monasteries. Buchanan and Spottiswoode follow Knox, but they both use Knox's book, and are not independent witnesses.

The biographers of Knox do not quote "The Historie of the Estate of Scotland," where it touches on the beginning of the Revolution, without disparaging the Regent's honour. We have another dubious witness, Sir James Melville, who arrived on a mission from France to the Regent on June 13; he left Paris about June 1. This is the date of a letter in which Henri II. offers the Regent every assistance in the warmest terms. Melville writes, however, that in his verbal orders, delivered by the Constable in the royal presence, the Constable said, "I have intelligence that the Queen Regent has not kept all things promised to them." But Melville goes on to say that the Constable quoted d'Elboeuf's failure to reach Scotland with his fleet, as a reason for not sending the troops which were promised by Henri. As d'Elboeuf's failure occurred long after the date of the alleged conversation, the evidence of Melville is here incorrect. He wrote his "Memoirs" much later, in old age, but Henri may have written to the Regent in one sense, and given Melville orders in another.

We find that Knox's charge against the Regent is not made in our earliest information, Croft's letter of May 19: is not made by the

Protestant (and, we think, contemporary) author of the "Historie," and, of course, is not hinted at by Lesley, a Catholic. We have seen throughout that Knox vilifies Mary of Guise in cases where she is blameless. On the other hand, Knox is our only witness who was at Perth at the time of the events, and it cannot be doubted that what he told Mrs. Locke was what he believed, whether correctly or erroneously. He could believe anything against Mary of Guise. Archbishop Spottiswoode says, "The author of the story" ("History") "ascribed to John Knox in his whole discourse showeth a bitter and hateful spite against the Regent, forging dishonest things which were never so much as suspected by any, setting down his own conjectures as certain truths, yea, the least syllable that did escape her in passion, he maketh it an argument of her cruel and inhuman disposition . . . " In the MS. used by Bishop Keith, Spottiswoode added, after praising the Regent, "these things I have heard my father often affirm"; he had the like testimony "from an honourable and religious lady, who had the honour to wait near her person." Spottiswoode was, therefore, persuaded that the "History" "was none of Mr. Knox his writings." In spite of this opinion, Spottiswoode, writing about 1620-35, accepts most of the hard things that Knox says of the Regent's conduct in 1559, and indeed exaggerates one or two of them; that is, as relates to her political behaviour, for example, in the affair of the broken promise of May 10. It may be urged that here Spottiswoode had the support of the reminiscences of his father, a Superintendent in the Knoxian church.

APPENDIX B.

FORGERY PROCURED BY MARY OF GUISE

In the writer's opinion several of Knox's accusations of perfidy against the Regent, in 1559, are not proved, and the attempts to prove them are of a nature which need not be qualified. But it is necessary to state the following facts as tending to show that the Regent was capable of procuring a forgery against the Duke of Chatelherault. A letter attributed to him exists in the French Archives, dated Glasgow, January 25, 1560, in which the Duke curries favour with Francis II., and encloses his blank bond, *un blanc scellé*, offering to send his children to France. *On January* 28, the Regent writes from Scotland to de Noailles, then the French Ambassador to England, bidding him to mention this submission to Elizabeth, and even show the Duke's letter and blank bond, that Elizabeth may see how little he is to be trusted. Now how could the Regent, on January 28, have a letter sent by the Duke to France on January 25? She must have intercepted it in Scotland. Next, on March 15, 1560, the Duke, writing to Norfolk, denies the letter attributed to him by the French. He said that any one of a hundred Hamiltons would fight M. de Seurre (the French Ambassador who, in February, succeeded de Noailles) on this quarrel.

There exists a document, in the cipher of Throckmorton, English Ambassador in France, purporting to be a copy of a letter from the Regent to the Duc and Cardinal de Guise, dated Edinburgh, March 27, 1560. The Regent, at that date, was in Leith, not in Edinburgh Castle, where she went on April 1. In that letter she is made to say that de Seurre has "very evil misunderstood" the affair of the letter attributed to Chatelherault. She had procured "blanks" of his "by one of her servants here" (at Leith) "to the late Bishop of Ross"; the Duke's alleged letter and submission of January 25 had been "filled up" on a "blank," the Duke knowing nothing of the matter.

This letter of the Regent, then, must also, if authentic, have been somehow intercepted or procured by Throckmorton, in France. It is certain that Throckmorton sometimes, by bribery, did obtain copies of secret French papers, but I have not found him reporting to Cecil or Queen Elizabeth this letter of the Regent's. The reader must estimate for himself the value of that document. I have stated the case as fairly as I can, and though the evidence against the Regent, as it stands, would scarcely satisfy a jury, I believe that, corrupted by the evil example of the Congregation, the Regent, in January 1560, did procure a forgery intended to bring suspicion on Chatelherault. But how could she be surprised that de Seurre did not understand the real state of the case? The Regent may have explained the true nature of the affair to de Noailles, but it may have been unknown to de Seurre, who succeeded that ambassador. Yet, how could she ask any ambassador to produce a confessed forgery as genuine?

LITERARY ANALYSIS

A Literary Analysis of John Knox and the Reformation by Andrew Lang

Introduction: Meeting the Man Behind the Myth

We often like our historical figures to be straightforward. We want heroes we can admire without reservation and villains we can condemn without a second thought. But what do we do with the difficult ones? The figures who are towering and transformative, yet also deeply flawed and unsettling? These are often the most fascinating people in history, and few are more compellingly difficult than John Knox.

If you want to understand the man who arguably forged the soul of modern Scotland, you could pick up any number of histories that paint him as a flawless Protestant saint. Or, you could do something far more interesting: you could read _John Knox and the Reformation_ by Andrew Lang. Published in 1905, this book is not a simple biography; it's a critical, psychological, and refreshingly skeptical investigation. Lang, a renowned Scottish man of letters, approaches Knox not with blind reverence, but with the sharp, inquisitive eye of a literary critic. He peels back layers of myth to question the man beneath, making this one of the most significant and enduring studies of Knox ever written.

Plot: The Anatomy of a Revolution

Since this is a biography, its "plot" is the remarkable and turbulent life of John Knox himself. Lang guides us through a narrative that has all the drama of a political thriller. We begin with Knox's obscure origins and follow his transformation into a fiery preacher of the new Protestant faith. The early acts of his life are filled with high drama: his capture by French forces and his brutal enslavement as a galley rower—an experience that undoubtedly hardened his resolve and his heart.

Upon his release, we follow him into exile in Geneva, where he studies at the feet of John Calvin, absorbing the rigid, systematic theology that would become his primary weapon. The core of the book, however, details his explosive return to Scotland. Lang masterfully chronicles Knox's campaign to dismantle the Catholic establishment, his "thundering" sermons that incited riots and inspired lords, and his legendary confrontations with the young Mary, Queen of Scots.

The plot isn't just a sequence of events; it's the story of how one man's iron will, coupled with a nation's political and social discontent, created a revolution. Lang makes it clear that Knox didn't just seek to change religion; he aimed to fundamentally remake the nation in his own ideological image.

Characters: A High-Stakes Ensemble

Lang's book shines in its portrayal of the key players, presenting them not as historical chess pieces, but as complex, driven individuals.

John Knox: Lang's Knox is a figure of immense and terrifying power. He is courageous, intelligent, and possesses an unshakeable belief in his divine mission. Yet, Lang refuses to ignore the darker side of this zeal. He presents a man who was dogmatic, intolerant of any opposition, and perhaps dangerously convinced of his own righteousness. Lang critically examines Knox's claims to be a prophet, suggesting he was a masterful political operator who skillfully used religious fervor to achieve his goals. He is neither a saint nor a simple villain, but a complex zealot who changed the world.

Mary, Queen of Scots: Mary is Knox's great antagonist, and in Lang's hands, she is a tragic and compelling figure. She represents everything Knox despised: Catholic authority, the "monstrous regiment [rule] of women," and a more refined, European courtly culture. Their famous face-to-face debates are the dramatic heart of the book. While Knox saw her as a devious idolater, Lang allows the reader to see her as a young, intelligent queen trapped by circumstance, trying to navigate a kingdom being torn apart by the very man standing before her.

Supporting Cast: Figures like the calculating regent Mary of Guise (Mary, Queen of Scots' mother) and the influential theologian John Calvin are sketched effectively, providing the rich political and intellectual context against which Knox's drama unfolds. They help us understand the forces Knox was up against and the ideas that fueled him.

Themes: More Than Just a Biography

Lang uses Knox's life to explore themes that remain incredibly relevant today.

The Line Between Faith and Fanaticism: This is the book's central question. At what point does profound religious belief curdle into dangerous, uncompromising fanaticism? Lang constantly prods at Knox's certainty, forcing the reader to consider how a man so convinced he is doing God's work can justify political rebellion, intolerance, and verbal brutality.

The Theocratic Impulse: The book is a fascinating case study of the eternal struggle between church and state. Knox's goal was not a "free church in a free state"; his goal was to make the state subservient to his vision of the church. Lang explores the profound dangers and seductive power of theocracy—the belief that one's own religious doctrine should be the law of the land for everyone.

The Power of Personality in History: Was Knox a "Great Man" who single-handedly bent history to his will, or was he simply the right man at the right time, giving voice to a revolution that was already brewing? Lang wrestles with this question, presenting Knox as both a product of his chaotic times and a unique force of nature who irrevocably shaped them.

Deconstructing a National Myth: Perhaps the most unique theme is Lang's own project of historical revisionism. He is consciously writing against the heroic, one-dimensional image of Knox that was prevalent in his day. The book is as much about how history is written and how myths are made as it is about John Knox himself.

Style and Technique

Andrew Lang was a man of letters, and it shows. His prose is not the dry, dusty language of an academic textbook. It is learned, elegant, and often laced with a subtle, biting irony. He writes with the confidence of a well-read intellectual who is unafraid to pass judgment and share his own witty asides with the reader.

His primary technique is critical analysis of the primary sources, particularly Knox's own History of the Reformation in Scotland. Lang doesn't take Knox's self-assessment at face value. He reads between the lines, points out inconsistencies, and questions Knox's motives. For example, when analyzing Knox's justifications for his actions, Lang might dryly note the convenient alignment of divine will with Knox's political objectives. This skeptical approach is his most powerful tool, turning the biography into an act of historical detective work.

Historical Context and Modern Relevance

Written at the turn of the 20th century, Lang's work is a product of its own time—an era increasingly influenced by psychology, secularism, and a scholarly desire to question national myths. He was applying a modern, more critical lens to a figure from the past.

The book's relevance today is startling. In an age where we grapple daily with the consequences of religious extremism, political polarization, and the rise of charismatic leaders who claim to speak absolute truth, Knox's story is a powerful cautionary tale. Lang's analysis of how Knox used powerful rhetoric to mobilize a populace, demonize his opponents, and consolidate power feels incredibly contemporary. It reminds us that the battle over truth, faith, and political authority is a timeless one.

The Modern Reader's Experience

Reading this book today is an intellectually rewarding experience, but it requires some commitment. Lang's Edwardian prose can be dense, and he assumes a certain level of familiarity with British history. This is not a light, breezy read.

However, the payoff is a profound and nuanced understanding of a pivotal historical moment. You will come away feeling not just informed, but intellectually stimulated. It challenges you to think critically about how history is shaped and how it is told. You might not "like" John Knox by the end, but you will understand him and his impact in a way that a more reverential biography could never allow.

Why It Still Matters

John Knox and the Reformation matters because it was a landmark in the art of biography. It helped shift the genre from mere hero-worship to critical, psychological analysis. It matters because it provides an essential, humanizing counterbalance to the myth of a national hero, reminding us that our historical figures are always more complex than the statues we build of them. Most importantly, it is a timeless study of power—how a single, determined personality can harness the forces of social and religious discontent to change the world, for better and for worse.

Reading Tips (for contemporary audiences):

Don't Expect Hagiography: Go in knowing that Lang is a critic, not a fan. His goal is to analyze, not to praise.

Pay Attention to Tone: Lang's genius is often in his subtle irony and skepticism. Notice where he questions Knox's own account of events.

Embrace the Challenge: If the prose feels dense, slow down. The ideas are worth the effort. Think of it as a rich, complex meal rather than fast food. It is more rewarding for the effort it demands.

Conclusion

Andrew Lang's John Knox and the Reformation does not offer the easy comfort of a simple hero's tale. It offers something far more valuable: a brilliant, incisive, and deeply human portrait of a difficult man who lived in difficult times. It challenges you, it engages you, and it ultimately leaves you with a profound understanding of the relentless forces that shape history. If you are ready to move beyond the myth and meet the man in all his fierce, flawed complexity, I cannot recommend this book highly enough. It is a rewarding intellectual journey you will not soon forget.

ABOUT THE AUTHOR

Andrew Lang: The Polymathic Scholar and Chronicler of Scottish History

Andrew Lang (1844-1912) was a truly extraordinary figure in late Victorian and Edwardian letters – a man whose intellectual curiosity knew few bounds. A prolific Scottish poet, novelist, literary critic, anthropologist, and historian, Lang's vast output spanned an astonishing array of subjects, from mythology and folklore to classical literature, historical biography, and even psychical research. While he is perhaps most popularly remembered today for his enchanting "Fairy Books," his more scholarly and historical works, such as "John Knox and the Reformation," published in 1905, reveal a meticulous  researcher and a keen analytical mind deeply engaged with the complexities of his native Scotland's past.

Born in Selkirk, Scotland, on March 31, 1844, Andrew Lang was the eldest of eight children to John Lang, the Sheriff-Clerk of Selkirkshire, and Jane Plenderleath Sellar. His upbringing in the Scottish Borders imbued him with a lifelong love for Scottish history, folklore, and literature, themes that would reappear consistently throughout his career. From an early age, Lang displayed prodigious intellectual gifts and a voracious appetite for reading.

He received his early education at Selkirk Grammar School and then at the Edinburgh Academy. His academic brilliance led him to St Andrews University, where he excelled. He then moved south to England, securing a scholarship to Balliol College, Oxford, one of the most prestigious colleges at the time. At Oxford, he further distinguished himself, becoming a Fellow of Merton College in 1868. His time at Oxford exposed him to a wide range of classical literature, history, and nascent anthropological theories, shaping his interdisciplinary approach to scholarship.

Upon leaving Oxford, Lang embarked on a literary career that was nothing short of prodigious. He settled in London and became a leading figure in the literary world. His output was immense, often juggling multiple projects simultaneously across various fields. He was a regular contributor to Longman's Magazine, The Daily News, and numerous other periodicals, showcasing his versatility as an essayist and critic.

While his "Fairy Books" (starting with The Blue Fairy Book in 1889), which compiled and retold folk tales from around the world, brought him widespread fame and continue to delight children, Lang's intellectual rigor extended far beyond the realm of enchanting narratives. He was a pioneering folklorist and anthropologist, deeply interested in comparative mythology and the origins of cultural practices. His works like Myth, Ritual, and Religion (1887) were significant contributions to these emerging academic fields. He also translated Homer's Odyssey and Iliad with S. H. Butcher and Walter Leaf, respectively, demonstrating his profound classical scholarship.

However, it was his unwavering commitment to Scottish history that drove some of his most significant, albeit sometimes controversial, works. Lang was fascinated by the pivotal figures and dramatic events that shaped Scotland. His biography, "John Knox and the Reformation," is a prime example of this dedication. Published in 1905, this work delved deeply into the life and impact of John Knox, the fiery and influential leader of the Scottish Reformation.

In "John Knox and the Reformation," Lang adopted a critical yet scholarly approach. Unlike many previous biographers who tended towards hagiography or outright condemnation, Lang sought to present a balanced, thoroughly researched portrait of Knox, drawing extensively from primary sources. He examined Knox's complex personality, his theological convictions, his political maneuvering, and his lasting legacy on Scottish society, religion, and national identity. Lang was not afraid to challenge conventional narratives or to highlight the less savory aspects of historical figures, even those as revered (or reviled) as Knox. His work was characterized by meticulous attention to detail and a vigorous, often witty, prose style. He immersed himself in the historical documents of the period, providing context and analysis that elevated his historical biographies beyond mere recounting of facts.

Lang's historical works often sparked debate, as he was unafraid to express his interpretations, which sometimes ran counter to established views. His other notable historical works include The Mystery of Mary Stuart (1901), where he engaged with the controversial figure of Mary Queen of Scots, and James VI and the Gowrie Mystery (1902). Through these works, Lang demonstrated his profound engagement with the complexities and ambiguities of historical inquiry.

Andrew Lang passed away on July 20, 1912, in Banchory, Aberdeenshire, Scotland. He left behind an astonishing literary legacy that reflects a truly encyclopedic mind. His contributions to children's literature, folklore, and classical studies alone would secure his place in literary history. Yet, his rigorous historical biographies, particularly "John Knox and the Reformation," reveal a scholar deeply committed to understanding and interpreting the past, especially the dramatic unfolding of Scottish history. Lang's work reminds us that intellectual curiosity, combined with a tireless work ethic, can lead to a lifetime of profound and lasting contributions across an almost unimaginable range of disciplines.

Printed in Dunstable, United Kingdom

76242317R00121